SOCIAL SCIENTISTS AS ADVOCATES

SAGE FOCUS EDITIONS

SOCIAL SCIENTISTS AS ADVOCATES
Views from the Applied Disciplines

edited by
George H. Weber and
George J. McCall

 SAGE PUBLICATIONS   Beverly Hills/London

For information address:

SAGE PUBLICATIONS, INC.
275 South Beverly Drive
Beverly Hills, California 90212

SAGE PUBLICATIONS LTD
28 Banner Street
London EC1 Y 8QE

Printed in the United States of America

Library of Congress Cataloging in Publication Data

Main entry under title:

Social scientists as advocates.

(Sage focus editions ; 4)
Contributions from a symposium held in
San Diego at the April 1977 meeting of the
Society for Applied Anthropology.
   1. Social scientists — United States — Congresses.
2. United States — Social policy — Congresses.
I. Weber, George Henry, 1921-   II. McCall,
George J. III. Society for Applied Anthropology.
IV. Series.

H53.U5S65   300'.973   77-26798
ISBN 0-8039-0943-8
ISBN 0-8039-0944-6 pbk.

FIRST PRINTING

CONTENTS

FOREWORD

It is an American paradox: pervasive skepticism of lawyers, yet a preoccupation with and affection for law and litigation. This country has converted many of the great moral issues of our time into constitutional disputes; we ask not is it good or bad, fair or unfair, but rather how will the Supreme Court hold on problems of race relations, poverty and welfare, education, housing — much that most concerns the collective life. Surely no other country so relies on litigation, no matter how dilatory, to settle personal, commercial, and governmental disputes.

One important positive value in this litigious cast of mind and habit of practice is that the social scientist is forced back to a role too long neglected, that of a deeply involved social reformer.

The comforting expectations of the nineteenth century have not been fulfilled; increasing knowledge of social organization allied to universal suffrage has not led inexorably to a larger social justice. The social scientist who raises his eyes and mind from whatever is his laboratory is thus pressed to engagement in social reform. In this most interesting collection of essays, the diversities of that engagement in social work, law, psychology, urban planning, anthropology, and sociology are organized around the concept of advocacy. Advocacy in this analysis ranges from helping those in need to express or plead their own cause, to intercession on their behalf before any bar of public opinion or any agency of regulatory or legislative change, to forensic involvement in the representation of a client or a class in litigation. As George McCall demonstrates in a concluding study, which draws together the cross-disciplinary themes that emerge from the six essays forming the body of this book, advocacy is an important method of applied social science.

George Weber's Introduction sets advocacy in the intellectual context of social science and social reform — the slow movements to acquire knowledge of community organization and to turn that knowledge to the achievement of a more just society.

One does not have to believe in the perfectability of man to find this an important book; but one does have to be willing to cast back to a great tradition, now somewhat unfashionable, of the intellectual as a passionately concerned citizen, who cares deeply for the diminution of human suffering and indignity, and is willing to use the knowledge and skill he has for the attainment of social justice.

— *Norval Morris*
University of Chicago

INTRODUCTION:
SOCIAL SCIENCE PERSPECTIVES ON ADVOCACY

Advocacy, according to Webster (1967), is the act of pleading the cause of another, or defending a cause or proposal. Though precise, Webster's definition points mainly to advocacy as it has traditionally been practiced in law and does not include the recent innovations in legal advocacy or the current uses of advocacy by the social and behavioral sciences.

As a manifestation of the social activism of the 1960s, advocacy in the current decade has been seen as a politically controversial, professionally daring, and conceptually divergent practice modality within several applied disciplines. Although never a prevalent modality, advocacy remains today an enterprise of considerable vitality and promise.

The profession of social work (NASW Ad Hoc Committee on Advocacy, 1969) suggested that advocacy be employed by its members to secure the necessary resources for their clients. A number of innovations followed. For example, Brophy, Chan and Nagel (1974) argued that clients should be helped, through counseling, to serve as their own advocates. Brager (1968), on the other hand, suggested that active political strategies be employed by social workers in behalf of the disadvantaged. Further, Gilbert and Specht (1974) point out that advocacy is being used to refer to a broad range of activities from civil rights and social protest pursuits through consumer education.

Community psychologists have indicated the need for psychology to broaden its helping techniques, its theory, and its professional role definitions (Fairweather, 1967; Cowen, 1973). That need has generated the suggestion that practicing psychologists work as generalists and focus their skills on solving a variety of problems (Sarason, 1976), as coordinators and "signal callers" in the community (Cowen, 1973), as human helpers (Reissman, 1965), and as advocates in specific settings (Davidson and Rapp, 1976).

Until the 1960s urban planning drew most of its direction from the community elite whose concerns were rationalized as being "disinterested" and in the "public interest." However, the 1960s fervor for social reform called for the opening of institutions and opportunities to all citizens and making planning encompass the broader interests and values of the community (Blecher, 1971). The illusion of value-free planning, which permeated the earlier philosophy of planning as a scientific technology, was rejected by Davidoff (1965). He urged planners to invite debate on the various actions that could be taken on a problem, to make known the values that underlie the possible course of action, and to be an advocate for that action each deems proper.

Applied anthropologists have used their cross-cultural perspective and research findings in serving as expert court witnesses (Stewart, 1973, and Lurie, 1955), program developers, and technical advisors and assistants to Indians (Tax, 1958; Peterson, 1973). Peattie (1960) points out that the Fox Project (Tax, 1958) developed a complex action strategy of "concerned interference" to assist the Fox Indians to increase their areas of free choice. Further, applied anthropologists have used advocacy as government consultants and liaison officers with the native population in the post-war administration of the United Nations Trust Territory of Micronesia (Barnett, 1956) and as "anthropologists-patrons" of a hacienda leased by Cornell University from Peruvian owners for the purposes of research and development (Holmberg, 1965).

Maintaining an academic stance, sociology has mainly focused its concerns about social problems on theory and research (Rubington and Weinberg, 1971). Thus its major contribution to advocacy has been in producing theories (like those of Comte, Ward, Weber, Marx) which have been used to develop rationales for social change and in producing research findings that have been used to effect change: Stouffer (1949) on the military, Myrdal (1944) and Frazer (1966) on the American Negro, Roethlesberger and Dickson (1943) on industrial management, and Coleman (1966, 1972) on school desegregation. Sociologists also have made contributions to advocacy strategies and procedures. Lundberg (1961) encouraged the sociologist to maintain his role as scientist — researching and making relevant data available to others — while in his role as citizen he might advocate and participate in practical affairs to effect change. Alinsky (1946), having complete faith in people, urged the development of people's organizations and an uncompromising war against poverty, misery, delinquency, disease, injustice, hopelessness, despair, and unhappiness.

While other professions have only recently begun to employ advocacy as a deliberate procedure to assist their clients, law has always relied on advocacy techniques. The lawyer's advocacy armamentarium has traditionally included intimate familiarity with legal rules and procedures, skills to present and argue a case, and skills to help his client organize his ideas, bring out the facts that may help him, and bolster his readiness to face the officialdom. The advocacy of lawyers, however, is not restricted to the courts and allied settings or to the interests of individuals. Rather it extends to a broad range of other legal and quasi-legal situations, including consumer problems, welfare rights, environmental protection, and other public interest issues.

But what is the state of the art of advocacy within these disciplines today? And what can we expect of advocacy as a practice modality in the years ahead?

Toward the end of answering these questions, leading representatives of advocacy from each of these six disciplines were asked to contribute parallel analyses of advocacy as it is practiced within their own fields to a symposium at the April 1977 meetings of the Society for Applied Anthropology in San Diego (supported by a National Institute of Mental Health contract, PLD-0399-77).

Contributors were asked not only to analyze their discipline's concepts of advocacy but to relate these concepts to the field's beliefs about a just society and to advocacy's historical roots within the discipline's panoply of responses to social injustice and social problems. Contemporary strategies and tactics of advocacy as practiced within the discipline were to be recounted and to be exemplified through two or three detailed case illustrations. Finally, contributors were asked to project what the next steps might be in the further development of theory, research practice, and training in advocacy efforts within their disciplines.

This symposium was organized not so much as a basis for the preparation of a theory or model of advocacy (or the plural of these), but rather as a set of materials which would encourage the careful spelling out of diverse conceptions of advocacy and facilitate cross-disciplinary comparisons. I believe these objectives have been met in rather splendid fashion. The representatives of the six disciplines have provided very thorough and remarkably informative analyses of the theory and practice of advocacy as conducted within their fields. In reviewing these materials, the reader cannot miss the fact that there is no "party-line" concerning either the theory or the practice of advocacy. Disciplinary divergences in approaches to advocacy are both abundant and coherent, yet a number of important themes emerge with striking regularity.

Perhaps surprisingly, the two most elaborated and most highly contrasting conceptualizations are those from social work and from sociology, which respectively open and close this set of disciplinary contributions. The tension between these end-pieces is mediated and elaborated by the analyses of four other disciplines and some further rationale for the order of presentation may be in order.

The three more clinical and individually oriented disciplines are presented as a group, with law unexpectedly emerging as a strategic bridge between social work and community psychology. Within the set of disciplines less frequently advocating for individuals, the order of presentation follows that of extent of practice orientation — urban planning, applied anthropology, and sociology.

The volume concludes with an analytical commentary by the second co-editor, with the complementary aims of identifying major common themes in advocacy as social science practice and of drawing out cross-disciplinary comparisons.

— George H. Weber

REFERENCES

Alinsky, S.D. (1946) *Reveille for Radicals.* Chicago: University of Chicago Press.

Barnes, H. E. (ed.) 1948) *An Introduction to the History of Sociology.* Chicago: University of Chicago Press.

Barnett, H. G. (1956) *Anthropology in Administration.* New York: Harper and Row.

Blecher, E. M. (1971) *Advocacy Planning for Urban Development.* New York: Praeger Publishers.

Brager, G. A. (19) "Advocacy as Political Behavior." *Social Work,* 13 (April): 5-15.

Brophy, M. C., Chan, A., and Nagel, R. J. (1974) *The Advocate Counseling Model,* University of Wisconsin. Available from the author.

Coleman, J. S., et al. (1966) *Equity of Educational Opportunity.* Washington: U. S. Government Printing Office.

Coleman, J. S. (1972) *Policy Research in the Social Sciences.* Morristown, N.J.: General Learning Press.

Cowen, E. L. (1973) "Social and Community Interventions." *Annual Review of Psychology.* Palo Alto: Annual Review.

Davidoff, P. (1965) "Advocacy and Pluralism in Planning." *Journal of American Institute of Planners,* 31 (November): 331-333.

Davidson, W. S., and Rapp, C. (1976) "Child Advocacy in the Juvenile Justice System." *Social Work,* 21 (May): 225-232.

Fairweather, G. W. (1967) *Methods for Experimental Social Innovation.* New York: John Wiley and Sons, Inc.

Frazer, E. F. (1966) *The Negro Family in the United States.* Chicago: University of Chicago Press.

Gilbert, N., and Specht, H. (1974) *Dimensions of Social Welfare Policy.* Englewood Cliff: Prentice Hall.

Holmberg, A. R. (1965) "The Changing Values and Institutions of Vicos in the Context of National Development." *American Behavioral Scientist,* 8 (July): 3-8.

Lundberg, G. A. (1961) *Can Science Save Us.* New York: McKay.

Lurie, N. O. (1955) "Anthropology and Indian Claims Litigation: Problems, Opportunities and Recommendations." *Ethnohistory,* 2: 357-375.

Marx, K. (1936) *Capital.* New York: Modern Library.

Myrdal, G. (1944) *An American Dilemma.* New York: Harper and Brothers.

National Association of Social Workers Ad Hoc Committee on Advocacy. (1969) "The Social Worker as Advocate: Champion of Social Victims. *Social Work,* 14 (April): 16-22.

Peattie, L. R. (1960) "The Failure of the Means-Ends Scheme in Action Anthropology." In F. Gearing, R. M. Netting, and L. R. Peattie (eds.) *Documentary History of the Fox Project.* Chicago: University of Chicago Press.

Peterson, J. H. (1973) *The Anthropologist as Advocate.* Paper presented at the American Anthropology Association, November, 1973. Available from author.

Reissman, R. (1965) "The Helper Therapy Principle." *Social Work,* 10 (April): 27-32.

Roethlisberger, F. J., and Dickson, W. J. (1943) *Management and the Worker.* Cambridge: Harvard University Press.

Rubington, E. and Weinberg, M.S. (eds.) (1971) *The Study of Social Problems — Five Perspectives.* New York: Oxford University Press.

Sarason, S. (1976) "Community Psychology, Networks, and Mr. Everyman." *American Psychologist,* 31 (May): 317-328.

Stewart, O. C. (1973) "Anthropologists as Expert Witnesses for Indians: Claims and Peyote Cases." J. Henry (ed.) *Anthropology and the American Indians: A Symposium.* Indian Historical Press.

Stouffer, S. A., et al. (1949) "Studies in Social Psychology." In *World War II, The American Soldier: Adjustment During Army Life.* Princeton University Press. Vol. 1.

Tax, S. (1958) "The Fox Project." *Human Organization,* 17: 17-19.

Weber, M. (1930) *The Protestant Ethic and the Spirit of Capitalism.* Translated by Talcott Parsons. London: George Allen and Unwin.

Webster's Seventh New Collegiate Dictionary. (1967) Springfield, Massachusetts: G. and C. Merriam Company.

1

ADVOCACY AND SOCIAL WORK

Herb Kutchins
Stuart Kutchins

THE JUST SOCIETY: MORALITY, NOT UTOPIA

Social workers are not utopian thinkers, they are moralists. In the
professional journals there are a great many expressions of indignation
or outrage at the misfortunes that people, particularly disabled and
disadvantaged people suffer, but not much discussuion about what an
ideal, just society would be like. As it is practiced, social work does not
head toward the development of an ideal state, but tries to ameliorate
the suffering of people living in an unkind world.

This description of the role of social work by Scott Briar (1974:
518), editor of *Social Work,* the leading professional publication in the
field, appeared in a recent issue of that journal devoted to the future of
the profession:

> The mission of social work, which is to enhance the quality of life
> for all persons, requires no apology, but why is it surprising that
> this mission is difficult to define? After all, ideas of the good life
> vary and change, as they should. What can be defined are the
> injustices and obstacles that damage and destroy the quality of
> life, and we know enough to name names, poverty, racism,
> sexism, drug abuse and a host of others. We keep working on
> these problems, often person by person, because they undermine
> and cause ruin. The problems are still there, but sometimes we do
> help some persons to be rid of them, which is no small
> achievement.

The nature of their profession commits social workers to a very pragmatic stance in the remedy of immediate social and personal problems. They are motivated to act not so much by a concept of a just society as by a sense of injustice. The relationship between justice and the sense of injustice is explicated in the work of a legal philosopher, Edmond Cahn (1964:13). He says that

> justice almost inevitably brings to mind some ideal relation or static condition or set of perceptual standards, while we are concerned on the contrary with what is active, vital, and experiential in the reaction of human beings. Where justice is thought of in the customary mode or condition the human response will be merely contemplative, and contemplation bakes no loaves. But the response to a real or imaged instance of injustice is something quite different; it is alive with movement and warmth in the human organism. For this reason, the name "the sense of injustice" seems to be preferrred. What then would be meant by "justice". . . ? The answer would appear to be: not a state, but a process; not a condition but an action.
> "Justice," as we shall use the term, means the *active process* of remedying or preventing what would arouse the sense of injustice.

According to Cahn (1964:22), the sense of injustice is triggered by denials of:

1. Equality;

2. Just desert, which means that the law will not be used to exculpate the guilty or punish the innocent;

3. Human dignity; embodied in the prohibition against cruel or unusual punishment;

4. Conscientious adjudication;

5. Confinement of government to its proper functions; and

6. Fulfillment of common expectations.

The experience of injustice is like having a fever. When the body temperature is normal, about 98.6°F, we are not concerned. When the condition of the body varies substantially from 98.6°F we say we have a temperature or a fever. Similarly, only when the social temperature varies and there is a fever caused by injustice are we concerned about justice.

The visceral experience of injustice, rather than utopian strivings, moves social workers to engage in advocacy and other forms of social action. This is not to say that social workers lack any vision of what a just society should be; there follow descriptions of two ideas about the just society which social workers share. But these visions must be understood as just that — inchoate views full of contradictions. These views shape the responses social workers make to injustice.

TWO CONCEPTS OF THE JUST SOCIETY

The Society of Equal Opportunity. The predominant social work ideal is equality of opportunity. There is sentiment in the profession that the ultimate goal is a society in which no one is prevented from accomplishing his ambitions because of personal attributes like race, economic background, or physical or emotional handicaps.

This sentiment, as it is embodied in social work, gives impetus to two types of activity — casework and community organization. In casework, a social worker attempts to assist an individual in solving some social or emotional problem. There is no one approach to casework used exclusively by all social workers, but as Briar (1967:21) reports,

> The dominant preoccupation of social casework over the past thirty-five to forty years has been devoted to the development of the therapeutic functions of social casework or what has come to be called "clinical" casework.

The clinical casework strategy is to assist clients to rid themselves of personal disabilities which interfere with their capacity to take advantage of opportunities. Although the impact of environmental factors may be acknowledged, the locus of change is the individual.

Community organization focuses on social rather than personal change. Norman Moore (1970: 225) describes it as

> A method of effecting social change in all or any part of a community through the modification of the behavior of its institutions and its ways of using social resources in social welfare matters.

There are two major aspects of community organization — one, the community planning approach and the other, generally referred to as grass roots organizing (Galper, 1975: 111).

Community organization was not initially concerned with organizing for social change but rather grew out of the Community Council and United Fund movements. Its focus was on organizing social agencies in relationship to one another to help them avoid competition and facilitate their fund raising efforts. Eventually it adopted a planning perspective that at one time was encapsulated in the idea that community organization was primarily concerned with encouraging an improved balance of community needs and community resources . . . From this perspective community organization was a help to the network of social service agencies that had become increasingly bureaucratized. Community organization moved into grass roots organizing over time.

Grass roots organizing came to public attention in the fifties and early sixties with the work of Saul Alinsky (1946) in organizing workers in Chicago ghettos and with the efforts of CORE and SNCC to organize southern Black communities. The fundamental premise of this approach to community organization is that the poor can accumulate power if they are organized into groups and that this power can be deployed to destroy the barriers to equal opportunity.

The ideal of equal opportunity is not peculiar to social workers; it is shared by many, perhaps a substantial majority of Americans. It is the ideal of the good America, the America of the Founding Fathers, in which all men are created equal with inalienable rights to life, liberty and the pursuit of happiness. Of course, the Founding Fathers had a limited view of who "all men" are — white male property owners — a view that is still in the process of considerable revision, but the condition of equal opportunity has been an important American ideal.

The most recent attempt to operationalize the ideal of equal opportunity was the War Against Poverty, which was promoted in some measure by social workers and was based on the premise that it is possible to achieve "The Great Society" without a single major program to redistribute wealth or income, simply by providing opportunities to those who are poor.

The Welfare State. It has been argued that society should provide more for its members than equal opportunity to compete for valued goods and services, that the state has an obligation to assure that certain minimum needs of all its citizens will be met — basic nutrition, shelter, health care and education. This is the concept of justice embodied in the idea of the welfare state: All members of society must be provided basic needs as a matter not of privilege but of right and this must be done in a regular, lawful, and even-handed way. It doesn't require that resources be divided equally, only that everyone gets enough to keep him alive and in shape to take advantage of opportunities.

This is the prevailing liberal view, one that is shared by a large number of social workers (Shottland, 1967; Titmuss, 1958). Harry Hopkins and other social workers played a significant part in the process which started in the thirties, of developing this approach into public policy (Schlesinger, 1957:25). Although there are still social workers playing similar roles (formulating policy, drafting legislation, etc.), other professions — economics, law, and public administration — with more sophisticated training and skills in this area are progressively eclipsing the contributions of social work to the development and operation of the welfare state (Rein, 1970). Nonetheless, social workers as professionals widely subscribe to the concept of the welfare state and their professional organizations have continued to lobby for and to promote social welfare programs and services (Galper, 1975: 12).

In Summary. The social work conception of the just society consists of commitment to (1) the provision of basic needs for everyone as a matter of right and (2) the guarantee to everyone of equal opportunity to compete for the society's goods and services. To clarify the picture delineated by these commitments it is helpful to indicate what is excluded. Social workers do not have a Hobbesian view of society and do not feel that government is a Leviathan which is inherently corrupt. They feel equanimity at the provision of increasing services by the government. When confronted by the prospect that increase in government services may increase the public regulation of citizens, the welfare state solution is not to limit services and programs in the interest of preserving privacy and liberty, but to build into government programs, policies and provisions that will provide protection from (unnecessary) incursions on individual rights.

There is little commitment among social workers to the Jeffersonian principle that the government which governs best is that which governs least. And there is little fear of an inherent danger that the expansion of government even to accomplish benign ends requires the sacrifice of individual freedom.

While on the one hand the social work concepts of the just society do not reflect the conservative view, neither do they accord with Marxist ideology. Marx's principle of distributive justice, from each according to his ability, to each according to his need, is not generally shared by social workers. Although there is a growing interest in

Marxist theories (Knickmeyer, 1972) among a small group, many social workers distinguish their political commitments from their professional practice (Rein, 1970). Although there are a few notable exceptions to this, particularly Galper's (1975) effort to formulate the idea of social work practice from a socialist perspective, social work as a profession has not been significantly affected by the major radical socialist reformulations of the last decade.

THE CONCEPT OF ADVOCACY AND SOCIAL WORK

THE HISTORY OF SOCIAL WORK ADVOCACY

Roots. Advocacy in the broadest sense of pleading a cause is an honored tradition in the history of social work. Social workers recall the efforts of Dorothea Dix on behalf of the mentally ill in the last century (Cohen, 1958: 35). The work of the turn-of-the-century reformers including Jane Adams and her associates at Hull House in Chicago and those at New York settlement houses, was clearly advocacy as we understand it today. They helped people, usually immigrants from Eastern Europe, to secure benefits and to negotiate with local governments and exploitative employers (Cohen, 1958: 56).

Nor was advocacy limited to individual cases. Social workers were deeply involved in a variety of activities, including the passage of child labor legislation and juvenile court laws, which they felt would improve conditions for the poor. The Goldmark sisters (Morris, 1971: 478) did the research and mobilized the data that were used in the original Brandeis brief, an important innovation in legal advocacy for social causes.

These are only a few of many examples of the practice of advocacy by early social workers in community, judicial, and legislative settings. Though this is a tradition that social workers take to be an important aspect of their history, advocacy had disappeared as a significant aspect of their professional activities by 1960 (Cloward and Epstein, 1965). This was due principally to three factors: repeated political purges within the profession; a commitment to the medical model of problem-solving and the psychoanalytic mania; and employment in agencies which were unsympathetic to change.

By the beginning of the sixties professional concern and training of social workers focused firmly on clinical methods of treatment. Briar (1967: 22) characterizes clinical casework as follows:

I know that many caseworkers are quick to insist on the difference between clinical casework and psychotherapy, but it is demonstrable that the theory and techniques of treatment that inform clinical casework were not developed independently but carry a heavy debt to psychotherapy, and to psychoanalytic psychotherapy in particular.

It was the caseworker's job to be a neutral therapist (Brager and Specht, 1967: 138), to allow clients to express confusion and distress, to help clarify how clients felt about problems and what actions clients might reasonably take to accomplish the solutions that the clients decided upon. Implicit in this sort of casework are the theories that the just society is our society and that inequality stems from the disability of the client.

This is a very passive, nondirective role, what my colleague Ivor Kraft likes to call "the talking cure." Clients often found themselves out doing battle with unyielding bureaucracies; social workers were often perceived (Brager and Barr, 1967), not by their clients alone, as unresponsive bureaucrats who did nothing.

The Re-Emergence of Advocacy in the 1960s. In 1961, Cloward and Ohlin of Columbia University's School of Social Work made the argument in *Delinquency and Opportunity* that certain groups had problems that did not proceed from their deficiencies but from the structure of society. Focusing on Black and Brown teenage gang members, Cloward and Ohlin pointed out that these youths shared the American Dream of success which they were prevented from realizing by social rather than personal deficiencies. Lacking legitimate means to achieve legitimate ends, the gangs took advantage of illegitimate means — they would be good Americans even if they had to be crooks to do it.

The implications of this argument, really the fruition of a long development of sociological thought from Durkheim and Weber through Merton and Sutherland (Moynihan, 1969: 53), is that the lack of equal opportunity is the cause of delinquency and other social problems and that the solution to these is to create legitimate opportunity structures.

For a while opportunity theory seemed to promise the transformation of professional social work activity from a casework approach to community organization. Social workers from the Henry Street settlement on the Lower East Side of New York City, with Cloward and Ohlin and help from the Ford Foundation, organized Mobilization for Youth. The goal was reduction of crime and delinquency through a planned, coordinated strategy which included casework, education, vocational training and, especially, community organization to open legitimate opportunities (Mobilization for Youth, 1961). Shortly thereafter opportunity theory and the MFY model of community action were used in framing the strategy for the War on Poverty (Moynihan, 1969). This campaign, embodied in the Economic Opportunities Act of 1964, was the last attempt to implement a coherent policy on a national scale to deal with domestic problems of poverty and deprivation.

Criticism of opportunity theory has come from many sources (Moynihan, 1969: 171-178), but many social programs and much effort by social workers are still based on commitment to the assumption that without racial, economic, or social discrimination to bar the way to the top, or at least to the middle, the just society will be achieved.

The current interest in social welfare advocacy emerged in no small part from the Mobilization for Youth and War on Poverty experiences (Marris and Rein, 1969: 164-191; Moynihan, 1969). Although not a clearly planned part of either, legal services spurred general enthusiasm for advocacy among social workers involved in Mobilization for Youth; and legal services became one of the two most popular programs of the War on Poverty (Johnson, 1974). Cloward (1967) and others (Grosser, 1965; Brager, 1968) quickly seized on the potency of advocacy as an approach for social work and other helping professions.

It is a matter of particular interest that the primary targets for these advocates were welfare agencies. They found that many of the programs were operated according to policies and procedures that were illegal, and in some cases unconstitutional (Reich, 1963; 1964; 1965; tenBroek, 1966). Some programs were operated in violation of their own rules, according to the personal dictates of those administering them (Handler, 1966). The net effect was widespread discrimination against members of minorities, the poor, the illegitimate; often those who were most in need of assistance were excluded as matter of preference or policy. Lampman (1966: 221) reported that in the mid-1960s income maintenance payments totaled

> $36 billion per year and go to over 30 million people. This class of income is 40% of the income of the poor population, yet most of it goes to the non-poor, and at least half the poor do not receive it.

THE SOCIAL WORK CONCEPTION OF ADVOCACY

When the idea of social work advocacy was reintroduced in the sixties, it was eagerly embraced by many groups within the profession. However, it is necessary to say at the outset what will be demonstrated shortly: that for social workers "advocacy" is essentially an undefined term that is used to refer to all kinds of social action. Social workers have not thought out the nature and full range of their commitments and therefore, as may be expected, have difficulty in performing advocacy. In fairness to the discipline, it should be added that examination of other professions does not yield a much different picture.

The National Association of Social Workers appointed an Ad Hoc Committee on Advocacy which, in 1969, offered in their position statement a definition of the advocate, starting with two quotations of dictionary definitions. The first (Ad Hoc Committee, 1969: 16) is, "one who pleads the cause of another," which, the Committee noted, reflects the traditional notion of the lawyer-advocate who is

> his client's supporter, his adviser, his champion, and, if need be, his representative in his dealings with the court, the police, the social agency, and other organizations that (affect) his well being.

The second dictionary definition, "one who argues for, defends, maintains, or recommends a cause or proposal," the Committee associated with "the political meaning in which the interests of a class of people are represented; implicitly, the issues are universalistic rather than particularistic." This, they said, fit Brager's (1968: 6) description of an advocate-reformer who

> identifies with the plight of the disadvantaged. He sees as his primary responsibility the tough-minded and partisan representation of their interests and this supersedes his fealty to others. This role inevitably requires that the practitioner function as a political tactician.

The Ad Hoc Committee's effort to define advocacy represents the general understanding of the term among most professional social workers. However, while the dictionary definitions of advocate — arguing a cause and representing another's interests — are quite reasonable, the Committee's amplification of these two basic points does little to illuminate the practice of advocacy as a professional activity and does a great deal to confuse the discussion.

Four major problems are discernible: first is the tendency to use romantic language like "champion", "tough-minded", "fealty", "hired-gun", to create an excitement about advocacy, which only obscures the need for greater conceptual clarity; second, the assumption is made that an advocate is a good guy, that to be an advocate means that the social worker will deal with the "plight of the disadvantaged"; third, a false dichotomy is introduced by the Committee's nonsequitur that "one who argues for a cause or proposal" implies that "the issues are universalistic rather than particularistic"; and, finally, the association of this false dichotomy with Brager's description of the advocate reformer results in an apparent expansion of the meaning of advocacy to encompass the full range of social action for worthy causes. These problems are, if anything, exaggerated in other widely circulated attempts to define advocacy.

The Family Service Association of America formulated the following definition of family advocacy (Manser, 1973: 3):

> Professional service designed to improve life conditions for people by harnessing direct and expert knowledge of family needs with the commitment to action and the application of skills to produce the necessary community change.

In the FSAA manual, advocacy is described as the entire range of activities of community organization.

In the report of a nationwide research project conducted by Alfred Kahn (1972: 62), a well-known social work planner and his associates, child advocacy is defined as "intervention on behalf of children in relation to those services and institutions that impinge on their lives." Kahn, et al. (1972: 66) observe that

> A multiplicity of interest groups interacts with these formal branches of the government in attempting to define the public interest. Child advocacy may be the way of assuring that children are adequately represented as such interest groups play their parts. Child advocacy is more, however, since its objectives also involve the individual child and his personal needs rather than public policy.

This definition does not even limit the kind of intervention to community organization and, since almost all services and institutions in society may impinge on children's lives, it is clear that virtually every form of intervention can be considered child advocacy. Examination of the "child advocacy" programs they investigated reveals an even wider range of settings, activities, and objectives than does the FSAA. Included are everything from a citywide council of youth groups in San Francisco to the Comprehensive Neighborhood Program at New York's Wiltwyck School for Boys, to Action for Children's Television in Newton, Massachusetts. Recently, Gilbert and Specht, (1976: 288) observed that,

> one finds the word [advocacy] used to describe consumer education, civil rights, and social protest actions, referral and social brokerage activities, and a big brother program for the developmentally disabled.

One cannot formulate a coherent concept of social work advocacy from such an aggregation of definitions, descriptions, and postures. It must be seen simply for what it is — the Tower of Babel.

The Demystification of Advocacy. Virtually all the discussion in the social work literature assumes that everyone knows what an advocate does, an assumption that has confused the role and the value of advocacy and has obscured the need for developing the technical skills for its practice. To define advocacy as a professional activity rather than a posture, it is useful to refer briefly to that discipline in which advocacy has its longest history and best developed place — the profession of law.

In the practice of law, advocacy as a professional activity entails (1) pleading a case or a cause, one's own or another's, (2) in an appropriate forum, (3) to accomplish a specific goal (e.g., to resolve a specific conflict or to redress a specific grievance). Departure from this basic idea leads to the confusion of advocacy with a wide range of other activities and with certain political commitments.

Advocacy for the Poor and Disadvantaged. For example, advocacy is often confused with working for the poor. One of the activities which social workers have most frequently identified with advocacy is helping clients obtain welfare benefits. Federally financed public assistance programs mandate fair hearings, quasi-judicial administrative proceedings which review agency decisions to refuse benefits, at which non-lawyer advocates may represent welfare applicants (Briar, 1966). This is a situation where social work advocates have been instrumental. But for every social worker acting as advocate for the underdog, there is soneone else, usually a social worker, acting as advocate for the Welfare Department.

Advocacy is a politically neutral activity. The decision that advocacy for the disadvantaged is an appropriate activity for social workers may be a step toward providing more realistic assistance for clients, but the commitment to work for the disadvantaged does not define the nature of advocacy, arguing a cause, or the goals of advocacy, winning the argument.

Advocacy and Community Organization. Another persistent confusion is the equation of advocacy with community organization. This equation is the result, at least in part, of historical circumstance. Advocacy and community organization were intimately linked in the War on Poverty and the civil rights movement in the 1960s.

The flowering of the civil rights movement in the 1960s was a result of advocacy, legal advocacy which generated major court decisions, particularly in *Brown* v. *The Topeka Board of Education* (1954), the landmark school desegregation case. It became a popular civil rights strategy in the South to engage in community organization in order to rally groups to test laws and local practices, promoting conditions in which legal advocacy could be employed to secure civil rights.

For example, organizers would go into southern towns to organize people to stage a voter registration drive and to appear at the polls on election day. When they were turned away, the grounds were established for advocates to go into court and press voters' rights cases. In this way community organization was used to promote advocacy.

In the War on Poverty, advocacy was initially used to promote community organization. An important technique for building a grass roots organization was helping people secure welfare benefits or other assistance from public agencies. This demonstrated the value of participating in the local group. In the one case, advocacy served community organizing; in the other case, the opposite obtained. In both cases they were linked and this led to the false equation of advocacy, pleading a cause, with grass roots community organization, building a group.

Advocacy and Social Action, Change, and Reform. Just as "advocacy" has been confused with "advocacy for the disadvantaged," and has been equated with community organization, so it has been confused with social action, social change, and social reform. Advocacy is a form of social action, but it is not the only form.

Advocacy may be a way of achieving social change but in fact, advocacy is probably best suited to prevent social change. Even in the area of advocacy for the disadvantaged, the advocate who represents his client in administrative hearings is not asking for social change. He is arguing that everyone would follow the rules. This is an inherently conservative position, demanding that bureaucracies be less flexible, more rule bound and that discretion in dispensing benefits be curtailed in the interest of order or due process. The goal is not social change but conformity.

Social reform is a kind of social change, usually thought to be positive. If the use of advocacy is of limited value in achieving social change, its usefulness for achieving reform may be still less. As Edgar Z. Friedenberg (1971) observed of social reform through court action, it is like sailing into the wind: one may reach the destination by tacking back and forth, but the route is very long and indirect. Advocacy may be a useful tactic in struggles for social change or reform, but it is unlikely to provide an overall strategy and, in any case, cannot be equated with either.

Pulling the Tiger's Teeth: The Normative Advocate. On the one hand, the failure to adequately define advocacy has discouraged development of a reasonable perspective of its value and limits for social work. On the other hand, the manner in which the limits for the practice of social work advocacy are spelled out in the literature undermines the ethics not only of advocacy but of social work itself. These limits on practice are set forth by the NASW Ad Hoc Committee. in the resolution of two dilemmas — the problem of competing claims and the conflict between case and cause.

What does an advocate do when he discovers that his client's claim for goods or services is competing with other claims on behalf of people equally or more deserving? The Ad Hoc Committee (1969: 19) dealt with the problem in this way:

> Suppose, for instance, that a child welfare worker has a client, a child who is in need of care that can only be provided by a treatment institution with a limited intake. Does he then become a complete partisan in order to gain the admission of his client at the expense of other children in need? What of the public assistance worker seeking emergency clothing allowances for his clients when the demand is greater than the supply? Quite clearly, in either case the worker should be seeking to increase the real availability of the scarce resources. But while working toward this end, he faces the dilemma of competing individual claims. In such

a situation professional norms would appear to dictate that the relative urgency of the respective claims be weighed.

That these problems are real or that they can be soul-wrenching cannot be denied. But they pose a dilemma for the advocate only when the definition of advocate is transformed from his client's representative to "champion of the underdog." If it is understood that the role of the advocate is to argue his client's cause, there can be no basis for demanding that the advocate adjudicate his client's claims. A social worker might decide not to be an advocate for a client, but once he has, he cannot be his client's tough-minded champion so long as there is no one more deserving.

The second dilemma arises from the dichotomy of case and cause. Should the client's short-range benefit be sacrificed in the interest of long-term goals? The Ad Hoc Committee (1969: 19) answers this by saying,

> One cannot arbitrarily write off any action that may temporarily cause his client hardship if he believes the ultimate benefit of his action will outweigh any initial harm.

This is the same sort of mistake, made for the same sort of reasons discussed under the problem of competing claims. It substitutes the advocates's judgment for the client's decision. This does violence to the ethics of advocacy and of social work.

Client Self-Determination. A basic principle of professional social work is that the client has the right to self-determination, that the professional cannot decide on behalf of the client what he or she is to do. In traditional casework, when a client comes in with a problem, let us say, about her spouse, the caseworker is to be non-directive, to help the client express her feelings about her spouse and her conflicts with him and to explore the problems, both emotional and practical, in leaving or staying, balancing the risks and possible benefits of all the alternatives. What the worker is not to do as a professional is to decide for the client what she is to do, whether to stay or go. It is the client's right to decide this, the right to self-determination.

Honoring the commitment to this principle is frequently difficult for social workers. For example, our hypothetical caseworker might be employed by a social service agency sponsored by a religious organization that prohibits divorce; if agency policy prohibits employees from counselling divorce, the caseworker might be prevented from helping the client to explore the full range of alternatives. But, however strained by agency policy, the social worker's overriding obligation is to the client's right to self-determination. This dilemma is clearly not a conflict of professional principles but a conflict between professional principle and the conditions of employment (or religious principle).

Therefore, it is rather surprising to read that, if the advocate is faced with the problem of competing claims, "professional norms would appear to dictate that the relative urgency of the respective claims be weighed." Professional ethics would appear to dictate that it is the client's decision, and the client's decision alone, whether or not to press the claim. The same principle applies equally to the case/cause dilemma: it is the client's right, not the advocate's, to decide which course to follow.

The Deserving Poor and The Public Interest. The betrayal of the principle of client self-determination in the resolution of these two dilemmas entails two concepts that were roundly criticized by social workers long before the term "advocacy" gained its present currency.

One is the concept of the deserving poor, that those in need should be evaluated on the basis of who is most deserving (Mandell, 1975: 5-19). This is a notion that predates this century and social workers have been arguing for a long time that clients should qualify for assistance not on the basis of whether they are deserving but on the basis of whether they meet the eligibility requirements for assistance.

Historically, the judgment that a poor person was undeserving hinged on whether he was lazy or irreligious. The Ad Hoc Committee's distinction hinges upon the severity of the disability of the client. They both involve substituting the social worker's judgment for available eligibility criteria for who should receive benefits.

The concept of apportioning benefits on the basis of who is deserving gave way at the turn of the century to the idea that programs should be developed in the public interest (Hofstader, 1955). Embodied in the Ad Hoc Committee's idea that the advocate has to develop priorities among the needy is the notion that he operates not on behalf of any one client, but in the public interest.

People began to realize a decade ago that programs carried out "in the public interest" frequently best serve the interests of those who control the program. So, for example, urban renewal programs in the public interest often prove to be of benefit to downtown business interests and adverse to inner city ghetto interests (Davidoff, 1965).

Public welfare was historically seen as a program for the poor conceived of by citizens operating in the public interest; Piven and Cloward (1971) have recently argued that these programs were actually designed to prevent public disorder and maintain the work force. One may say these goals are in the public interest, but, given the oppressive nature of these programs, they seem to serve the interests of employers rather than those of the poor.

One of the reasons that many professions embraced the concept of advocacy is that it provided an alternative to the public interest fallacy. The concept of the public interest has been superseded by the concept of pluralism, that there are competing interests of different groups. The purpose of advocacy for the disadvantaged in a pluralistic society is to promote the interests of individuals and groups which have heretofore lacked the resources to make themselves heard.

Thus the Ad Hoc Committee's idea of limiting the efforts of advocates for the sake of the deserving poor or in the public interest are both ethically unsound and politically confused.

The foregoing is an introduction to some of the basic themes and problems of social work advocacy presented in the professional literature. To develop a fuller picture of social work advocacy and, particularly, of the way the concept has evolved over the last fifteen years, we shall next describe two examples. The first, welfare rights advocacy, typifies the practice of advocacy prevalent in the 1960s, advocacy linked to grass roots organization contributing to the development of a mass movement. The second, an advocacy system for the developmentally disabled, represents the style of this decade, advocacy as a governmental system. Together these two illustrate the shift from advocacy from below to advocacy from above.

EXAMPLES OF SOCIAL WORK ADVOCACY

ADVOCACY AND SOCIAL WORK IN THE WELFARE RIGHTS MOVEMENT

The Mobilization for Youth experience made the importance of advocacy very clear. The strategy was to improve conditions for low income people by providing opportunities for training, education, and jobs and to mobilize the resources of the ghetto community through community organization (Mobilization for Youth, 1961). But the problems of implementation were far more complex than had been anticipated (Marris and Rein, 1969). Not only were low income people the victims of rapacious businessmen (Caplovitz, 1963), employers (President's Commission on Income Maintenance, 1969: 24; Allen, 1975: 32), and landlords (Purcell and Specht, 1965; Sax and Heistand, 1967), but they were subject to equal or greater abuse from public programs on which they depended for support (Reich, 1963; 1964; 1965; Handler, 1966; tenBroek, 1966; Wald, 1965).

For example, someone on welfare might enroll in a job-training program which provided a subsidy for personal maintenance and transportation, only to find the family's public assistance check reduced by the amount of the subsidy. This obviously made it impossible for the person to attend the training program for which the money was provided since the subsidy had to be used for food which had previously been purchased with the now-reduced welfare grant.

MFY and War Against Poverty workers organizing in impoverished areas came across the same complaints repeatedly. A substantial amount of their time was spent in negotiating adequate arrangements so that people would not be penalized for taking advantage of the opportunities they were there to provide. Lawyers were called in to find ways around the endless regulations which hemmed in the poor; non-lawyers – social workers and others – gained considerable expertise as advocates in securing benefits from welfare agencies (Weissman, 1969).

These efforts became very important as a basis for contact with low income people and for organizing them. A fundamental problem of community organization is to create interest in the group, which is done by convincing people that they have something to gain. MFY and, subsequently, War on Poverty programs brought groups of people together around the deprivations they commonly suffered at the hands of the public assistance agencies by delivering concrete and immediate benefits to those who joined.

In New York City, welfare programs provided not only for basic "subsistence allowances," but for extra benefits called "special needs." Special needs grants might be for a refrigerator, a crib for a new child or other items which went beyond the provision of food and shelter. It was generally agency policy that application was to be made only in cases of great emergency, if the house burned down, for example.

The question arose, what is an emergency? If a family had no refrigeration and their welfare grant was barely sufficient to pay for food, much less an expensive appliance, then they needed help to get a refrigerator. Did they have to wait until their house burned down to get the help they needed? When organizers read the regulations, they found that special needs were not tied to catastrophe. It was just a matter of policy to keep expenditures for special needs at a minimum by not advising recipients that they were available. When recipients asked for special needs, they were granted, if only under the watchful eye of a welfare rights advocate.

The work of the War on Poverty and allied community organizers began by employing tactics of negotiation and advocacy in dealing with public agencies on behalf of welfare recipients. These tactics were well suited for the early tasks of recruiting individual members and provided groundwork for later efforts at mass organization. In one very famous example, a mass meeting was held at which mimeographed sheets listing all the categories of special needs were distributed and everyone in attendance was asked to check off their needs. The signed lists were subsequently presented en mass to the Welfare Department. Because of tactics like this, additional payments for special needs of more than ten million dollars per month were made to recipients in New York City (Grosser, 1973: 88).

The results of these welfare rights protests were not always positive. When welfare departments were called upon to eliminate discrimination in the administration of benefits they often did it by simply eliminating the benefits. This was especially true when benefits were dependent on local regulations rather than federal law, as was the case with special needs provisions. In fact, discretionary allowances for special needs were eliminated in many places as the availability of benefits became more widely known to recipients and the costs increased.

As organizers and advocates continued to challenge local welfare departments, both the extent of the problems and the strategy for action began to change. It was clear that local governmental units, dependent on property taxes and sensitive to local business interests, were unresponsive to problems of poverty and had inadequate financial and other resources for the poor. Attention turned to the federally mandated programs and strategy refocused on tactics that would lead to a guaranteed annual income.

There were significant shifts in organization which accompanied this shift in focus, and the National Welfare Rights Organization was formed. Grosser (1973: 88) described the shift from local, sporadic activities carried on by poverty workers to a national movement:

In the spring of 1966 the various discrete attempts at welfare-client organization came together for the first time in a coordinated national effort. This merging both reflected and was facilitated by the work of Richard Cloward and Frances Fox Piven, professors at the Columbia School of Social Work, who had published a major ideological statement on the movement. In their article, "A Strategy to End Poverty," Drs. Cloward and Piven (1966) set forth many of the theoretical, ideological, and programmatic issues surrounding the administration of welfare. Seeking to replace, rather than rehabilitate, the existing welfare system, they proposed a series of campaigns to be mounted by a coalition of civil rights groups, militant anti-poverty groups, and the poor. The activity of this coalition, they suggested, should be geared toward compelling the federal government to redistribute resources by some national guaranteed income plan, thus entirely eliminating the need for public welfare. The aim of ending the welfare system could be gained through the organization of welfare recipients to demand and receive their full entitlement under the law and through the organization of the eligible poor who were not receiving the benefits available to them under existing legislation. Estimates made by the authors and others indicated that such a campaign could double the welfare rolls and create a demand for higher budgets and supplementary benefits whose cost would mount to hundreds of millions of dollars. This, they claimed, would bankrupt the welfare system and enforce its replacement.

The politics of welfare became more complex. The arena of struggle shifted to Congress; the political decisions involved a major redistribution of wealth and, with it, power. Advocacy, in the sense of effective persuasion, was only a small part of the battle. The situation now demanded the technical skills needed to plan a guaranteed annual income program, and the political skills to mobilize power — grass roots organizing, developing a national organization, forming alliances with organized labor, civil rights organizations, and other humanitarian groups that supported welfare reform.

The implementation of a guaranteed annual income involved technical questions in the area of social planning, which the welfare rights advocates and their allies could not answer satisfactorily (Moynihan, 1973). This discouraged policy-makers, even those committed to change, and the power of the National Welfare Rights Organization was not sufficient to keep the effort alive.

There were many reasons why the NWRO was unable to mobilize adequate political support to force radical change. The very notion of basing a national movement on welfare recipients, particularly AFDC mothers who were the backbone of the organization, was faulty. Although some people are on welfare for long periods of time, the general stay is short, and those who are most likely to provide leadership are also most likely to stop being recipients most quickly.

This inherent instability of its political base was only one of the political problems which beset the welfare rights movement. Along with many other social protest movements, it disintegrated as the suppression of dissent increased in the 1970s.

The history of the welfare rights movement illustrates important issues about the role of both social workers and advocacy in social action. Advocacy for the disadvantaged played a significant part in the struggle for welfare reform. Advocacy was often productive as a specific tactic in a coherent strategy, but the usefulness of advocacy depended on the orchestration of many techniques in an organized social action approach to reform.

Social workers, both as theorists and as practitioners, played a major role in the welfare rights movement. They worked as organizers and as advocates, trained recipients as advocates, helped plan strategy, and later, through their professional organizations, supported the fight for a guaranteed annual income. However, social workers did not work alone, but as members of teams that included representatives of other professions. And social workers were involved on both sides of the struggle; one early attack was on the provision of casework counseling by social workers in lieu of money and other direct benefits. Ultimately this lead to Social Security amendments separating public assistance and social services.

For better or worse, welfare rights organizing and the welfare rights movement were inextricably tied to the profession of social work and to its traditions.

DESIGNING AN ADVOCACY SYSTEM FOR
THE DEVELOPMENTALLY DISABLED

Developmental Disabilities (DD) is a legal category, not a medical one, which includes mental retardation, cerebral palsy, epilepsy, autism, and some other less known central nervous system disorders. It is the most favored category of the despised disabilities. In California, over $800 million per year is spent on DD programs. A great amount of this money is spent on custodial care in state hospitals, but many other services are also subsidized. In fact, a survey (Kalmanoff, et al, 1977: 7) of the services available is like a complete catalogue of services that social planners can think of to deal with social problems.

This is not to say that services are adequate, but only that they are provided to some degree throughout the state — always, it appears, to a lesser extent than needed. A measure of the inadequacy of services is that the state is now investigating over a hundred unexplained deaths in state hospitals for the DD, some of which may have resulted from neglect or outright brutality.

In 1975, Congress passed Public Law 94-103; Section 113 mandated a statewide advocacy system for the developmentally disabled. The law requires: (1) that the system be established by October, 1977, as a precondition to the further receipt of any federal funds for DD; (2) that the advocacy system have independent authority from the state to pursue any appropriate course, presumably including the authority to sue the state; (3) that in order to prevent conflict of interest, those involved in delivery of services may not be involved in operating the advocacy system.

Rolf Williams is a professional social worker. He was executive Secretary of the California State DD Council, a state planning board consisting of a number of public officials and private citizens appointed by the governor. Williams has cerebral palsy and is one of the few people afflicted with a developmental disability who has a significant role in planning or providing social services.

Last year, Williams sought consultation with one of the authors. He explained that there were several very different groups interested in the federal advocacy funds. On one end of the spectrum was Citizen Advocates, part of a national movement of zealous parents and volunteers, whose concept of advocacy (Wolfensberger, 1972: 72) calls for volunteers to work on a one-to-one basis with developmentally disabled people. This program has been frequently characterized as a "big brother" program (Gilbert and Specht, 1976: 288), and the idea of citizen advocates playing Brager's (1968) tough-minded partisans stretches the imagination. At the other end of the spectrum was a group of attorneys trying to set up a specialized legal service (Haggerty, 1976; Herr, 1976) for the DD.

Confronted with competition between advocacy programs, the typical solution adopted in other states has been to give everyone some piece of the action, the size of the shares varying with political strength. Williams wanted to do something different, to create a coherent advocacy system. He felt both groups were seriously limited in their approaches. Both were very insulated and neither reached the vast population of the DD who were not already actively involved in the existing services.

Among those not reached were those most in need, the minority and poverty populations (International Technical Services, Inc.). The families of the DD in these populations do not have the time or the sophistication that enables middle-class families to seek out services; social or cultural stigma sometimes prevents them from even acknowledging the nature of the disability.

Williams was also concerned about the fact that services were provided to the DD almost exclusively by specialized agencies. He favored developing access to "generic" social services both for economic reasons and as a strategy to reduce isolation and stigma. In very practical terms, this means that if a swimming pool is needed for recreation, an advocate's task might be to assure that the YMCA or the city recreation department make provision for the use of existing pools by the DD rather than to force the construction of specially built pools.

The jobs of outreach to the unserved DD and of establishing programs in generic agencies involve advocacy as part of a community organization effort. There is very little of that in the state; advocacy efforts have generally been turned inward, to existing programs for the DD on behalf of those already participating in such programs.

Williams had watched with interest for several years a special project run by United Cerebral Palsy (Hansen, 1975) which used advocacy as a part of a campaign to involve Chicanos in programs for the DD. The UCP program employed a model of advocacy developed by the author and implemented by one of his students in a community organizing campaign. This model is based on the premise that advocacy is the use of persuasion to win a favorable decision in a conflict between two parties over valued resources. The conflict is decided in an adversarial system; if the advocate knows the elements of the system and their significance, his role as an advocate is clarified and his chances of winning — the goal of advocacy — are enhanced. In this model, advocacy is understood as a technique for winning conflicts and nothing more; the technique can be used as a tactic in community organizing without confusing organizing and advocacy.

Williams hoped that somehow the virtues of the various approaches — Citizen Advocates' use of lay volunteers, the technical expertise of the legal service proponents, and the community organizing and advocacy principles operative in the UCP project — could be combined to develop a statewide system of advocacy.

A small consultant team was assembled whose members were skilled in social work, law, planning, and social sciences. All had independently studied advocacy in various settings for a number of years; none had any significant prior experience in the field of DD. It was felt that this last was a positive quality in that none of the consultants had any stake in any existing program; conflict of interest is rampant in the DD field.

The team began without preconception of what the system should be, but with a shared concept of advocacy as a technique rather than a program which was presented (Approach Associates, 1976) as part of the contract for services. The consultants worked with the California DD Council's Advocacy Committee which included representatives from all the conflicting groups. The first step was to obtain agreement that the basis for advocacy funding would be problemsolving.

A survey (Kalmanoff, et al, 1976) was made of existing DD services and advocacy needs and activities. It was agreed that there was in fact a great deal of advocacy activity throughout the state and that with the amount of money available that it would not be wise to set up a program de novo to do all the advocacy needed. The result was a plan (Kalmanoff, et al, 1977) to establish a small agency to provide training and evaluation, to coordinate ongoing activities, to identify problems and to contract with new or existing programs to address the problems.

By this means a number of difficulties were averted and some positive tendencies promoted. By contracting for services it was assured that the advocacy funds would not be consumed by supporting groups in other than their advocacy activities. Secondly, since any one group might have the capability of doing a part but not all of a job, consortiums might form among existing programs and/or existing programs might be encouraged to seek new resources among generic agencies. Third, the plan promoted healthy competition that would encourage careful planning and improvement of services; this was reinforced by the adoption of a policy of refunding only two thirds of the projects each year.

By establishing the definition of advocacy by contract and conditioning funding on solution of specific problems, the planners prevented conflict among groups which would have interfered with planning of the system. Whenever a committee member attempted to argue the advantage of, say, legal services over citizen advocates, he was reminded that the plan would only specify the type of problem to be addressed; after the system was established, proposals could be entertained from anyone who wanted to address a problem and then would be the time to argue the merits of one approach or another.

Although the planning of the system was accomplished virtually without struggle, the real fight is shaping up over implementation — who will control the system. It has been proposed that the agency be established as an independent entity with a board of directors appointed initially by the DD Council, subsequent vacancies to be filled by the incumbent board.

This proposal has met resistance from many sides. Some members of the DD Council have objected, wishing to preserve the right to fill vacancies. Other attempts have been made to subsume the agency under various state mandated advocacy programs or other ongoing state agencies such as the Public Defender's Office or the Consumer Affairs Agency. Some of these attacks on the protection and advocacy agency's autonomy have been repulsed by virtue of statutory provisions for independent authority to pursue legal action against the state and prohibitions against conflict of interest. These federal regulations may be sufficient to finally assure agency autonomy, but it seems clear that the nature of the advocacy performed may be determined less by how the system is designed than by whom it is controlled.

ADVOCACY IN THE 1960s AND 1970s

These two examples illustrate the differences between advocacy as it was practiced in the last decade and in this. In the sixties, advocacy attracted attention among social workers as a tactic in grass roots community organization. Later, it helped foster a mass movement which increased awareness of the relationship between the distribution of power and resources on the one hand and the existence of poverty and of social welfare programs that perpetuated poverty on the other. This mass movement was a major factor in the effort to develop a guaranteed annual income which would have required a major reorganization of many of our governmental, economic and social institutions.

In the seventies the trend is towards advocacy systems rather than programs. But advocacy is useful only when there is a shared formulation of the problem, determined by a constitutency with a recognized self-interest. Initially, the enthusiasm for advocacy stemmed from its potential as a technique to challenge institutions and policies, so it may prove counterproductive to develop government controlled advocacy systems. When programs pursued the interests of the disadvantaged aggressively, there were bitter fights over support for them from the federal government (Grosser, 1973: 28). The price of stability in funding has been a decreased impact on welfare institutions.

Now the government is preempting the field entirely. The governmental advocacy system is likely to share the weaknesses of the welfare and social service systems it is supposed to challenge: minimal level of support; sacrifice of recipient interests to the interests of those who determine policy; and institutional sanctions to prevent the use of advocacy to strengthen organizational power of the poor and deprived, which was the greatest contribution of advocacy in the sixties.

THE FUTURE OF SOCIAL WORK ADVOCACY

RESEARCH

Much of the discussion about advocacy has been exhortative, to convince social workers that it is their duty to be advocates, or has concerned the ethical dilemmas (really the political problems) that social workers face if they decide to do advocacy. There has been very little attention paid to gathering systematic information which will help advocates do their work. Two types of research are needed: research which will outline the nature of problems which social work advocates can profitably address themselves to, an advocacy agenda; and, secondly, research about the ways in which advocacy can be practiced most effectively. (We are not considering here the research that must be done in the practice of advocacy per se, but research about advocacy.)

An Advocacy Agenda. A model for an advocacy agenda for social workers can be found in the work of the sociologists Carlin, Howard, and Messinger (1966), done at the time when the War Against Poverty's legal services program began. They surveyed and mapped the range of problems involving civil litigation which could benefit the poor.

The work of Carlin and his associates really concerned the activities of lawyers on behalf of the poor, so it has limited use for social workers as advocates; and since many of the problems have been altered due to legal services and other reform efforts in the past decade, its initial value is still further reduced. Nonetheless, it serves as a model of programmatic analysis and direction for advocates to plan their efforts and maximize the use of their resources.

Effective Advocacy. The second problem that requires research is how advocacy activities can be organized in a way that is likely to prove most effective. Some preliminary work by Briar which was never carried through suggests some ways in which research could help shape advocacy practice. There was a general feeling that the appellate process in public assistance programs mandated by the federal government was really a form of red tape in which the odds were stacked against the recipient. Briar's (1967: 29) research, which was confirmed by others, indicated this was not so:

> A substantial proportion of recipients who obtain fair hearings win their appeals. And the recipient's chances of winning are doubled if he brings someone along to represent him. The recipient can select anyone he wants as his representative; rarely does he bring a lawyer, but the hearings are informal and a lawyer's skills and knowledge are not necessary to represent the client.

Briar found that fair hearings were a severely neglected opportunity for effective non-lawyer advocacy. Less than one-tenth of one percent of all recipients took advantage of fair hearings even though the rate at which welfare officials erred against clients, creating grounds for appeal, was staggeringly high. The failure of clients to appeal illegal rulings was surprising since the stakes were very high, involving food, shelter and other necessities. Briar concluded that very few recipients appealed because most did not know about the availability of fair hearings.

This one small piece of research had important implications for social work advocacy. First, the success rate demonstrated that it was a fertile ground for advocacy; second, the relatively low use of easy appeal procedures which could greatly augment benefits indicated a need for attention in this area; and, finally, the ignorance of clients indicated that one of the first steps for social work advocates should involve a massive campaign to make clients aware of the procedure.

This is not the only substantive area in which research needs to be done. Nor is this the only type of research that needs to be done. For example, Blecher (1971) has studied different ways in which advocates can deliver services. He evaluated three models, one where there were advocates assigned to an ongoing agency program, a second where there was a distinct advocacy unit, and a third where advocacy services were provided by an independent contractor. He concluded that the last approach produced the best results.

There are many other questions of an organizational nature which need attention. Should advocacy services be provided by lawyers, social workers, non-professionals, or some combination of all three? How can advocates avoid becoming exhausted very quickly, since advocacy programs are marked by the prevalence of what they refer to as the "burn out" syndrome which decimates their ranks. These and a variety of other questions about the delivery of advocacy services can usefully employ the time and attention of researchers.

The future of social work advocacy seems dependent less immediately upon research than on clarification of what advocacy is and of the context in which it is to be performed. Critical issues must be addressed in three areas: the theory of advocacy, the politics of social work, and the theory of justice.

THEORY

Theory of Advocacy. The role of the advocate must be distinguished from the concept of the good social worker set forth in the NASW Ad Hoc Committee's (1969) formulation. The social worker as an advocate cannot weigh competing claims, cannot sacrifice his client's interests for any cause. The Ad Hoc Committee's formulation must be rejected. The advocate can only represent his client's interests as the client defines them. When the social worker stops doing that, he stops being the advocate for that client (Hoshino, 1971).

At issue here is not how a social worker-advocate should act, but whether or not social workers are to be advocates for the disadvantaged. The commitment to conflict strategies to accomplish client's goals depends on decisions about the relationship of social work practice to the political order.

The Politics of Social Work. The politics of social work in the last twenty years has been subject to severe reinterpretation. Political historians, inside the profession and outside, have argued that public welfare (Piven & Cloward, 1971), mental health (Foucault, 1965), and correctional programs (Rusche and Kirchheimer, 1968; Platt, 1969) are institutions used to regulate the poor, maintain the labor force and suppress political dissent. That the social worker who is an agent of these programs is acting as partisan of the disadvantaged or champion of the underdog is hardly a tenable notion.

Just taking up the cudgel of advocacy does not change this — advocacy is only a technique and cannot answer the questions of what or whom to advocate for. The community organizing of the opportunity theorists has been characterized, like the case work of the tradition that it challenged, as victim-blaming (Galper, 1975). Critics have pointed out that there is unequal distribution not just of opportunities but of rewards. Furthermore, advocacy itself has been criticized (Piven, 1970) for diverting attention and energy from political efforts to gain needed resources to petty quarrels over meaningless projects.

It seems clear that advocacy as a technique can be useful as an aspect of a program for social change, but only when the agenda for social change is formulated. As a first step, a more sophisticated theory of justice must be developed as a basis for social work practice.

Theory of Justice. The role of social workers as agents of repressive social institutions, the inexorable frustration of the needs and aspirations of the disadvantaged, the unending exploitation of the unfortunate — these are grim facts, painful to look at. They do not proceed from the ruthlessness of social workers, from a failure to respond positively to the sense of injustice or from a reluctance to operationalize theories of justice. It may well be that the prevailing theories of justice are inadequate; indeed, they seem to have broken down.

Although Americans have committed themselves to equality of opportunities and to racial equality, we are witnessing the way in which these two principles can be mutually contradictory. Affirmative action quotas for minorities are being attacked because they are based on principles of racial discrimination. But without affirmative action it seems that there will be no way of assuring that minorities begin to achieve equal representation. Either way, we are involved in a violation of one of the basic principles of justice, equality. How can we resolve this dilemma?

A solution may lie in Rawls' recently published *A Theory of Justice* (1971), a revolutionary contribution to legal philosophy. In an excellent review of this work Lewis (1973) described Rawls' approach to the problem of discrimination to achieve equality for minorities and the poor:

> In general, all social primary goods, liberty and opportunity, income, and wealth and the bases of self-respect are to be distributed equally unless an unequal distribution of any or all of these goods is to the advantage of the least favored.

Lewis, attempting to apply Rawls' principles of justice as fairness to social work, makes a strong argument for social workers to adopt the principle of fairness enumerated by Rawls as a standard for practice, replacing standards of practice (normative) or from practice (the best of what we do). This standard for practice would be an instrument for measuring our actions based on an ideal of justice. The need for such an instrument increases as we move from a passive role (employing the talking cure) to an active one (employing advocacy and other forms of social action). A standard for practice may help avert the kind of harm which social workers and others in the helping professions can cause when they set out with warm hearts and conflicting commitments.

PRACTICE AND TRAINING

The subject of practicing advocacy and training advocates deserves considerable discussion, but the major questions about advocacy in social work have not been how to do advocacy but when and where and why. This is not so much because social workers are adept at advocacy, but that setting and purpose are prior questions. As has been indicated, social work has generally been practiced in an agency setting, supported by government funds or private charity. Thus, the sanction and support for social work has generally been from the very institutions and elements of society which are most likely to be adversaries of the poor and the oppressed. So long as such agencies remain the locus for social work support, the potential for advocacy is limited to accomplishing things which will not seriously offend those controlling the funds.

Under these circumstances it is a matter of indifference whether social workers are good or bad at advocacy since their goals are defined not by their clients' interests but by their employers'. Again, this does not arise from a lack of concern about the causes of poverty. When power elite theories (Mills, 1956; Domhoff, 1967) are presented in graduate classes for professional social workers, they seldom object to them. When the ideas that public welfare, mental health or correctional programs are institutions used to regulate the poor, maintain the labor force and suppress political dissent are examined, students are often in enthusiastic agreement; and those who are employed in the programs being criticized are often among their most vociferous critics.

Why, then, are students willing to participate in institutions and activities that they believe to be oppressive? Two answers are given: one is that they need the work and the other is that they do not know what else to do. Obviously, the starting point for social work advocacy practice and training is the search for new settings. There are very few ways to generate financial support and at the same time represent client interests unfettered by agency constraints. Some social workers do engage in private practice, but they are usually therapists.

One experimental setting that offers some promise has been developed as a part of the graduate program in social work at California State University, Sacramento. A student has been allowed to develop an advocacy field placement associated with a law collective. Her task is to prepare social work documents, to provide testimony and to perform related tasks which are commissioned by the collective's clients.

There are a variety of circumstances under which social work reports are used — divorce and custody cases, juvenile and adult presentence evaluations, to name a few. One of this student's major activities has been the development of alternative sentencing reports. The information available to judges often comes from probation officers who, from lack of time, pro-prosecution orientations, the need to anticipate and accommodate to the idiosyncracies of the judge for whom the report is prepared, and a desire to protect their agency from criticism by law-and-order taxpayers, often prepare reports in which information is erroneous and in which the sentencing recommendations are extremely harsh. Although the reports are supposed to be the result of independent fact-finding by a neutral professional, they are not, in reality, unbiased. The student's job, recognizing the adversarial nature of the proceeding, is to prepare an alternative report which as skillfully as possible presents the case for the most desirable sentence for her client.

This placement doesn't solve all the problems of social workers as advocates. One of the concerns of social workers has been to establish themselves as independent professionals. A major issue is that they have served as handmaidens to doctors for many years in mental health clinics. A placement like this, and in fact, many activities which occupy social work advocates, threaten to turn them from junior psychiatrists into junior lawyers. Since lawyers have not proved more successful in solving the major social problems of our times than psychiatrists, this tradeoff is not particularly desirable.

The student's assignment is not simply to provide a service to the law collective but to establish an independent business where she will be paid on a fee-for-service basis. The law collective to which she is assigned supports this approach and has publicized her services. Other attorneys have shown an interest in her work and the demand for her services is growing. Although forensic services have been performed for a long time by psychiatrists and psychologists, this is an unfamiliar area for social workers, and each new step has involved new discoveries.

Despite the obvious subservience to lawyers, the approach suggested here has some promise. It clarifies the social worker's relationship to the client. It can be fee-generating and it provides an alternative to the traditional agency-bound activities of social workers. It is perhaps this last factor which makes this example so important. If advocacy is to succeed it will require social workers to invent new ways of working with clients in order to break loose from the traditional constraints which prevent social workers from performing advocacy in an effective way.

Other assignments have been developed at CSUS which involve advocacy. The university is located in the capital of the largest state in the country, where the potential for legislative advocacy is second only to Washington, D.C. Systematic attempts have been made to place students in positions related to the work of the legislature and the governor's office, with legislative committees and with public interest lobbying groups. These are not novel assignments, but are relatively ignored possibilities for social work positions, promoting involvement in the formulation of public policy and in the legislative process.

SUMMARY

Advocacy is nothing more than a technique. Technical innovations are inadequate to remedy the social problems which gave impetus to advocacy in the last fifteen years — poverty, racism and related deprivations. Nothing less than fundamental reorganization of American society will do. Unless we intend to continue our drift toward a major social disaster, we must develop a society which will operate without poverty and racism, something that American society as it is now constituted will not do.

Since a new vision of society must entail a substantial redistribution of resources and other values, a concept of justice must be adopted which will facilitate this redistribution. Problems of political theory and justice are not simply technological issues. They are issues that involve values, commitments and desires. They involve the entire spectrum of questions about how to organize human existence.

It is true that advocacy is a better technique for promoting social, political and economic change than the technique for solving social problems which has most frequently been used by social workers. Advocacy should be taught and practiced. But only by developing the context in which advocacy can be freely practiced and by formulating the goals for which the advocate should strive, can teaching the technique of advocacy have significant impact on the problems we need to solve.

REFERENCES

Ad Hoc Committee On Advocacy. (1969) "The Social Worker as Advocate: Champion of Social Victims." *Social Work* 14,2 (April): 16-22.

Alinsky, S. D. (1946) *Reveille for Radicals.* Chicago: University of Chicago Press.

Allen, H. L. (1975) "A Radical Critique of Federal Work and Manpower Programs, 1933–1974." Pp 445-457 in B. R. Mandell (ed.) *Welfare in America: Controlling the "Dangerous Classes."* Englewood Cliffs: Prentice Hall.

Approach Associates. (1976) *A Proposal for Planning the Development of a Statewide Advocacy Program for the Developmentally Disabled.* Oakland, Ca.: Approach Associates.

Blecher, E. M. (1971) *Advocacy Planning for Urban Research.* New York: Praeger.

Brager, G. and H. Specht. (1967) "Social Action and the Poor: Prospects, Problems and Strategies." Pp 133-150 in G. Brager and F. Purcell (eds.) *Community Action Against Poverty.* New Haven: College and University Press.

––– and S. Barr. (1967) "Perceptions and Reality: the Poor Man's View of Social Services." Pp 72-80 in G. Brager and F. Purcell (eds.) *Community Action Against Poverty.* New Haven: College and University Press.

––– (1968) "Advocacy and Political Behavior." *Social Work* 13, 2 (April: 5-15

Briar, S. (1966) "Welfare From Below: Recipients' View of the Public Welfare System." *California Law Review* 54 (May): 370-385.

––– (1967) "The Current Crisis in Social Casework." Pp 19-33 in *Social Work Practice.* Columbus: National Conference on Social Welfare.

––– (1974) "The Future of the Profession." *Social Work* 19,5 (September): 514-518.

Brown v. The Topeka Board Of Education. (1954) 347 U.S. 483.

Cahn, E. (1964) *The Sense of Injustice.* Bloomington: Indiana University Press.

Caplovitz, D. (1963) *The Poor Pay More.* New York: The Free Press.

Carlin, J., J. Howard and S. Messinger. (1966) "Civil Justice and the Poor." *Law and Society* 1, 1 (February): 17-21.

Cloward, R. and L. Ohlin. (1961) *Delinquency and Opportunity.* Glencoe, Ill.: Free Press.

――― and I. Epstein. (1965) "Private Social Welfare's Disengagement from the Poor: The Case of Family Adjustment Agencies." Pp 623-644 in M. Zald (ed.) *Social Welfare Institutions*. New York: Wiley.

――― and F. F. Piven. (1966) "The Weight of the Poor: A Strategy to End Poverty." *The Nation* (May 2): 510-517.

――― and F. F. Piven. (1967) "Birth of a Movement." *The Nation* (May 8): 582-588.

Cohen, N. (1958) *Social Work in the American Tradition*. New York: Dryden Press.

Davidoff, P. (1965) "Advocacy and Pluralism in Planning." *Journal of the American Institute of Planners* 21 (November): 331-338.

Domhoff, W. (1967) *Who Rules America?* Englewood Cliffs: Prentice Hall.

Donovan, J. C. (1967) *The Politics of Poverty*. New York: Pegasus Press.

Foucault, M. (1965) *Madness and Civilization*. New York: Pantheon.

Friedenberg, E. Z. (1971) "The Side Effects of the Legal Process." Pp 37-54 in R. P. Wolff (ed.) *The Rule of Law*. New York: Simon and Shuster.

Galper, J. H. (1975) *The Politics of Social Services*. Englewood Cliffs: Prentice Hall.

Gilbert, N. and H. Specht. (1976) "Advocacy and Professional Ethics." *Social Work* 21, 4 (July): 288-293.

Grosser, C. F. (1965) "Community Development Programs Serving the Urban Poor." *Social Work* 10,3 (July): 15-21.

――― (1973) *New Directions in Community Organization*. New York: Praeger.

Haggerty, D. E. (1976) "Legal Advocacy." Amicus 1,4 (May): 11-13.

Handler, J. (1966) "Controlling Official Behavior in Welfare Administration." California Law Review 54: 479.

Hansen, R. (1975) *Child Advocacy Project: Seven Reports on Component Processes*. Palo Alto: UCPA of San Mateo/Santa Clara.

Herr, S. (1976) *Advocacy Under the Developmental Disabilities Act: Summary of a Discussion Paper on Implications of Section 113, PL 94-103*. Washington, D.C.: DHEW, Office of Human Development, Developmental Disabilities Office.

Hofstader, R. (1955) *The Age of Reform*. New York: Vintage Books.

Hoshino, G. (1971) "The Public Welfare Worker: Advocate or Adversary?" *Public Welfare* 29,1 (January): 35-41.

International Technical Services, Inc. (n.d.) *Prevention Services for Developmental Disabilities in Urban and Rural Poverty Areas: An Assessment of Needs*. San Rafeal: ITS, Inc. (mimeo).

Johnson, E., Jr. (1974) *Justice and Reform: The Formative Years of the OEO Legal Services Program*. New York: Russel Sage Foundation.

Kahn, E. J., S. B. Kamerman and B. McGowan. (1972) *Child Advocacy*. New York: Columbia University School of Social Work.

Kalmanoff, A., H. Kutchins, M. Aaronson and S. Dudley. (1976) *Preliminary Findings and Options Regarding the California Protection and Advocacy System*. Oakland, Ca.: Approach Associates.

―――, et al. (1977) *The Plan for the California Protection and Advocacy System for the Developmentally Disabled*. Oakland, Ca.: Approach Associates.

Knickmeyer, R. (1972) "A Marxist Approach to Social Work." *Social Work* 17, 2 (July): 58-65.

Lampman, R. J. (1966) "Ends and Means in the War on Poverty." in L. Fishman (ed.) *Poverty and Affluence.* New Haven: Yale University Press.

Lewis, H. (1973) "Rawls' 'A Theory of Justice.' " *Social Work* 18,4 (July): 113-116.

Mandell, B. R. (ed.) (1975) *Welfare in America: Controlling the "Dangerous Classes."* Englewood Cliffs: Prentice Hall.

Manser, E. (ed.) (1975) *Family Advocacy, A Manual for Action.* New York: Family Service Association of America.

Marris, P. and M. Rein. (1969) *Dilemmas of Social Reform.* New York: Atherton Press.

Mills, C. W. (1956) *The Power Elite.* New York: Oxford University Press.

Mobilization For Youth. (1961) *A Proposal for the Prevention and Control of Delinquency by Expanding Opportunities.* New York: Mobilization For Youth, Inc.

Moore, N. (1970) "The Practice of Community Organization." Pp 226-243 in R. Klenk and R. Ryan (eds.) *The Practice of Social Work.* Belmont: Wadsworth Publishing Co.

Morris, R., et al. (eds.) (1971) "Goldmark, Josephine Clara (1877-1950)," *Encyclopedia of Social Work* 16,1: 478-479. New York: NASW.

Moynihan, D. P. (1969) *Maximum Feasible Understanding.* New York: Free Press.

Piven, F. F., et al. (1970) "Whom Does the Advocate Planner Serve?" *Social Policy I,* 1 (May, June): 32-37 and I,2 (July, August): 33-42.

––– and R. Cloward. (1971) *Regulating the Poor.* New York: Vintage.

Platt, A. M. (1969) *The Child Savers.* Chicago, University of Chicago Press.

President's Commission On Income Maintenance. (1969) *Poverty Amid Plenty.* Washington, D.C.: U. S. Government Printing Office.

Purcell, F. and H. Specht. (1965) "The House on Sixth Street," *Social Work* 10,4 (October): 69-76.

Rawls, J. (1971) *A Theory of Justice.* Cambridge: Harvard University Press.

Reich, C. (1963) "Midnight Welfare Searches and the Social Security Act." *Yale Law Journal* 72: 1347.

––– (1964) "The New Property." *Yale Law Journal* 73:733.

––– (1965) "Individual Rights and Social Welfare: The Emerging Social Issues." *Yale Law Journal* 74: 1245.

Rein, M. (1970) "Social Work in Search of a Radical Profession." *Social Work* 15,2 (April): 13-28.

Richan, W. (1977) "Serving Clients and Society Simultaneously." *Social Work* 22,1 (January): 64-65.

Rusche, G. and O. Kirchheimer. (1968) *Punishment and Social Structure.* New York: Russell and Russell.

Sax, J. L. and F. J. Hiestand. (1967) "Slumlordism as a Tort." *Michigan Law Review* 65: 869.

Schlesinger, A. M., Jr. (1957) *The Age of Roosevelt: The Crisis of the Old Order, 1919-1933.* Boston: Houghton.

Shottland, C. I. (ed.) (1967) *The Welfare State*. New York: Harper and Row.

tenBroek, J. (1966) *The Law of the Poor*. San Francisco: Chandler.

Titmuss, R. (1958) *Essays on the Welfare State*. London: Unwin University Books.

Wald, P. (1965) *Law and Poverty, 1965*. Washington, D. C.: National Conference on Law and Poverty.

Weissman, H. H. (ed.) (1969) *Justice and the Law in the Mobilization for Youth Experience*. New York: Association Press.

Wolfensberger, W. (1972) *Citizen Advocacy for the Handicapped, Impaired, and Disadvantaged: An Overview*. Washington, D.C., GPO, DHEW Publication No. ((S) 72-42.

2

ADVOCACY AND THE PUBLIC INTEREST LAWYER

Marshall Patner

A JUST SOCIETY

The lawyer by trade (or profession) is an advocate, a "mouthpiece" for one side or the other in a dispute. Out of resolution of these disputes in courts the law moves along, sometimes bringing about reform. Meanwhile, the job of the lawyer as advocate of the client's interest remains. It is in this indirect way that the lawyer-advocate contributes toward a just society.

Justice Holmes (1881) viewed the law as a method of dealing with society:

> The life of the law has not been logic; it has been experience. The felt necessities of the time, the prevalent moral and political theories, institutions of public policy, avowed or unconscious, even the prejudices which judges share with their fellow men, have had a good deal more to do than the syllogism in determining the rules by which men should be governed. The law embodies the story of a nation's development through many centuries, and it cannot be dealt with as if it contained only the axioms and corrollaries of a book of mathematics. (Holmes, 1881: 1)

Thought of in this way, the law is seen as a method — and as such those trained in the law are traditionally prepared for an adversary system, one in which "you represent one side, I'll represent the other — and we'll let the judge and jury decide." Persons trained in this way do not debate abstract principles of what is a "just society."

The law is a method of problem solving. Excellent texts on ethics generally deal with only what conduct is allowed to lawyers (Bishkin and Stone, 1972). Courses in ethics taught in law schools went begging, at least at most schools, until the bar examiners, in the post-Watergate wave of morality, began to pose questions about legal ethics; but still, legal ethics deal with what a lawyer should or shouldn't do, and not with the concept of a just society.

Yet lawyers do have their own concepts of a just society. They do not, however, get those concepts fed to them in law school, because professors in law schools do not generally take sides or directly attempt to shape thinking on such questions. If one student wants to represent the environmentalists against the polluters, or (in this commercial era) more likely the other way around, his choice will come from a course background based on materials attacking such problems from the side of the plaintiff and of the defendant. The law school course would be rare that would dwell on an alternative not raised by the parties to the litigation but which might produce a more just society. In law practice the lawyer generally follows the client's interest, and lawyers tend to be identified quickly with one side or the other of the fence. Since lawyers do not raise issues without a client's cause, the law, as a profession, plays a dependent role; it reflects social values, shaping them only as the result of the decision in a controversy between two parties, the resolution of which has a spill-over effect on society.

A stranger to the law, looking to find its conception of its role in attaining a just society, might well form this opinion: the law's role is to keep the means to social change open and such means are to be found in fair procedure; no more is necessary. The lawyers can think this way because out of the resolution of disputes within the adversary system for or against their clients comes decisions that serve as guidelines for future conduct in society.

In this context, the law school experience is a good way to train public interest lawyers, although this point of view is not common. In addition to its method of attacking a problem from the vantage point of opposing litigants — with whatever limitations this approach may also carry — the student, and fledgling public interest lawyer, is exposed to myriad precedents to be overcome in the field and to the minds of fellow students who will be their opponents in these confrontations.

Thus, lawyers feel that they contribute to a just society by representing the interests of their clients — advocating or defending their causes. Lawyers in public interest practice, presumptuously, as they will agree, seek a more direct role. They seek a just society directly through their advocacy. To these lawyers, their skills and techniques — their services — should be available to protect precious natural resources from despoliation, improve conditions for the poor, foster integration, compel public officials to perform their duties (in providing housing, education, employment, transportation, and administering justice), and to influence other broad issues of social concern. But if public interest lawyers presume that they can recognize important issues, they are merely seeking to counterbalance the lawyers who have traditionally helped to maintain the right of their clients to quietly continue their long-established patterns of conduct on the "other side" of those issues.

Except for the involvement of public interest lawyers, these issues might not be raised or, if raised, might not be fully litigated or otherwise pursued in the normal course of private law practice. This is because a private lawyer often reaches the point when the client's best interest is served by settlement or litigation, as a matter of dollars-and-cents weighed against risk. It is not common, however, for a public interest case to be settled instead of litigated. The interests taken on are generally deeply entrenched and therefore change must be accomplished by court decree. This is consistent with the public interest lawyer's concept of the ideal client's interest: the achievement of the ruling with the broadest, positive effect on social change and in the interest of some segment of society that includes but is not limited to the client. The public interest lawyer, therefore, must break the mold of ordinary client representation, and his ideal client is therefore the person or group with such an objective in mind.

RECTIFYING INJUSTICE

You may have your belief of what is just, and I may differ with you. Unless our legislature has seen fit to pass a law that fits precisely to our concern, we will have room to differ, and to do so is our right in a democracy. But in a democracy neither of us can force our viewpoint on the rest of society, not without a court ruling that will affect the others.

The law is at once a good and a poor avenue to rectify injustice. It is good because as a system it lends itself well to resolution of specific conflicts, at least within many situations. It is not so good because it is expensive, time-consuming, and depends a great deal on the quality of the lawyer representing the aggrieved and on other limitations inherent in any human system. It is poor in that it is not set up to take on broad societal causes but contributes to them only as a spillover from resolution of specific cases. Moreover, the entire process seems to work on an ad hoc basis.

When the system works, it works very well indeed. But it is most often put into motion in response to some evil; it is rarely used to anticipate and head off problems. That function is supposedly left to the legislature, and even the executive — but like the advocate in the courts, they too seem to act responsively.

An illustration is the case popularly known through Anthony Lewis's (1964) *Gideon's Trumpet.* The decision in this one case had a ripple effect on all similar cases. The handwritten petition to the United States Supreme Court of Gideon, a destitute Florida prisoner who had been convicted in a trial without the aid of counsel, resulted in the award of a new trial. The broad effect of the decision, however, was that the states across the country had to provide indigent defendants counsel in criminal cases. This ruling was applied first to the most serious, and later to all criminal cases, affecting most of the criminal litigation in the country. And the principle of the Gideon case is being argued as to civil cases as well.

The system, however, is slow to adapt to changing societal demands. Courts, for example, are not easily accessible to litigants trying to save precious national resources (Stone, 1974) or to make corporations socially responsible (Stone, 1975). This is because the system does not allow for intervention of lawyers into causes in which the issues they want to raise are not being litigated. Since courts address only those problems brought to them by litigants, there is another problem: inadequate legal services, not only for the poor, but for those just above the line set for provision of free counsel. If the members of these vast classes of people do not have representation, the issues that directly affect them do not get litigated, while those of the affluent do. Further, although lawyers do represent the interests of community groups in many subjects, and even though there are organizations represented by lawyers (such as the Sierra Club, the Legal Defense Fund of the NAACP, or the American Civil Liberties Union), legal services are rarely available for community groups on the same day-by-day representation available to members of the business community. These community groups might be organized around purely local neighborhood issues, or they might be focused on common issues such as health care, schools, local transportation, police relations, new versions of urban renewal, and other social problems.

The use of the law to achieve a just society is the public interest lawyer's objective. It is a method, using advocacy to represent rights, but not, however, working toward a definition of a just society. In the process the public interest lawyer represents the community's conscience, serves as a gadfly, and is a form of ombudsman.

The role of raising the community's conscience is the presumptuous role; for who is to say what is in the best interest of the community? But the lawyer does not decide the determination of the issue; he or she merely raises it. Whatever the position, because of the nature of our adversary system, the position presented is opposed. And it is the court, not the parties, which makes the decision. Therefore, in the end the activity of the public interest lawyer is not truly presumptuous. The public interest lawyer who achieves a favorable ruling has done nothing more than the lawyer representing a business client; i.e., hammered an issue into acceptable shape for a decision by a court.

Gadfly sometimes means to flit about. Doing so can be for the public good. Instead of lying back, waiting for history to address a problem, drawing an issue into the public eye so that others will take it up as a legal cause is a useful gadfly function. Public interest lawyers (who cannot handle every aspect of every issue) started the revision of the legal relationship favoring landlords over tenants in this country, and those lawyers who challenged the legal favoritism of creditors over debtors started movements taken up by others in the courts. Working in this way, starting on one subject and moving on to another, the public interest lawyer can multiply effectiveness and so get a great deal accomplished despite limited resources. The lawyer in a more standard practice is saddled with continuing client relations – doing no more than the client wishes – and with social pressures within law firms or the legal community itself not to stir up trouble.

An ombudsman in Denmark, the country of origin of the term, is a government employee, working from the inside out. That concept has never taken in this country. And the public interest lawyer has taken on the role, but working from the outside in. An ombudsman working within a governmental unit, according to our cynical view of bureaucracy, would soon lose the advantage of an insider with knowledge and understanding of the operation, succumbing to the erosive pressures of conformity and protection. An outsider, in contrast, while dependent on others for information, is independent of those forces, and by being independent of them is free to question, challenge, and suggest.

CONCEPTION OF ADVOCACY

Advocacy is the lawyer's fare, and advocacy implies two sides to a question. The lawyer knows that "in almost every case except the very plainest, it would be possible to decide the issue either way, with reasonable legal justification". (Lord MacMillan, as quoted from *The World of Law* (1960). London Ephriam, ed. New York: Simon and Schuster, p. 14.) The lawyer is therefore a detached spokesman for one side, and though lawyers do tend to specialize, and in doing so, to lean toward plaintiffs or defendants, they are trained to, and could, argue either side. (Indeed, that is the essence of Moot Court, a law school training technique in vogue in the Litchfield Law School in the early 1800s, Kimball, 1966. 539.) Lawyers can do so because out of their training for the adversary system they see emerging from the process one improved principle after another.

Persons in the various social science disciplines represented in this symposium might not be so detached. To some the rightness of their cause is going to be clear. To the lawyer, what is clear is that the client is entitled to legal representation, hopefully the best available, and that the job to be done is to make the best presentation of the client's case and to do the best job of blocking the opponent's.

The lawyer-advocate gathers facts, constantly testing them to see whether they will hold up against cross-examination. He analyzes the facts against legal principles that seem to apply, tries other principles until satisfied with the fit, considers procedural avenues and hazards, and anticipates the opponent's case (and it is fair to say the opponent's case even if the work is on a will or a contract, drafted at the desk — for the lawyer's job is to do work that will stand the test of an opponent's attack). The product is the synthesis of each of these steps.

The process is essentially the same whether the problem arises under a statute adopted by a legislature, a rule of a court or an administrative agency, a constitutional provision, or an earlier appellate court decision. The lawyer draws the principles out of the prior case decisions and applies them to the principles of the current problem, and it doesn't matter whether the facts in the cases are similar or remote: it is the principles that count in this process known as legal reasoning:

> I told him it was law logic — an artificial system of reasoning, exclusively used in courts of justice, but good for nothing anywhere else. (John Quincy Adams, as quoted from a letter to William Wirt, Attorney General [1819])

If the principles apply, the prior case is a precedent, carrying the binding effect of law. Anastaplo (1975: 114) cites Langridge's *Case, Common Bench* (England) 1345, finding some inherent quality in these decisions so that "no precedent is of such force as that which is right."

And Justice Cardozo (1921) stated the virtues of a system dependent on precedent:

> One of the most fundamental social interests is that law shall be uniform and impartial. There must be nothing in its action that savors of prejudice or favor or even arbitrary whim or fitfulness. Therefore in the main there shall be adherence to precedent.

Ambrose Bierce (1957) had seen such an opening as "in the main" and raised this problem in his *Devil's Dictionary:*

> PRECEDENT, n. In Law, a previous decision, rule or practice which, in the absence of a definite statute, has whatever force and authority a Judge may choose to give it, thereby greatly simplifying his task of doing as he pleases. As there are precedents for everything, he has only to ignore those that are against his interest and accentuate those in the line of his desire.

But Jonathan Swift (*Gulliver's Travels,* chapter 5) saw a problem in the predictability of precedent:

> It is a maxim among these lawyers that whatever has been done before may legally be done again; and therefore they take special care to record all the decisions formerly made against common justice and the general reason of mankind. These, under the name of precedents, they produce as authorities.

And the venerable Justice Holmes (1897: 469) added this dimension:

> It is revolting to have no better reason for a rule of law than that it was laid down in the time of Henry IV. It is still more revolting if the grounds upon which it was laid down have vanished long since and the rule simply persists from blind imitation of the past.

The point is that precedent is subject to argument (Llewellyn, 1951), and argument is advocacy.

The trial of a dispute, pitting one advocate against another as part of the adversary system, is sometimes said to be a quest for truth and justice. Justice Jerome Frank (1949), a thoughtful man, saw the system as a "fight theory" rather than a "truth theory," and worried about the inequality between the adversaries and the resources of their clients. He thought that lawyers tended toward surprise and the withholding (even the distorting) of evidence. No one has been able to come up with a better system (not even Judge Frank), and some would say that the system is there to resolve disputes, not to get at truth or justice:

> Mr. Glacier met Mr. Roger and Mr. Plumb in the law courts and thanked them for their help. "But what a lot of time and money," he said, "it has cost to arrive at the truth." "The truth?" said Roger, "No one in Court said anything about arriving at the truth." (Henry Cecil)

Clarence Darrow (as quoted from *The World of Law* (1960). London Ephriam, ed. New York: Simon and Schuster, p. 13) is equally direct: "litigants and their lawyers are supposed to want justice, but in reality there is no such thing as justice either in or out of court. In fact, the word cannot be defined."

Trials resolve disputes subject to rules of procedure and of evidence (and each is vulnerable to challenge). The rules of procedure often seem to be applied harshly in the name of order. The rules of evidence seem to be unpopular, but if they don't contribute toward truth-getting, at least they help to eliminate undependable testimony. And discovery (the court process that allows considerable power to either side to delve into the files and to question the witnesses of the other before trial) buttresses the effectiveness of these rules.

But the lawyer-advocate, accepted in England in the reign of Edward I (Kimball, 1966: 519), began to be licensed in the reign of Henry IV because of "a great number of attornies, ignorant and not learned in the law." The same pattern followed here in the United States, first restricting new attorneys from the profession, because of the "unskillfulness and covetousness of attorneys, who have more intended their own profit and their inordinate lucre than the good and benefit of their clients" (Act of 1655, Virginia, cited in Kimball, 1966: 531), and later allowing voters "of good moral character" to practice law in all courts in Indiana from 1851-1853. Today most cases in courts require legal representation, but the increased dependency on lawyers in a complex society has also meant an increase in licensing controls. Canons of ethics prohibit lawyers from soliciting clients, and without a client a lawyer cannot intervene in a court dispute.

A lawyer who wants to advocate a cause must do so, at least in the forum of a court, through a client. And the cause is secondary to the client's interest, even if the client wants to push the cause instead of such an interest. In an example, a group of environmentalists wrapped strips of bedsheets around trees slated for destruction for a highway, were arrested under an ordinance making it illegal to hang rags on city trees, and were convicted. On appeal their lawyer raised an issue that he had initiated on his own at the trial: the strips were symbols of speech, a protest to the mayor, and as such the free speech conduct of the environmentalists was constitutionally protected against the provisions of the ordinance. The group liked that argument and wanted it pushed on appeal. On the appeal the lawyer also raised another issue, one he had not discussed with the clients: since the trees were on park district land and the park district was a separate governmental unit, the city ordinance did not apply. The case was won on that point – courts don't like to reach constitutional issues if they can dispose of a case on other grounds – and the clients were angry with their lawyer.

While some disciplines have to overcome tradition to intervene, lawyers, who by tradition are advocates and spokespersons, are further restricted from entering into causes by canons of ethics against solicitation of legal business. Perhaps it was not anticipated that these canons would be used to inhibit noncommercial clauses. But even if involved in a court case, the lawyer may be limited in pursuing a cause. Courts consider only issues that can be supported by the facts in a case – and a client with a community-wide problem may want more to be considered by the court, although the court is not an open forum for community issues.

And perhaps more important, the public interest lawyer lacks the financial means to serve the community group, above the poverty line but below the affluent, which by its nature develops the need for such representation. Public interest law is a very limited phenomenon because it depends on outside sources for financial support; clients cannot afford to support issue-oriented litigation.

Whatever these limitations, the concept of the public interest lawyer is to use the existing legal machinery to seek to achieve positive social change. The public interest lawyer conceives of advocacy as a means of generalizing principles of social concern. Theories are explored to uphold a litigant's right to sue (called "standing to sue" in the legal field), to expand the scope of suits that have broad application (tax payers' actions and class suits, the former of limited application, the latter not in favor with the courts outside of the commercial area), and in doing so, to seek to improve conditions of life for the largest number of people the scope of the case can support.

Traditional methods and techniques apply: investigation, discovery (court-authorized examination of the opponent's files and witnesses), and court orders and decisions. Traditionally, using these steps, such action has been taken by state and federal attorneys general; the public interest lawyers are seeking to take on that role, and there is always conflict about their authority to do so, particularly from the interests who seem to oppose them on specific cases.

But some public interest lawyers go beyond the lawyer's traditional methods and techniques. They use public disclosure (achieved through investigation, provisions of the federal Freedom of Information Act, and discovery), disseminated through reports or even through newspaper advertisements (often paid for by the public responding with small contributions) — none of which means is within the style of the private lawyer.

Public interest lawyers have also used lobbying as a technique. Until recently there was enough confusion about whether such activity was permitted under tax codes that there was relatively little work done in the area. The Tax Reform Act of 1976 has changed that. It is now clear that lobbying is allowed, up to a specific portion of a tax exempt organization's expenditure of time.

And the public interest lawyer operates under an assumption, expressed not long ago in a speech to the Chicago Council of Lawyers by Chief Judge Swygert of the United States Court of Appeals in Chicago: "It will often take at least three trips to the courthouse to succeed in undoing established doctrine, as oppressive as it might be."

CASE ILLUSTRATIONS

Case histories of the lawyer as advocate will not contribute as much as case histories of where the lawyer was unable to serve effectively as an advocate. This is so because the lawyer is advocate almost by definition, and because the lawyer's skills, techniques, and services should be — but are not — available to the other disciplines. This may sound like a claim of monopoly; it isn't. Perhaps it is nearsightedness:

> People specializing in a particular study area tend after a time to think of their area as being at the center of the universe. You have perhaps seen the humorous drawing of a New Yorker's view of the United States — in which the Eastern seaboard dominates the map, while the Midwest, mountain States, and Far West are an almost undifferentiated glob of shrunken territory off to the left. When your life is bound up with the law, you may tend to think of it as hovering over everything else, like some "brooding" omnipresence in the sky. (Mermin, 1973)

But the important point is to share experiences — if those in the disciplines become advocates, they may act on their own, using lawyers' paraphernalia; or, depending on the nature of the problem, they may have occasion to adapt to the rules, as witnesses or even as clients.

The first of several case histories cited here deals with the social worker and the law: the diminishing chasm between social workers and lawyers in neglected and dependent child, and in abused child proceedings. It is an example of the need within the disciplines to understand and, in so doing, to accept the way the lawyers play the game. That is, they ought to do so if they have a client interest — and want to win.

There are many methods of solving disputes, and many forums other than the courtroom. But when a dispute is one that is going to go to court, one in which the state has taken an interest and provided the court as the forum, the lawyer's world becomes critically important to the participants.

In these two case areas court proceedings over the past ten years have changed. All of the parties are represented by attorneys. This new step is the result of a series of court challenges; to social workers, when the new step was taken, the court became a house of strangers. Reports were rejected as hearsay, recommendations were rejected as conclusory statements, and each was inadmissible.

At first the new step was seen to be a conflict between professions (Tamilia, 1971). Then schools of social work began to offer legal training, in-service training in the law, and legal consultation for social workers engaged in child protection work (Bell and Mlyniec, 1974).

Without intending the myopic view noted above, the social workers began to learn to prepare their cases so that they would stand up to the rules of evidence. This is the same lesson learned by expert witnesses who offer up opinion testimony, and it is the same process applied to the police. Although social workers had a strong belief in the professionalism behind their work, when they were exposed to the possibilities (or probabilities) of the unfairness of a criminal conviction based on hearsay evidence that by its nature could not be tested on confrontation or by cross-examination, they began to gather direct evidence or to be prepared to testify as an eyewitness themselves.

When the social workers saw that an opinion could as well be used against their cause (without being tested) and learned the limits and uses of opinion evidence, they learned about patterns and practice, about how to abstract the principal problem of the case, and to see the value of opinion evidence limited to more general situations (that would encompass the case they were interested in) without reducing the evidence involved to best guessing.

Lawyers contributed to this process. But in order to do so, they too had to learn something. For lawyers sometimes take their rules and jargon as being understood by those they work with. The lawyers had now to learn how to explain, how to slow down and find out just what the social workers had to offer, and to explain their system to the social workers in terms that made sense to them. In doing so, the lawyers learned a lot about the social work field and about how to present their cases. And with the informed cooperation of the social workers, they presented cases to win but were also in a position to present cases so as to make a clear record of the issues for an effective appeal if they were to lose. The second case history to be cited here is quite different from the first, in that the lack of mutual understanding between lawyer and client was never successfully resolved.

In the late 1960s a wave of protest by blacks seeking to enter the construction industry moved through major cities in the north and into Washington, D.C. The groups claimed discrimination in membership to unions and in employment practices controlled by unions and builders. In Chicago, the Coalition of United Community Organizations, members of a coalition of black groups, surrounded federally funded projects, a tactic used in other cities, and the white workers left the sites and refused to return to work. The builders and unions, working in harmony, obtained court injunctions against further demonstrations. The injunctions, fought by lawyers called in on a crisis basis, brought the black groups into the mayor's office and then to the negotiating table — and threw them into contact with lawyers serving them in such a role for the first time.

At the mayor's meeting leaders of the group spoke up; the two lawyers involved were asked by the leaders to stay in the background. Afterward the mayor asked one of the lawyers to stay behind. The mayor had explained to the lawyer that he did not personally know the members of the group, and asked whether the lawyer thought he had touched upon the issues that were important to them. The group was suspicious; however, lawyers are used to stepping into such difficult situations, where it is understood by their clients that they continue to maintain their loyalties — only one of many factors not understood by the Coalition, which was unfamiliar with lawyers and their ways.

Later on, as the parties were drawn to the bargaining table the Coalition leaders took the front seats. At first they did not want to let their lawyers into the negotiation sessions at all. However, across the table they saw the builders and unions represented by spokesmen — their lawyers with whom each had a long-standing relationship. The lawyers for the Coalition were therefore invited into the room but were seated in the back. Session by session the Coalition leaders asked the lawyers to move up, a little closer each time. Notes were passed to them, ideas sought, and finally they were drawn into the process. But they never became the spokesmen for the group. The leaders were not willing to give up that role, nor were they ever able to focus on issues that started the protest in the first place.

When the negotiating session broke, the lawyers tried to set up discussions with the Coalition leaders and to huddle, just as the unions and builders were doing with their lawyers, about objectives and alternatives. The Coalition leaders saw the lawyers' efforts as competing with their own. When it came time to submit a draft agreement for settlement, the Coalition leaders wanted to start negotiations over again each time any of their demands were accepted: they thought that if anything happened to be accepted that they should have asked for more, and were ready to do so. And when their lawyers put down the terms for an agreement, the Coalition wanted to change them, or suspected the lawyers of giving away a chance to negotiate further.

The constant renegotiation by the Coalition weakened their position. The builders and unions began to lose respect for them, and they took advantage of internal dissension that followed among the blacks, while the builders and unions maintained a strong united front. It was their lawyers who did the talking for them — they had no constituency to worry about; their people were trained to understand the lawyer's role, the relationship of that role to their leadership, and to themselves. The blacks could not accept a lawyer to talk for them; spokesmen were to be the leaders, not the outsiders.

Not surprisingly, the Coalition did not get anywhere in the negotiations, and the black groups slowly drifted away. Some time later the lawyers for the Coalition won a reversal of the injunction (mentioned above) that had thrown them into contact with the Coalition leaders months before. But by the time of the formal victory there was no more organization, and there were no demonstrations, even though they would have been legally protected as a result of the lawyers' efforts.

Without any tradition of relating to such groups, lawyers lack the background of communication, understanding, and trust necessary to develop issues and seek solutions. Being called in on an emergency basis has little promise of longterm success, especially if the work to be done will be outside of the courtroom (courtroom work being commonly accepted as lawyers' work). Lawyers representing a business, on an ongoing basis, would get to learn the business and to know its chief personnel. The lawyers would then be in a position to anticipate and head off problems. The lawyer called in for the first time under emergency circumstances might be able to solve a courtroom problem, but in dealing with people unfamiliar with the process would find that such people would identify the lawyer with any unsatisfactory ruling by the court (the injunction for example).

Thus the lawyers seeking to serve as advocates for the Coalition started out with little chance of success. But what made it certain that they would not succeed was that the leaders were operating to maintain organization itself, while the lawyers continually tried instead to get to the objective of the organizational drive.

Case histories of successful advocacy by public interest lawyers might also be cited, however, to illustrate something of the range of strategies and tactics that have been employed in this field.

The first of these is an example of classical lawyering (i.e., through litigation) — a case that a public interest lawyer has carried on for over eleven years (first as a volunteer while a member of a large law firm, and afterward as a staff member of a public interest law firm), the case did not have a client who could pay and the client's own interest would have been but a miniscule piece of the issue presented. The larger issue was whether the City Council had the authority to veto all sites for Chicago public housing projects within the city. Suit was brought for Mrs. Gatreaux, an applicant for public housing, and at the end of the first stage a court order voided the Council's veto power and converted that decision into an affirmative order against the Chicago Public Housing Authority, requiring it to build on scattered sites for the purpose of integrating the City (*Gatreaux v. Hill* [1976], 425 U.S.284).

The issue of whether a public housing applicant could get into public housing became a test of whether that applicant could get a court to rule where public housing was to be built — out of a ghetto; and later, whether a court would go further and require such housing to be built in a metropolitan-wide area to avoid segregation within a city.

The case was then converted into a metropolitan-wide effort, by bringing H.U.D. into the case *(Gatreaux v. Hill)*. The purpose was to integrate the suburbs around Chicago, and to prevent flight of whites from the city. A little over a year ago the Burger Court unanimously upheld the order against H.U.D. to build public housing projects on scattered sites in the suburbs. The case was continuously controversial. Columnist Patrick Buchanan, once a Nixon speech writer, was incensed at "the tyranny" of the decision; while the *Baltimore Sun* thought the decision might someday exceed *Brown v. Board of Education* in importance. The decision is being followed up with other integration efforts by an agreement with H.U.D. — implemented by the Leadership Council for Metropolitan Open Communities.

I will close with two less traditional examples of advocacy on community issues, in which the strategies and tactics were those of public disclosure and public awareness, totally without litigation.

A few years ago, Mayor Daley proposed to build an airport in Lake Michigan, a proposal opposed by many for the horrendous environmental effects it would have. Public interest lawyers in Chicago undertook a public advertisement campaign, built on extensive research, featuring cartoons depicting dozens of ills that the project would cause: a fish wore a clothespin on its nose; a diver, descending to retrieve a vehicle that fell over the edge, had windshield wipers on his goggles; congestion of every kind, everywhere. The caption read: DON'T DO IT

IN THE LAKE. Once bumper stickers appeared with this legend — and they seemed to be everywhere — the project was dropped.

Around the same period, Sears, Roebuck and Company built in Chicago the World's Tallest Building, widely resented because it caused ghosting in over a quarter-million television sets in the vicinity. In the end, Sears Tower built television transmitters, contrary to its original plans, which alleviated the rebound and ghosting effect it had been causing to signals from other locations. This came about after a series of television announcements by a public interest lawyer on a station that did not take advertising. The first was, "Hey, when Sears sells its television sets, is it going to put a great big label across the tube that says, 'This set won't work because we want the world's tallest — and fanciest — building'?" That announcement was followed by a series debunking the company's claims that it could cushion the TV signals by application of various coating materials. After one final announcement, the company gave in. It had published a revisionist map of the areas in which the ghosting occurred, and this time the announcements went: "How does it feel to live in (naming some) cities that Sears has wiped off the map?" Sears received enough telephone calls cancelling charge accounts and its Allstate insurance to get the message.

These are illustrations of a wide number of inventive uses of advocacy that have succeeded toward public interest goals, and which might be used, adopted or participated in by members of the interested disciplines.

NEXT STEPS FOR DEVELOPMENT OF ADVOCACY

Lawyers could well extend their expertise in the field of advocacy to others. They should be able to make their training, skills, and techniques and themselves known to the other disciplines. They should be open to learn where their services are needed (without waiting for a client to lead them to that need), and they ought to be clever enough to develop ways of providing those services. The lawyers should be able to develop ways to represent the unrepresented middle gap of society. And they should learn from the other disciplines what these fields know and need to know about advocacy, and be able to assist them in self-help programs. Lawyers should either be advocates for, or help to train lay advocates in, the other disciplines.

In theory, lay advocates can take the place of lawyers. In practice that may not work. Or, it may not work without at least some working relationship with a lawyer.

Lay advocates will constantly be needed, for lawyers need not get into every problem — and, because of limited resources and conflicting demands, won't be able to do so. But lay advocates, in addition to learning the nature of the advocate's role, must learn the responsibilities it carries. Perhaps the harshest criticism of public interest lawyers is that they may use their clients to experiment, to further their own causes. Another criticism is that public interest lawyers deliver false promises. Setting up a community facility as a research facility by a discipline, and dismantling it once the research is in, would be an example of both irresponsibilities. Don't be guilty of either. Use advocacy justly for a just cause.

REFERENCES

Anastaplo, G. (1975) *Human Being and Citizen.* Chicago: Swallow Press.

Bell, C., and W. J. Mlyniec (1974) "Preparing for a Neglect Proceeding: A Guide for the Social Worker." *Public Welfare* 32 (4): 22-30.

Bierce, A. (1957) *The Devil's Dictionary.* New York: Hill and Wang.

Bishkin, W., and C. Stone (eds.) (1972) *Law, Language and Ethics.* New York: Foundation Press.

Cardozo, B. N. (1921) *The Nature of the Judicial Process.* New Haven: Yale University Press. Frank, J. (1949)

Frank, J. (1949) *Courts on Trial.* Princeton, N. J.: Princeton University Press.

Holmes, O. W. (1881) *The Common Law.* New York: Macmillan.

––– (1897) "Path of the Law." 10 *Harvard Law Review* 457, 469.

Kimball, S. L. (1966) *Historical Introduction to the Legal System.* St. Paul: West Publishing.

Lewis, A. (1964) *Gideon's Trumpet.* New York: Random House.

Llewellyn, K. N. (1951) *The Bramble Bush.* Dobbs Ferry, N.Y.: Oceana.

Marks, F. R. (1972) *The Lawyer, the Public and Professional Responsibility.* Chicago: American Bar Foundation.

Mermin, S. (1973) *Law and the Legal System. Boston: Little, Brown.*

Stone, C. (1974) *Should Trees Have Legal Standing? Toward Legal Rights for Natural Objects.* Los Altos, Calif.: W. Kaufmann.

––– (1975) *Where the Law Ends: The Social Control of Corporate Conduct.* New York: Harper and Row.

Tamilia, P. R. (1971) "Neglect Proceedings and the Conflict Between Law and Social Work." *Duquesne Law Review* 9:585.

3

ADVOCACY AND COMMUNITY PSYCHOLOGY

William S. Davidson II and
Julian Rappaport

PSYCHOLOGY: THE ADVANCEMENT OF SCIENCE, PROFESSION, AND HUMAN WELFARE

In order to more clearly understand the crisis of community psychology as it applies to notions of advocacy, it is necessary to review the development of its conceptual base. Community psychology has its roots in the field of psychology and more specifically in the field of clinical psychology. As such, it has strong academic and professional ties to psychology's stance on the definition of human welfare. Psychology has historically had an investment as a profession in a triadic goal. Each month the American Psychological Association publishes a reminder of its organizational goal for its members in the inside cover of the *American Psychologist* (the field's most popular journal): "The purpose of the APA is to advance psychology as a science, as a profession, and as a means of promoting human welfare." While the formal face of the organization has subscribed to notions of promoting the human welfare, the field in no way has a unitary definition of what human welfare is or further how psychology ought to contribute to its promotion. This is indeed intriguing for a discipline which has placed major emphasis on the development of reliable definitions of variables.

In fact, the continuing debate concerning the acceptable definition of human welfare has been intertwined with the development of specific conceptual and theoretical positions within the field. Most relevant to our discussion here is the influence of these issues on the development of the field of community psychology. Various authors have suggested that community psychology arose out of a crisis within the field over what definition of the human welfare ought to be sub-scribed to and to what extent psychology should be active in attempts to alter the status quo human welfare (Fairweather, 1967; Fairweather, 1974; Cowen, 1973; Kelly, 1977; Rappaport, 1977a).

The formal beginnings of a psychology of the community are generally associated with a conference held in Boston in 1965 (Bennett, Anderson, Cooper, Hassol, Klein and Rosenblum, 1966). As with many movements towards theoretical, paradigmatic, or professional role innovation, the community psychology movement was a reaction to a perceived crisis and an attempt to provide an alternative to traditional psychological positions (Cowen, Gardner, and Zax, 1967; Zax and Specter, 1974; Rappaport, 1977b). At issue were the accepted domains and modes of inquiry, the political responsibility or neutrality of the psychologist, the strategies and tactics of intervention procedures, and the scope of professional roles.

A central issue was serious questioning of the dominant view of human behavior and the resultant role implications for psychologists. Psychology had historically — as well as by definition — placed nearly exclusive emphasis on the role of individual variables as determinants and definers of the phenomena of interest. It was argued that this conceptual or paradigmatic position led to a rather passive, status quo supporting role for psychological research and change procedures (Rappaport, 1977b). Community psychologists argued strenuously that sterile consideration of individual difference phenomena led to far too simplistic, and therefore impotent, conceptual frameworks. The most eloquent detailing of this position was provided by Ryan (1971). His major thesis was that the resulting individual difference approaches to research and intervention supported malignant social programming and the inequitable distribution of human and economic resources. Other authors (e.g., Kamin, 1974) provided strong evidence of the interplay of psychological research on intelligence and the political needs of the power structure. In short, if documentation of covariation between social problems and individual incompetence could be demonstrated, status quo distribution of resources could be supported. Along a similar line, the questionable efficacy of psychotherapy procedures – cited by community psychologists as the major mode of psychological reaction to human suffering – were innately adaptation-oriented rather than supportive of social change efforts. While debatable from a variety of perspectives, the ineffectiveness of individual therapeutic procedures, regardless of theoretical orientation, led to the questioning of predominant scientific and professional positions and assumptions.

A second issue was the utility of professional criteria as indicants of competency to carry out psychological interventions. The argument was that even if individual therapeutic procedures were maximally effective, the field could not hope to train sufficient numbers of doctoral level professionals to meet the increasing demand for human services (Albee, 1968). In addition, there was evidence presented that nonprofessionals, particularly when similar in social status and life experiences to the target group, were as or more effective than highly trained professionals (Poser, 1966; Rappaport, Chinsky, and Cowen, 1971; Seigel, 1973). These issues provided the beginnings of the opening of the professional role definition for community psychologists and help lay the ground work for the emergence of the advocacy alternative. One effect was the dethroning of the psychologist as the aloof and apparently politically neutral expert. The systematic problem-solving generalist with specific ends-oriented goals was suggested as an alternative (Sarason, 1976). A second effect was to suggest a coordinating and signal-calling role for the psychologist in relation to a variety of services and change agents (Cowen, 1973). A third effect was to dramatically expand the groups used as change agents. The human helper movement has now embraced nearly every human problem area which has come to our attention (Reissman, 1965).

A third issue was a redefinition of the human problem areas to be embraced by the psychologist. In response to both the societal crises of the sixties and the perceived crisis in psychological conception, the community psychology movement argued from the beginning that individually based conceptions of human problems were severely restrictive (Kelly, 1970; Kelly, 1973; Fairweather, 1967). In a similar way that politicians and policy makers had turned to the physical sciences for solution of the technological and educational crises created by "Sputnik", social scientists were called into the social problem arena in the 1960s. Faced with this situation, community psychologists, among others, were quick to point out that multi-level conceptions and interventions were necessary if social problem solution was to be attempted. It was recognized that the influence of individuals, as well as groups, communities, institutions, organizations, and societies, must all be considered. Others suggested that in fact previous "errors of logical typing" in identifying the appropriate level of intervention had led to misguided intervention approaches (Watzlavick, Weaxlund, and Fisch, 1974). If particular human problems were actually a function of economic resource distribution and intervention approaches were focused on individual therapeutic or behavioral change, a positive outcome could hardly be expected. This kind of thinking had a particular impact on the community psychology movement and its call for multi-level conceptions of human behavior and multiple focus interventions. Individual change and social system implications were demanded.

The most dramatic outcropping of the community psychology movement for an advocacy model was the explicit dealing with value and political questions. There were actually two related issues involved. The first is the demand for explication of the values involved in community psychology investigation and interventions. As will be detailed in the next section, even attempts at pure science within psychology can have grave value-oriented implications. The second is the development and adoption of a new paradigmatic position for community psychology. Prominent notions of victim-blaming and environment blaming are rejected in favor of social goals which respect diversity and seek ways of economically and culturally supporting diversity.

Table 3.1, adapted from Rappaport (1977a), describes how the suggested paradigm fits with existing prominent positions. It includes the dimensions of psychological-cultural goals and environmental support. The value positions outlined represent distinct traditions within psychological investigation and intervention. The direct inter-play with intervention strategies will be further described in the next section. Briefly, the stereotyped conservative position is closely affiliated with the prediction paradigm of psychological testing. Prediction of the status quo is the goal. The bootstrapper is related to a position which would not involve the psychologist in social interventions directly. Rather, individuals should adhere to a single standard,

TABLE 3.1

Alternative Value Positions for Community Psychology

(Adapted from Rappaport, 1977)

	Psychological — Cultural Goals	
Environmental Resources Support	Traditional Individualistic-Conservative	Traditional Social Welfare-Liberal
Traditional Individualistic-Conservative	**A. THE STEREOTYPED CONSERVATIVE** Individual diversity respected. Every individual makes it on their own as a function of individual abilities. Traits, evolution, social Darwinism emphasized as reasons for differences.	**B. THE BOOTSTRAPPER** Melting pot system prevails. Individual is less important than the social good. Everyone should adhere to the same standards but should make it on their own. Individuals must overcome environmental differences.
Traditional Social Welfare-Liberal	**C. THE COMMUNITY PSYCHOLOGY VIEWPOINT** Diversity, strengths of differences emphasized. Ecological perspective seeking and advocating a fit between persons and environments. Social responsibility emphasized with shared resources being equitably distributed.	**C. THE STEREOTYPED LIBERAL** Conformity to a common culture and value system. Everyone should be similar. Interventions should provide assistance in adapting to society and altering the environment to facilitate adaptation.

but are left to their own devices for accomplishing compliance. The stereotyped liberal adequately describes most compensatory or therapeutically oriented intervention systems. Training, enriching, therapizing, treating, etc., individuals to the norm is the goal. The community psychology viewpoint provides a mix of the traditional liberal and conservative positions on the two dimensions outlined. On the one hand, individual and subgroup differences are respected, supported, and viewed as assets. Further, those differences which do exist are to be supported by society and particularly by intervention programs. Notions of cultural amplifiers, the creation of alternative settings, and opening the range of groups and individuals which have access to advocates of their position are all implied (Rappaport, Davidson, Wilson, and Mitchell, 1975).

The emergence of this value position within community psychology laid very critical groundwork for the advocacy position. The realization that psychologists had been active and passive supporters of specific subgroups of society led to the suggestions that the resource generation capability of psychologists ought to be systematically made available to usually ignored groups. Given adherence to this position, a number of alternative modes of intervention are possible.

ALTERNATIVE MODES OF HUMAN INTERVENTION

As alluded to earlier, the development of community psychology and the role of the advocacy model was as much a reaction to the conceptual as the technical models available in psychology. The prescribed mode for psychologists had been one of passive scientific inquiry (Hebb, 1974). The model involved the systematic generation of knowledge on the variables influencing behavior, phenomenological events, etc. Some have even gone so far as to restrict psychology's appropriate role to the investigation of essentially biological reductionist pheonomena (e.g., Hebb, 1974). Any attempt at human intervention or social change is seen as outside the role of the psychologist per se. Even those psychologists who wandered into studying phenomena which have direct social policy or political implications have protested suggestions that they are responsible for the application of their research findings (e.g., Jensen, 1969). If the results of such investigation are to be applied to human intervention or change procedures, the consumer of psychological data is left to his/her own devices in making such applications. Within this strictly pure science view, the technique of human intervention is only the generation of scientifically credible information. It is nonapplied and apolitical in nature. From the view presented here, this is a "head in the sand approach" to human problems. The notion that scientific inquiry exists in such a socially and politically sterile sense is incomprehensible to the community psychologist. The pure scientist is influenced by social, political, and economic forces whether they are actively engaged in or not. The selection of phenomena for investigation, the kinds of variables which funding sources are willing to consider worthy of investigation, and the interpretation of findings by government or private agencies all have social policy implications. Dealing with such forces in a passive way does not deny their existence or impact (Rappaport, 1977a).

For example, the laboratory work on environmental deprivation in animals provided a strong rationale for the deficit-oriented compensatory educational programs of which Head Start was the prime example (Hunt, 1961). Rather than take a passive stance to the subsequent use of their findings, psychologists could be active in investigating phenomena which are of interest to usually defined "out groups" and systematically working towards application in advocating human rights. Obviously, this demands an expansion of the current boundary conditions placed on the role of the scientist and the form in which research reports are presented. The modes of advocating for financial support of scientific investigation could as well be used as modes of advocating for the implications for oppressed groups:

A second prominent mode of human intervention could be characterized as applied science. Here the basic tenets of purely scientific psychology are merely taken into applied domains. Again, social or individual change is not viewed as part of the activities of the psychologist. Probably the most common method is the construction of a variety of psychometric procedures in the areas of academic achievement, intelligence, personality characteristics, interests, attitudes, etc. The major paradigm has been the prediction of future performance on the basis of test scores. There is now little question that, whether intentionally or not, such procedures have major implications for social policy and human change procedures. Kamin (1974) has graphically described the use of psychological tests in determining immigration procedures, selecting and screening armed services recruits, contributing to career choices, determining educational philosophy, and selecting candidates for college entrance. It would appear that such intervention modalities are intrinsically status quo oriented. If maximum predictability is to be maintained, it is helpful if environmental conditions are not altered. Further, the original prediction scheme is directly related to existing social groupings and classifications. Such tests are generally constructed according to the ability of items and scales to discriminate criterion groups of interest. The continued utility of the strategy is intertwined with the notion that existing criterion groups will continue to be important.

The most commonly considered modes of human intervention in the armamentarium of the psychologist include individual and group psychotherapy procedures. While a complete review of the variety of specific psychotherapeutic modalities is well beyond the scope of this paper, some categorical comments and observations on the viability of the therapeutic model are important for considering the advocacy alternative. While the variety of specific therapeutic modes is considerable, in general terms each relies heavily on the development of an interpersonal therapeutic relationship as providing a "mini-environment" in which individual change can take place. Specific modes place relative importance on the development of insight, rearrangement of psychic forces, alternative coping strategies, clarification of interpersonal perceptions, and specific restructuring of cognitive propositions. The overriding assumption of these specific strategies is that individual adjustment to development breakdowns, learning deficits, environmental stress, etc. is the desired goal. In short, the assumption is that individuals should adjust to the demands of their life situations and the demands of the larger society (Rappaport, 1977a). A related dimension is the manner in which interventions are delivered to troubled individuals. Again, we observe a relatively passive strategy of waiting for patients to be committed, referred, or to experience sufficient levels of discomfort to self-refer (Rappaport and Chinsky, 1974). The community mental health movement was an original attempt to deal with such problems. Essentially, the goal was to move traditional mental health therapeutic services into new "community" settings, to increase the reach of mental health services to groups previously unserved, to reduce the need for long-term hospitalization, and to expand the role of the mental health worker to include concerns beyond the individual level (Hobbs, 1964). The result, according to a recent NIMH evaluation of community mental health centers (Windle, Bass and Taube, 1974), has been the nearly exclusive use of individual psychotherapeutic procedures as the intervention of choice. Within the perspective presented here, psychotherapeutic procedures have by definition resulted in the perpetuation of victim-blaming ideologies and modes of intervention (Ryan, 1971; Halleck, 1974). On both conceptual and technical grounds such approaches are at odds with the position of community psychology.

A development within psychology over the last two decades was the systematic application of learning principles to human problems. The advent of behavior modification was heralded as a major breakthrough in providing a powerful technology for alleviating human problems (Ullmann and Krasner, 1965; Franks, 1969; O'Leary and Wilson, 1975; Neitzel, Winett, MacDonald, and Davidson, 1977). Conceptually and technically, great attention was paid to the role of environmental contingencies and the social relativity of deviance. A major thrust of the behavioral movement was the necessity of making the goals of intervention procedures highly specific and public. Hopefully, this would lead to a more honest representation of the political and value issues involved. At a conceptual level, the behavioral movement shared a great deal in common with community psychology (Davidson and Robinson, 1975). In terms of application, it is now obvious that the use of behavioral techniques has many times been for the benefit of the same groups which benefited from basic and applied science, the testing movement, and adjustment-oriented therapeutic endeavors (Winett and Winkler, 1972; Davidson and Seidman, 1974). Further, the assumed generality of the "laws of learning" into the applied situation inadvertently focused attention on individual levels of analysis and intervention.

For community psychology, it was the considerable dissatisfaction with these briefly reviewed modalities of social change that set the stage for the development of specific advocacy models. From one point of view, the notion of advocacy offered nothing new at all. Rather, it was only the realization that psychological intervenors had all along been advocates for particular groups. The importance of the advocacy stance was to make these assumptions and loyalties explicit. From another point of view, the delineation of advocacy models meant a tremendous break with traditional conceptions and role definitions of the field.

A MULTIPLE STRATEGY MODEL
OF ADVOCACY

ENVIRONMENTAL RESOURCES CONCEPTION

In contrast with previous conceptions, the environmental resources conception of human behavior takes a dramatically different stance in providing the rational base for advocacy efforts. It specifically does not concern itself with the eradication or amelioration of differences in individuals or target groups. At the very heart of the environmental resources conception is the notion that a wide variety of differences do exist in this society. From a statistical standpoint, given two comparison groups of sufficient size, there will be differences observed on a multitude of individual and environmental variables. Generally, social status, sexual, educational, racial, geographic and occupational groups have been compared. Covarying problems led to the conclusion that, to eradicate the observed differences, the major characteristics of the groups or individuals had to be altered. Within the environmental resources conception, such differences are to be viewed as the assets of a pluralistic society and such differences are to be supported rather than serving as the basis for exclusion from resource availability. From this point of view, the over-emphasis of individual and environmental differences has provided a basis for negative expectations for social interventions. Further, it has added to the lack of accountability to target groups among policy makers.

The environmental resources conception takes a universalistic rather than an exceptionalistic approach to social problems (Ryan, 1971). The universalistic approach assumes that the variety of unmet needs displayed by various troubled groups in our society are not exclusively housed within those identified groups and individuals. Rather, identified troubled groups are to be treated as all fully participating members of society. Some areas of lacking resources, given the proper timing and setting, meet with severe social or legal sanction. The process of identification often sets in motion a series of events which exacerbate rather than remedy the situation, while placing responsibility for such failure on the individuals in question. The alternative suggested by the environmental resources conception is that all individuals of this society have the right to have their collective and individual needs fulfilled. The vehicle of advocacy is suggested as a means of focusing intervention efforts on resource stimulation and generation rather than on individual repair (Davidson and Rapp, 1976).

Given this view of social intervention, the specific principles of advocacy-based intervention are prescribed. The general model for the strategy comes from various long-existing advocacy groups. Lawyers, for example, are charged with insuring that the position and needs of their clients are protected, labor organizations protect the interests of their members, neighborhood organizations are active in pushing for developments which protect the interests of the residents, and professional organizations lobby for resource distribution beneficial to their members. At the very heart of the advocacy position for community psychology is the notion that the information and resources of the field be used in behalf of often ignored groups. Politically potent groups are constantly engaged in activities which benefit their situation and undoubtedly enhance their mental health. However, many groups, often those also accused of having intra-individual problems, are left without a formal or informal advocate.

The multiple strategy model of advocacy is conceptually simple, yet potentially operationally complex. It is intended to draw on the informational, political, and technical resources of the advocate. The implications for professional roles include a relatively common view of the advocate as an individual or group who works for the benefit of a mutually agreeing constituent (Sarason, 1976). It is anticipated that the advocacy model could be applied in interventions directed at the individual, group, or organizational levels of intervention. The overall goal of advocacy efforts is to provide needed resources for the target individual or group.

OVERVIEW OF THE MODEL

The multiple strategy model of child advocacy is not at a point of technical development where a highly standardized set of procedures is specified. Rather, a general sequential problem-solving model is prescribed for the purpose of developing strategies for generating and stimulating needed resources. In many ways, the multiple strategy model of advocacy can be seen as encompassing a multitude of strategies. Its emphasis on environmental resources, sequential action-reaction cycles, and continual monitoring are all critical components of the model. It should also be pointed out that many of the specifics of the advocacy model provided a basis for a program aimed at diverting delinquent adolescents from the juvenile justice system. Our efforts in that project provide many of the operational principles of the model. A more detailed description of the advocacy model within the diversion project will be included in the following section. The model developed here has implications for political action, program development and administration, and individual case management.

The multiple strategy model is an attempt to provide a systematic framework for advocacy efforts. The conceptual framework includes notion of sequential problem-solving as a purposeful approach to generating environmental resources. By intention, the model is concrete and aims to provide a relatively simple framework for initiating advocacy-based programs. The multiple-strategy model includes a nine-step problem-solving format (Table 3.2), as originally presented by Davidson and Rapp (1976). The sequential steps involved are divided into primary assessment, strategy selection, and implementation. Each of these generic categories provides a set of sub-steps and a series of interrelated action-reaction feedback loops. Although each step is described separately for conceptual purposes, in actuality the nine steps are highly interrelated, dependent on information from preceding steps, and dependent on continual interaction with the specific social environment in which the advocacy effort is taking place. In short, the multiple strategy model is an attempt to construct an open systems model of intervention which includes a continuous process of evaluation, action, reevaluation, and reaction.

In selecting the strategies to be employed, careful consideration is given to the expected outcomes of a specific action sequence. However, rather than implying a lengthy construction of alternative futures in a highly deterministic sense, the model dictates a quick move into action-oriented components. Initial assessment as well as the wealth of information which can be gained from reactions to intervention provide the basis for continually upgrading and altering the strategy.

Selection of the advocate or advocate group might be ideally done best after one had an idea of exactly what was needed, through what mechanisms, in what settings, and so on. However, this is not at all feasible in an operational sense. Within the context of this paper, it is suggested that advocacy provides an alternative intervention mode for the community psychologist in social problem areas. This is not intended in a parochial or provincial sense, but stated only for the purposes of this symposium. In the more general sense, the advocacy

TABLE 3.2

Alternative Advocacy Strategies

	Advocacy Focus		
Advocacy Strategies	Individual Level	Administrative Level	Policy Level
Positive Approach	I. Advocate identifies individual teachers and seeks their agreement to make adjustments in classroom curriculum more conducive to the individual educational needs.	II. Advocate would contact educational administrator with a proposal for drafting an application for educational innovation funds to generate additional curriculum alternatives.	III. Advocate would lobby with state legislators to alter the statewide curriculum requirements.
Neutral Approach	IV. Advocate provides information to individual teachers concerning the educational goals and needs of the target youth.	V. Advocate would present information to the pupil personnel services concerning the rates of educational attainment among the target group and ensure that such information were made available to the media.	VI. Advocate would present state board of education and state superintendent of schools with dropout rates and preferences for educational alternatives and would highlight the right of all students to public education.
Negative Approach	VII. Advocate would have the local media cover the story about a young person's being denied a quality education due to irrelevant classroom rules.	VIII. Advocate would initiate a class-action suit against the school district for failing to meet its legislative mandate to educate all youth in the district.	IX. Advocate would enjoin a legislative committee to investigate the educational agency mandated to provide educational alternatives.

model is seen as providing an operational base for a variety of individuals. The important characteristics for the advocate are commitment to the target population, the commitment to working for the constituent group, and possession of the strategies to make the changes necessary to stimulate the needed resources.

Because of the nature of the multiple-strategy model, it is impossible to construct a list of the ideal characteristics for the advocate. What is critical is that advocacy efforts be initiated for a variety of groups in this society. At a minimum, the advocacy group should include professionals, members of the target group, and sufficient technical assistance when needed to deal with particular areas. Again, the emphasis is on drawing on existing individual and collective strengths to "make things happen".

A critical factor in forming an advocate group is the degree of freedom necessary on the part of the advocate. It is important that the advocate be politically and economically independent from potential targets of change. The first author was recently fascinated by a local State Department of Social Services suggestion that a youth advocacy council be formed in their office as advocates for incarcerated youth under the department's care and guardianship. Professionals interested in advocacy approaches need to be aware of potential constraints before adopting an advocacy strategy. A major source of sanction is the interaction between the formal and informal organizational processes — that is, the problem of incompatible loyalties; threats of being fired, sanctioned, or not promoted; responses to existing professional norms, relationship procedures, and channels. Responsibilities to an advocate's career, to his family or friends, limit the full range of strategies which might be considered. In most professional positions, compliance with existing norms and rules is rewarded. The important point is that a sound base of support must be established for the advocate.

PRIMARY ASSESSMENT

The initial phase of primary assessment includes the specific steps of assessing unmet needs, defining the needed resources, determining who is in control of the resources currently, and assessing the vulnerability of the individual or group currently controlling the resource. The accurate selection of resources and intervention strategies is dependent on the most accurate assessment of unmet needs possible from the perspective of the target group and the advocate.

Assessing Unmet Needs. In the first step of any advocacy effort, getting the perceptions of the target group is critical. This is not seen as excluding sources of information to verify the observations. Other individuals in the situation can also provide useful information and perspectives. For example, in advocacy efforts with adolescent groups, the perspectives of parents, potential employers, teachers, peers, etc., will need to be considered so that initial advocacy efforts are not misguided. These additional sources of information can provide an excellent way for clarifying the position of the target individual or group. From the very beginning, the advocate needs to be on the lookout for information which will be important at other steps in the process. Information about organizational contingencies, expectations, stated goals, and critical organizational individuals are all important areas to be informally assessed from the beginning. In this step, as in all of the steps, the target group must be the primary director of the intervention. In cases of information discrepancy, the position of the target group is to be the one which is acted upon.

Identification of Resources. The next step is to determine what resources are needed to alleviate the situation considered problematic by the target group. In many cases, this step is completely ignored because the advocates come with their favorite resource, program, or treatment regimen and ready to apply it. A very important aspect of the overall multiple strategy model is that available options are considered. The obvious resources may not include all the possibilities, nor are they often the best options. What is critical is that as many options as possible are generated and their probable outcomes assessed. This phase of the model can involve several tactics including interviewing, brainstorming, investigative reporting, legal research, and gaining information from individuals with technical knowledge of an area.

Isolating the Controlling Individual. This step in the model involves two sequential elements. The first is whether or not a resource is available. For those resources which are available, the organization or person in control must be specifically identified. In the case of resources which are controlled by organizations, it is particularly critical to identify that individual within the organization who is specifically responsible. For those needed resources not available, the task becomes one of figuring out a way in which it could be provided. As a starting point, other individuals interested in the general area or organizations with a related organizational purpose provide a starting point. As in the previous phases, it is essential to push the traditional limits. Often times, several individuals or organizations can provide a necessary resource. Careful selection on the basis of vulnerability and target group fit with the specific setting are all important. This step in the assessment process ends with the isolation of an individual, group, or organization that can provide the resource in question.

Assessment of Vulnerability. The final step in the assessment phase is also one which is commonly ignored: namely, specification of the conditions under which the individual or organization controlling the needed resource is likely to provide it to the advocate's constituency. The advocate needs to assess the applicability of a range of positive and negative approaches to the controlling individual. Example questions which must be answered in this phase include: does the individual or organization have a bias which would encourage or support the request to be made? Is there currently any interaction between the target group and the controlling individual? Does the controlling individual view the current interaction positively or negatively? What are the controlling individuals' immediate interests in the matter at hand? To whom is the controlling individual most responsible — i.e., does the individual answer to county supervisors, taxpayers, consumers, legislators, school boards? How is it possible to gain personal access to the controlling individual? Who are the controlling individual's potential allies and enemies in the decision? One possible outcome of this phase of the assessment is that it may become extremely obvious that the original individual isolated as being critical in providing a particular resource may actually be secondary.

This step has many implications for the effectiveness and efficiency of the overall strategy. Therefore, adequate time and effort should be devoted to developing an accurate and complete picture of the alternatives available. As indicated earlier, the compromise which has to be drawn is between endless assessment and premature misguided action. In general, the advocate is better off on the side of premature action since the reaction will provide invaluable information about subsequent alternatives. It should also be noted that an initial positive approach to the controlling individual may be necessary to gain the information to complete the vulnerability assessment.

STRATEGY SELECTION

The multiple strategy model of advocacy suggests three interrelated steps in selecting an intervention strategy to be carried out. The first deals with defining the alternative approaches available. This involves an interaction of the personal and available skills of the advocate and the target group members. This initial step is open and freewheeling in nature and encourages the advocate to push the limits of typical organizational change techniques. The second step is selecting a smaller number of the available strategies from the original set. The criterion used here is what strategies could reasonably be implemented in the situation. Finally, considering the information learned from the assessment phase, the advocate and target group need to select a particular strategy which is most likely to lead to the desired outcome. Basically what is attempted is a rough cost-benefit comparison. The general rule throughout is to maximize the gains made by the target group and to minimize the costs to them.

The strategy alternatives available to the advocate can be generally categorized along two continua. The first dimension ranges from positive, "salesmanship-oriented" approaches to aversive, threatening, or negative approaches. In order to generate or stimulate a needed resource, the advocate could select a positive or negative strategy or opt for a neutral approach. The points on the continuum include the following:

1. At the positive end, the advocate can attempt to gain the good favor of the controlling individual or organization.

2. At the midpoint, the advocate could select a neutral strategy, often referred to as consultation, in which information would be provided to the critical individual or organization about the level of the unmet need.

3. At the negative end of the continuum, the advocate could decide to take direct or indirect aversive action against the critical individual or organization. If the needed resource is not provided, threats to take such action are obviously a major component of this end of the strategy continuum.

The second strategy continuum at issue here is the organizational level at which the advocate decides to intervene. The range of alternatives varies from individual-level interventions to societal-level interventions. The decision which needs to be made is what level of impact is necessary to ensure resource availability to the target group. The points on this continuum include the following: (1) at the individual level, the advocate could identify the critical person in control of the needed resource and decide that gaining access to the resource was restricted to this individual case only, i.e., that broader changes were not necessary to ensure the durability of the desired change; (2) at the administrative level, the advocate could identify a critical agency in control of the needed resource and decide that gaining access to the needed resource necessitated an alternative of overall agency operations; (3) at the policy level, the advocate would identify the political or social system in which change was necessary prior to the needed resource becoming available.

As can be seen in Table 3.2, these two continua necessarily interact to provide the advocate a variety of strategic approaches. To add clarity to the table, example entries are included describing the alternative strategies for an educational resource advocacy effort. The actual combinations of strategies which could actually exist in a particular situation are practically endless, depending on the situation, the people involved, the resource being sought, and the person controlling the resource. Careful consideration of the options and the related costs and benefits is the necessary precursor of advocacy efforts per se.

IMPLEMENTATION

A critical component of the advocacy model is the selection of a strategy of sufficient potency to produce the desired effects. By necessity, this will have to be accomplished in each particular situation. As noted earlier, at the heart of the community psychology movement and the advocacy approach are the notions of individual rights and target participation in the control of environmental resources. In addition, the model of advocacy is in a real state of infancy in terms of its development. This means that it is not yet possible to provide an a priori prescription as to what resources are needed, which strategies are indicated, and who should carry out the actual advocacy effort. The advocacy model has been rather straightforward in detailing the fluid complexity involved in intervention efforts. Given this realization, it is unlikely that such intervention approaches are ever likely to achieve high levels of technical standardization. The action-reaction sequence can provide the most valuable information for selection of subsequent strategies.

A few generalizations about the relationship between the strategy used and the likely reaction can be proposed on the basis of previous work in this area. At any level of intervention, positive and neutral advocacy modes have little chance of causing short-range negative consequences. Many strategies include combinations of positive, neutral, and negative approaches. The crucial consideration which must be monitored and considered throughout is how to obtain the resource needed. At times negative backlash must be risked to insure that the position of the target group is not compromised.

Similarly, it is ill advised to engage in only single-level interventions. As reviewed earlier, most intervention programs to date have been unitary in their focus, ignoring the multi-level impact necessary for durable change. A major thrust of the universalistic position outlined earlier was the importance of policy and administrative level changes. A related issue is that the multiple-strategy model demands that the target group be actively involved in planning, executing, and monitoring the advocacy effort. This is particularly critical since the model does not place the advocate in a one-up position with the target group and because the model is intended to foster increased self-advocacy efforts.

As outlined here, the advocate will need to begin by actively assessing needs, identifying available and potential resources, selecting alternative strategies, monitoring the strategy's effectiveness in meeting the need, and finally making sure that the target group is aware of the general model employed to enhance continued self-advocacy. This goal is similar to suggestions made by Iscoe (1974) in his description of the competent community. He suggests that the goal should be the development of a community that "utilizes, develops, or otherwise obtains resources of the human beings." In the end, the target group needs full access to the rationale for the advocacy approach, the potential resources available, and the mode of selecting alternative courses of action. In one sense, the entire advocacy effort should be aimed at enhancing self-advocacy.

USING THE ADVOCACY MODEL: TWO EXAMPLES

This section will provide two concrete examples of the use of advocacy strategies in programs for youth. The first is a project initiated by the authors and their colleagues at the Community Psychology Action Center at the University of Illinois (Seidman and Rappaport, 1974; Davidson and Rapp, 1976; Ku and Bleu, 1977; Davidson, 1976; Davidson, Seidman, Rappaport, Rapp, Rhodes, and

Herring, 1977; Rappaport, Davidson, and Linney, in preparation). This project, referred to as the Adolescent Diversion Project, represents and attempt to apply the advocacy model as an individual approach to adolescent offenders diverted from the juvenile justice system. The second example is characteristic of other approaches to advocacy intervention. The Massachusetts Advocacy Project exemplifies the application of the model in a broader context.

THE ADOLESCENT DIVERSION PROJECT

In order to understand the operation of the advocacy efforts in the Adolescent Diversion Project it is necessary to put the Project in its actual context. The Adolescent Diversion Project was planned out of the conceptual position outlined in the first part of this article. The project was aimed at providing a constructive alternative to juvenile justice system processing for youth who were in jeopardy of court appearance. In order to implement such a project, a specific relationship was negotiated with the juvenile authorities in Champaign and Urbana, Illinois. The resulting agreement stipulated that the juvenile officers of these two communities would refer youth to the project in lieu of court processing and would allow careful experimental examination of the effectiveness of the project. The project itself operated as part of a larger effort being undertaken by the Community Psychology Action Center between 1972 and 1975 (Seidman and Rappaport, 1974). The larger effort involved an extensive National Institute of Mental Health research grant aimed at examining the efficacy of volunteer change agents with a variety of target groups. The Adolescent Diversion Project was one of four subprojects under this federal grant. Within the rationale presented here, the Adolescent Diversion Project sought to more adequately respond to the needs of identified adolescent offenders by averting their further envelopment in the juvenile justice rehabilitative system, providing them with an action-oriented intervention provided on a one-to-one basis by undergraduate college students.

The specific advocacy approach outlined in the Davidson and Rapp (1976) article referred to earlier provided the basis for the advocacy component of the Adolescent Diversion Project. As such the ADP involved several specific components of the overall advocacy strategy. At one level, the project involved the initiation of advocacy efforts of a positive nature focused on the policies of the local juvenile justice system in order to initiate the diversion project in the beginning. At another level, the project involved the application of the advocacy principles and procedures to individual youth diverted to the project. It is really this level of advocacy which was most fully developed in the Adolescent Diversion Project and which will provide the basis of the example reviewed here.

The specific model of advocacy applied was based on the notions of each youth's rights to community resources. This model provided the basis for the volunteer based intervention with adolescent youth diverted from the justice system. Prior to the initiation of the project, the student volunteers who were the change agents for the project received extensive training in the principles and strategies of child advocacy, the procedures and regulations of the local school system, the community services and resources available to youth in the local community, the labor laws of the state, and modes for getting to know adolescent youth. The emphasis was on identifying, generating, stimulating, or rejuvenating individual and community resources to meet the needs of the youth involved. Rather than specify general resources needed by all youth, the child advocacy approach focused on adapting the general model to each individual case based on an assessment of individual needs. The position taken was consistent with the basic individual rights conception of the advocacy approach.

The advocacy intervention used in the Adolescent Diversion Project can best be described as four sequential segments. The child advocacy approach involved an initial period of the student volunteer getting to know the youth to whom they were assigned. This initial two-week period also provided the framework for assessment, by the student together with the youth, of the areas of unmet need. Every attempt was made to include consideration of family, economic, vocational, educational, legal, and personal domains. Within this framework, such an assessment was in terms of unmet needs and the relevant individual or institutional resources.

A second phase involved mutual identification of who could provide the needed resource. Particularly critical at this step was mutual identification of important individuals in control of needed changes. This included identification of individuals in control of entrance to educational alternatives, in charge of vocational training or job placement programs, responsible for membership in recreational centers, etc. In many cases, the youth were charged with finding out the information necessary for zeroing in on the critical individual. Group

supervision provided the student volunteers with an additional source
of information about the important individuals.

After the initial assessment of areas of unmet need and mutual
selection of target individuals for change, the students were involved in
attempts at direct manipulation of resources for the youth in question.
The range of strategies available were construed in the same manner as
the alternatives outlined earlier in the general model of advocacy. The
first set of alternatives described various advocacy strategies ranging
from positive approaches to aversive or negative tactics. At the positive
end were such strategies as getting to know the director of the
alternative high school, providing information about the project, and
arguing for needed entree for the youth in question. The more neutral
approach was characterized by the straight provision of information. In
this instance, one case involved informing the basketball coach of the
availability of a particular youth who had recently moved to the
community. At the negative end of the continuum were strategies
usually characterized as more disruptive. In this instance, faced with the
suspension of a youth from school for nonattendance, the student
threatened to take to the central administration the information that
the youth had been absent for over a year without the youth's parents
ever having been informed. As detailed earlier, a second important
dimension included the level of intervention. For the most part, the
Adolescent Diversion Project involved efforts focused at the individual
level. However, in several specific cases more general changes had to be
sought. These included altering the entry criteria for the local
educational alternative program which had previously excluded delinquent youth, expanding the criteria for youth considered eligible for
work study programs, etc. Critical at this third phase of the advocacy
intervention was the selection of the strategy likely to produce the
maximum gain for the youth in question.

Following the selection of a strategy and its initiation, the critical
phase of monitoring its effects was undertaken. It is often one thing to
negotiate a needed change and quite another to actually make sure that
it is carried out. Here again, the major focus was upon keeping in
constant contact with the youth to make sure that the changes were
implemented to their satisfaction. It was also critical to check with
other critical individuals to ensure the durability of the change. Making
sure that educational alternatives did not become special education
dumping grounds, seeing that jobs promised were actually delivered,

monitoring the youth's participation in recreational activities, etc., were all examples of this phase of the advocacy effort. In many cases, alternative strategies or targets were selected on the basis of information gained.

A central component of the advocacy intervention used in the Adolescent Diversion Project was its ultimate focus. There has been some debate concerning the extent to which advocacy-based interventions should involve themselves in taking action for the target individual as opposed to instructing such individuals in taking such actions themselves. As described above, the first two phases primarily involved advocacy activities mainly initiated by the student volunteers. During the final phases of an 18-week program, the volunteer change agent purposefully switched gears into more direct efforts at executing advocacy activities with the youth. This also involved the beginnings of instructing, showing, and encouraging the youth in taking such action for himself/herself. The basis for this final phase was either an initial area of unmet need which was not sufficiently rectified, an additional area, or an area of projected future need. This phase saw the change agent working through the process with the individual youth. The basic techniques involved instructing the youth in assessing problem areas within an individual rights conception, showing the youth how to consider and select targets for change, determination of modes of strategy selection, and supporting the youth in such actions through actual practice sessions and actual encounters with critical individuals in the relevant social systems. Finally, the advocacy intervention involved the volunteer change agent assuming a more passive role and consulting the youth in carrying out his/her own advocacy efforts. Essentially the last month was aimed at preparing the individual youth for becoming his/her own advocate.

MASSACHUSETTS ADVOCACY CENTER

The Massachusetts Advocacy Center grew out of the experiences of a group of Boston citizen-advocates known as The Task Force on Children Out of School. In 1973 the group received a Ford Foundation Grant and became the Massachusetts Advocacy Center. The early development of the original group has been described by Peter Edelman in the Harvard Educational Review (1973). It is an interesting story in its own right. In that paper Edelman describes the involvement of Hubert Jones and Larry Brown, who brought to the attention of the people of Massachusetts the large number of children being involuntarily excluded from school because of discipline, pregnancy, physical and emotional handicap, or language problems. They organized a Task Force of lay and professional people who put together a report on the problem. The Task Force was composed of "nonestablishment" people, together with agency professionals who would have to respond to the report. It included, from the outset, those who lived in the neighborhoods most directly affected, as well as those who were less likely to be advocates, but who were both influential and willing to examine the facts. In the process they all became convinced of a need for change, and were able to support the report's widespread dissemination leading to specific changes in public school policy and programs throughout Massachusetts.

In 1974 a law went into effect in Massachusetts, calling for every school system to provide education for all children, aimed at whatever the individual needs of a child happen to be. This is the law which has served as a model for similar national legislation. The people at the Advocacy Center view one of their roles to be a monitor of its implementation. They have established citizen monitors in 280 of the state's 351 school systems, and provided the monitors with checklists of substantive issues to examine. They collect data, and follow up on schools which are in noncompliance with the law. They are training parents, as well as other case advocates, to assure that all children will get the full and intended benefit of the law. (Massachusetts Advocacy Annual Report, 1975)

In the context of describing the early work of the Center, Edelman points out several "rules" or tactics useful when engaging in the advocacy strategy:

1. Someone must identify the problem and set the process in motion.

2. The problem should be small enough to be possible to solve and comprehensible to the public, while evoking strong emotion.

3. One must be prepared to present specific remedies.

4. Some core of dedicated (paid) staff who will work day-to-day are required, after the initial issue is raised.

5. Fund raising may be necessary but only after people have gotten it off the ground. Volunteers may be crucial in the early stages.

6. "Mainstream" as well as "street people" can be incorporated into a task force.

7. After a report is written follow-up is essential. Implementation is the key step. This requires that the same people who collect the information be willing to work directly with appropriate agencies for administrative agreements and actual implementation of change.

This latter tactic describes the general style of the Massachusetts Advocacy Center. Following a clear documentation of a difficulty, and the dissemination of a report through the media, directly to legislators, and to other citizens, a climate is created which serves to allow the advocates to follow through. This means that much of the actual implementation is at the administrative level and they can begin with positive or neutral tactics (as described above) when working in each school district. Negative tactics, including adverse publicity, use of the courts, and pushing for legislative change, are not excluded, but it is often the case that laws already exist, and enforcement is the issue. What is required is often public attention to a difficulty and people who accept the responsibility for follow-through. These then are the key elements in the approach: 1) public attention which draws light on a general problem; 2) people who keep the pressure on specific agencies responsible by providing specific and constructive change suggestions; 3) implicit or explicit threats to focus the attention from the general difficulty to a specific setting in question; and 4) quiet negotiation with agency administrators, backed up by a potential for publicity which has already been demonstrated.

What Edelman refers to as administrative advocacy is not litigation, nor is it ideology. There is no formula or ritualized way to proceed. It requires flexible reaction to a local situation, and persistence. The exact content and style must differ from one locale to another. At the same time, various researchers and activists (Fairweather, et al., 1974; O. M. Collective, 1971; Alinsky, 1971; Rothman, 1974) seem to come to very similar suggestions for social change activities as we move toward a "theory of action" (Rappaport, 1977).

The Massachusetts Advocacy Center has now implemented its model in multiple problem areas, and has issued formal reports on topics such as *The Politics of Mental Health in Massachusetts; An Education Handbook for Students, Parents and Professionals;* a report on *Childhood Lead Paint Poisoning; Hunger in the Classroom; Special Education in Boston; The Drugging of Children;* and the *Juvenile Court.* The Center's staff (with a budget as of 1975 of $120,000, provided by various foundations) had expanded to eight full-time people and over thirty part-time volunteers, including attorneys, social scientists, educators and students. Staff continued to see their role as initiators of others into action. In the center's 1975 *Annual Report,* it is self-described as "monitoring the administrative process to direct attention of policy makers, the public, and community/professional organizations to the unmet needs of Massachusetts citizens, particularly children." They do not focus on one area such as education or mental health but rather on the view that law is not enough, and the rights of children must be functionally translated into administrative action in various social systems.

CONCLUSION AND FUTURE DIRECTIONS

The advent of a community psychology perspective clearly laid the groundwork for the development of the environmental resources conception and resulting model of advocacy intervention. The crises which existed concerning preferred theoretical perspectives, definitions of professional roles, the political nature of science, and the goals of psychology, all led to the development of new models of operation. The multiple strategy model of advocacy developed in this paper has several implications for the future direction in the field. These will embrace the areas of theory development, research strategies, professional role expectations, and training programs for future community psychologists.

The development of a psychology of the community really represented a paradigmatic break with past positions. The implications of such developments as the advocacy model will have the impact of expanding future theoretical formulations. In the first place, the variables considered relevant in theorizing about social problems have to be considerably expanded. The open-systems orientation calls into question the static, deterministic metatheory currently deeply entrenched in social science theory building. The advocacy model calls quite directly for the consideration and importance of systemic variables as well as those at the individual level. It also recognizes the importance of considering the interaction between any phenomenon of interest and the social environment in which it operates. What is needed is theory building which transcends existing disciplinary and philosophical boundaries. A second direction which needs to be witnessed in the construction of theoretical perspectives is an explicit handling of the political and policy relevant implications of the theoretical perspective constructed. Historical examples of the political convenience and hence inappropriate use of theoretical propositions highlights the need for becoming directly involved in the political translation of conceptual positions. In addition, the positions of all groups most likely to be affected by theoretical or paradigmatic positions must be included. To date, only certain segments of society have had their interests considered. What is suggested is that theoretical perspectives useful to a variety of groups be undertaken. In short, the current crisis created by dissatisfaction with existing theoretical positions has opened the way for innovative alternatives. The directions in which those new developments lead will be critical.

One could conclude the multiple strategy model of advocacy would lead to the rejection of research efforts. On the contrary, what is suggested is that the research methods available to the community psychologist provide a useful tool for generating credible information relevant to the interests of various target groups. Here again, the traditional models of social science investigation will need to be opened and altered considerably. The research models employed will have to be moved from the exclusively confirmatory tradition to include exploratory procedures (Davidson and Berck, 1977). A major change must include the criteria specified by the participants or target groups in examining the operation of social processes and the effectiveness of social programs (Goodwin, 1971). Measurement procedures will need to be constructed which take into account the perspective of the target group as well as the pet theory of the investigator. Probably most important, research approaches must expand beyond the individual difference or victim-blaming bias which has been observed (Caplan and Nelson, 1973). Systemic effects as well as individual effects must be examined. The advocacy model also demands the increased use of purposeful research approaches (Fairweather and Tornatzky, 1977; Campbell, 1969). Moving to research methods which systematically address themselves to the solution of a problem from the criteria of the target group is clearly indicated.

The professional role changes alluded to throughout are considerable. The advocacy model obviously involves a dethroning of the aloof expert or sterile researcher. It demands an explicit dealing with the practical applications of one's work and a clear specification of the value positions involved. In many ways, what is called for here also expands the role which professionals have been accustomed to playing. The movement is more in the direction of an active problem-solving generalist than increasingly narrowly defined specialists. The importance of the advocate's personal resources are elevated to an equal status with the individual's record of formal training or highly specialized technical skill (Sarason, 1976). A common observation is that the advocacy mode demands an increased tolerance for role ambiguity. As the conceptual position and professional roles are opened the options available to the community psychologist are increased dramatically. A critical issue is the securing of an institutional base of support for advocacy efforts. This problem has been pointed out in related innovative roles for psychologists (Tornatzky, 1976). What is to be expected and hopefully avoided is premature consummation of bonds with apparently new paradigms. The likelihood of experiencing the same old wine in the new shiny bottle would appear high.

REFERENCES

Albee, G. W. (1968) "Conceptual Models and Manpower Requirements in Psychology." *American Psychology* 23: 317-320.

Alinsky, S. (1971) *Rules for Radicals.* New York: Random House.

Bennett, C. C., Anderson, L. S., Cooper, S., Hassol, L., Klein, D.C., and Rosenblum, G. (eds.) (1966) *Community Psychology: A Report of the Boston Conference on the Education of Psychologists for Community Mental Health.* Boston: Boston University Press.

Campbell, D. T. (1969) "Reforms as Experiments." *American Psychologist* 24: 409-429.

Caplan, N. and S. D. Nelson (1973) "On Being Useful: The Nature and Consequences of Psychological Research on Social Problems." *American Psychology* 28: 199-211.

Cowen, E. L. (1973) "Social and Community Interventions." *Annual Review of Psychology* 24: 423-472.

———, Gardner, E. A., and Zax, M. (eds.) (1967) *Emergent Approaches to Mental Health Problems.* New York: Meredith.

Davidson, W. S. (1976) "The Diversion of Juvenile Offenders." Unpublished doctoral dissertation, University of Illinois.

———, and P. Berck (1977) "Research Methods for Community Psychology: A Method for the Madness." Unpublished manuscript.

———, and C. Rapp (1976) "Child Advocacy in the Juvenile Justice System." *Social Work* 21: 225-233.

———, and M. R. Robinson (1975) "Community Psychology and Behavior Modification: A Community-Based Program for the Prevention of Delinquency." *Corrective and Social Psychiatry and Journal of Behavior Technology Methods and Therapy* 21: 1-12.

———, and E. Seidman (1974) "Studies of Behavior Modification and Juvenile Delinquency: A Review, Methodological Critique, and Social Perspective." *Psychological Bulletin,* 31 998-1011.

———, Seidman, E., Rappaport, J., Rapp, N. , Rhodes, W., and Herring, J. (1977) "The Diversion of Juvenile Offenders: Some Empirical Light on the Subject." *Social Work Research and Abstract* (in press).

Fairweather, G. W. (1967) *Methods for Experimental Social Innovation.* New York: Wiley.

———. (1972) *Social Change: The Challenge to Survival.* Morristown, N. J.: General Learning Press.

———, Saunders, D., and Tornatzky, L. (1974) *Creating Change in Mental Health Organizations*. New York: Pergamon.

———, and L. Tornatzky (1977) *Experimental Methods for Evaluating Social Change*. New York: Pergamon.

Franks, C. L. (1969) *Behavior Therapy*. New York: McGraw-Hill.

Gergen, K. (1973) "Social Psychology as History." *Journal of Personality and Social Psychology*, 26: 309-320.

Golann, S., and C. Eisdorfer (eds.) (1972) *Handbook of Community Mental Health*. New York: Appleton-Century Crofts.

Goodwin, L. (1971) "On Making Social Research Relevant to Public Policy and National Problem Solving." *American Psychologist*, 26: 431-442.

Halleck, S. (1974) *The Politics of Psychotherapy*. New York: Random House.

Hebb, D. O. (1974) "What Psychology Is About." *American Psychologist*, 29: 71-79.

Hobbs, N. (1964) "Mental Health's Third Revolution." *American Journal of Orthopsychiatry*, 34: 822-833.

Hunt, J. Mc.V. (1961) *Intelligence and Experience*. New York: Ronald.

Iscoe, I. (1974) "Community Psychology and the Competent Community." *American Psychologist*, 29: 607-613.

Jensen, A. R. (1969) "How Much Can We Boost IQ and Scholastic Achievement?" *Harvard Educational Review*, 39: 1-123.

Kamin, L. (1974) *The Science and Politics of IQ*. Potomac, Maryland: Erlbaum.

Kelly, J. G. (1970) "Antidotes for Arrogance: Training for Community Psychology." *American Psychologist*, 25: 524-531.

———. (1972) "Moving to a Psychology for Community Service." *Inter-American Journal of Psychology*, 6: 121-130.

Kelly, J. G. (1977) "Social and Community Interventions." *Annual Review of Psychology*, 28: 323-362.

Ku, R., and C. Bleu (1977) *Out of the Ivory Tower*. U. S. Department of Justice: Washington, D.C.

"Massachusetts Advocacy Annual Report." (1975) Boston: Massachusetts Advocacy Center, Second Annual Report.

Nietzel, M., Winett, R., MacDonald, M., and Davidson, W. S. (1977) *Behavioral Approaches to Community Psychology*. New York: Pergamon.

O'Leary, K. D., and T. Wilson (1975) *Behavior Therapy: Application and Outcome*. Englewood Cliffs: Prentice-Hall.

O. M. Collective. (1971) *The Organizers Manual*. New York: Bantam.

Poser, E. G. (1966) "The effects of Therapists' Training on Group Therapeutic Outcome." *Journal of Consulting Psychology*, 30(4): 283-289.

Rappaport, J. (1977a) *Community Psychology: Values, Research, and Action*. New York: Holt, Rinehart, and Winston.

———. (1977b) "From Noah to Babel: Relationships Between Conceptions, Values, Analysis Levels, and Intervention Strategies." in I. Iscoe, B. Bloom, and C. D. Spielberger (eds.) *Community Psychology in Perspective*. New York: Hemisphere Press.

–––, and J. Chinsky (1974) "Models for Service Delivery: An Historican and Conceptual Perspective." *Professional Psychology*, 5: 42-50.

–––, Chinsky, J., and Cowen, E. (1971) *Innovations in Helping Chronic Patients.* New York: Academic Press.

–––, Davidson, W., Wilson, M., and Mitchell, A. (1975) "Alternatives to Blaming the Victim: Our Places to Stand Have Not Moved the Earth." *American Psychologist*, 30: 525-528.

Reigel, K. (1972) "Influence of Economic and Political Ideologies on the Development of Developmental Psychology." *Psychological Bulletin*, 78: 129141.

Reissman, R. (1965) "The Helper Therapy Principle." *Social Work*, 10: 27-32.

Ryan, W. (1971) *Blaming the Victim.* New York: Vantage.

Rothman, J. (1968) "Three Models of Community Organization Practice." *Social Work Practice*, : 16-41.

–––. (1974) *Planning and Organizing for Social Change.* New York: Columbia University Press.

Sarason, S. (1976) "Community Psychology, Networks, and Mr. Everyman." *American Psychologist* 31: 317-328.

Seidman, E., and J. Rappaport (1974) "The Educational Pyramid: A Paradigm for Training, Research, and Manpower Utilization in Community Psychology." *American Journal of Community Psychology*, 2: 119-130.

–––, Rappaport, J., Davidson, W. S., and Linney, J. (in preparation) *Changing Human Service Systems: Interventions with Children, Adolescents, Adults, and the Elderly.*

Siegel, J. M. (1973) "Mental Health Volunteers as Change Agents." *American Journal of Community Psychology*, 1: 138-158.

Sjoberg, G. (1975) "Politics, Ethics, and Evaluation Research." in M. Guttentag and E. L. Struening (eds.) *Handbook of Evaluation Research.* Beverly Hills, CA: Sage, 29-51.

Tornatzky, L. (1976) "How a Ph.D. Program Aimed at Survival Issues Survived." *American Psychologist*, 31: 189-191.

Triandas, H. C. (1977) "The Future of Pluralism." *Journal of Social Issues* (in press).

Ullman, L. and L. Krasner (1965) *Case Studies in Behavior Modification.* New York: Holt.

Watzlawick, P., Weakland, J., and Fisch, R. (1974) *Change: Principles of Problem Formation and Problem Resolution.* New York: Norton.

Windle, C., Bass, R. D., and Tabue, C. H. (1974) "P. R. Aside: Initial Results from NIMH's Service Program Evaluations Studies." *American Journal of Community Psychology*, 2: 311-327.

Winett, R. A. and R. C. Winkler (1972) "Current Behavior Modification in the Classroom: Be Still, Be Quiet, Be Docile." *Journal of Applied Behavior Analysis*, 5: 499-504.

Zax, M. and G. Specter (1974) *An Introduction to Community Psychology.* New York: Wiley.

4

ADVOCACY AND URBAN PLANNING

Paul Davidoff and
Linda Davidoff

Together with urban activism of all kinds — with the possible exception of neighborhood community organizations — planning advocacy has experienced a kind of "hunkering down," a period of learning to make do with limited resources of money and public support. The year 1977 will, we believe, establish a demarcation between this time of stabilization and one of renewed exploration into new territory. The reasons are obvious: an end to a swing of the business cycle, one which has been especially sharp and painful to urban enterprises; and a new national political landscape, with a renewed commitment to public intervention on behalf of the poor and the powerless.

HISTORY: ADVOCACY'S ROOTS
IN PLANNING PRACTICE

The American practice of urban planning began in the 1900s as an outgrowth of an elitist concept of urban political structure: the "good citizens" would swing their influence behind the formation of a Planning Commission for the city which would make long-range decisions about city growth and design, insulated from the crass self-interest and short-sightedness of the corrupt political machine. This 19th-century hangover was a salient feature of planning thought and practice right through the Kennedy Administration, which, in its Urban Renewal programs, wrote large the idea of the Master Plan drafted in the Public Interest, and channeled federal money into the execution of the experts' vision of the downtown commercial, real estate, and banking interests' plans.

City planning, traditionally, was oriented toward the physical city. Its history in our country and elsewhere has been centered on the physical approach, looking at the physical structure of the city, the means of transportation, the use of land. It looked to the capital budget rather than the operating budget, to the structures required for the facilities in which government would create its services. Until very recently urban planners were not concerned with the services to place within the facilities, only with their locations and physical characteristics and the ways in which the locations of public and private facilities could assist in meeting certain social, economic and political goals.

The ideal to which planning as a discipline, and practicing planners, looked was an ideal of the "highest and best use" of the physical space of urban communities. The ideal community was a community of orderliness, of hierarchy, in which land and buildings were used to their "highest" potential. The Daniel Burnham Chicago Plan of 1893, reflecting the Beaux Arts movement of Europe, was widely imitated; it relied on aesthetic perceptions of symmetry and order and of appropriate symbolism to create an urban plan expressive of the dominance of urban society by city government, big business, banks, and commercial establishments. At the same time, planning thought and approaches were influenced by the housing and settlement house movements, and the muckrakers and social critics who looked beneath the marble facades of the Beaux Arts plans. Mumford, Wright, and Stein and the Regional planning Association of America were writing in the 1920s about the need for a planning approach which dealt with the economics and social structure of an urban national society (Sussman, 1976).

During the period from 1900 to 1950, as planning departments and commissions became a standard feature of city governments throughout the United States and the Department of Housing and Urban Development came into being, the dominant tone of planning was of civic design and civic improvement, elevating the physical appearance of cities by tearing down the ugly and "unplanned." Social concerns, including the development of a sense of a "just society," were far from central to the common practice of urban planning.

Beginning in the late 1950s, city plans began to address service issues — issues of social planning. That was a healthy and, we believe, an important change in outlook. It took place during the course of the war against poverty and the civil rights movement, when it became increasingly clear that it was impossible for city planners to be concerned with the physical environment while ignoring the social repercussions of events that took place within that physical environment. After a period of years of pressure within the profession, a broadening of the definition of the role of planning took place.

Corresponding to this expansion of the scope of planning during the 1950s and 1960s, the planning profession, having grown considerably in size and in its independence from its origins in architecture and civil engineering, became concerned with the problem of self-definition. The complaint rose that there was very little thought in the field and in our graduate schools; planners had no concept of what they were about; and what it was that was planner-like about us. There was concern with how planners could improve their ability to deal with the issues of the urban community. The search for self-definition turned up a belief that Meyerson and Banfield (1964) had pronounced earlier, and that Herbert Simon (1976) and others had discussed. They took what was essentially a managerial or rational decision-making approach that planning was a process by which decisions could be made about how the resources of the future could be allocated and utilized in an effective manner to achieve the aims of the society. The planning process was viewed as a kind of recipe or set of instructions which identified the potential goals that were available to the body politic, urged the society to make choices among its potential goals, clarifying and making explicit what its goals were. Having made the goals explicit, the plan then could search for the appropriate means to achieve those goals. The goal-setting part was seen as a very important part of the planning process, because in the absence of specification of the goals to be achieved, it is very hard to follow through on planning. How does one know what one wants to achieve if the goals, the aims, are ambiguous or vague? The goal-oriented view of planning said that the rational process is to identify the range of means that are available to achieve a given set of goals; to compare the set of alternative means and try to evaluate the consequences that would flow from the implementation of these sets of means, in terms of which would be most suitable in achieving the goals sought. Meyerson and Banfield go to great length to identify different types of consequences, intended and anticipated, unintended and unanticipated, that planners can examine in searching for a comparison of alternate means. Having completed the process, the planner may divulge a best means, or a set of means. The next step is choosing the process by which those means can be implemented and overseeing the implementation to make certain that there is a constant pursuit of the goals through the means employed. And finally, there is the overall appraisal, or feedback mechanism, for the reconsideration of goals and means and methods of implementations.

This recipe for developing a rational pursuit of goals was very important for the development of planning theory in the historical setting of the late 1950s. In the time of Eisenhower and of Senator Joseph McCarthy, the language of societal movement and change had to be neutral, technical, and devoid of reference to discredited ideologies. A critique of the then-dominant standard master plan, the plan for downtown urban renewal, had to be couched in noninflammatory terms. It would be very important back in the 1950s and early 1960s to identify and make clear to the public what its alternatives were, because, in fact, the planning system and the urban development and urban renewal system weren't doing that. They were coming in with the answer, the way to do it. Those of us who were attuned toward thinking that the social and political system would be better served through redistribution of wealth, power, and access to social good and who saw no redistributional emphasis in planning and renewal proposals, came to the conclusion that a way to begin to explore the opportunities for redistribution was by working within the system to expose the opportunities that could occur through alternatives. The exploration of "alternatives" was an effort to find a way to open the system to more choices than the rather conservative system of the late 1950s was providing.

The rational pursuit of goals and of means and methods of implementation gave rise in planning thought to what now seems an obvious point: the method by which urban planners and theoreticians selected the issues to be chosen for study was itself culturally biased. It was necessary not only to explicate planners' biases and perspectives, but also to try to move beyond their biases by giving expression to the full range of choices in the rational pursuit of a better urban community. Planning issues were not matters of objective techniques or factual conditions that would automatically suggest appropriate courses of action. Planners had to understand that their perceptions were subjective and that their determinations of appropriate courses of action, too, were subjective, value-based, and, in a sense, political.

Another important issue of planning theory in the post-World War II period was the problem of creating a democratic planning process. The whole concept of planning was under strong attack in the 1930s and the 1940s. The argument was not against city planning, it was against national economic planning. In the American reaction against the Bolshevik Revolution, the concept of planning — the very identification of a plan of government — meant the denial of freedom to participants in the society. A plan meant that citizens had to adhere to the plan if it were to be carried out. These criticisms of planning (Hajek, 1944) as the opening wedge of totalitarian coercion are still valuable critiques of the nature of planning.

Planners continue to be greatly concerned with the question of reconciling planning with the norms of a democratic society. The realization that all planners make proposals in terms of their own personal, subjective evaluation of the urban situation was immensely important in a process of establishing the requirements for a democratic planning process. Planning is not a neutral, "scientific," technical process; it is a process of making and implementing subjective judgments about what is good for an urban community. A technician could perform a useful role by contributing information and analysis as a background to decision making. But no expert could come forth and prescribe a plan, because a plan should be a product of a democratic decision making process. No single person's or agency's judgment could be proxy for a democratic process of urban decision making — planning. As in other aspects of the development of advocacy in urban planning, Herbert Gans' (1962) book, *The Urban Villagers,* contributed valuable insights into the way that apparently neutral, technical decisions about the "best" use of parcel of urban land could be seen as exercises of bureaucratic insensitivity and even tyranny.

This recognition of the planner's necessarily limited role in formulating goals in a democratic society had a strong impact on the profession. In the Eisenhower and early Kennedy eras, with anticommunism and anticollectivism approaching the status of a national religion, planners who were "liberal" in their political learnings felt safest not in confronting conservative attitudes on the part of elected public officials head on, but in trying to enlarge the sphere of discussion by identifying new alternatives so that the Master Plan could educate the public as to what the real alternatives were. The public could then engage in debate and in consideration of what its own desires were. Within the profession, it was assumed that the debate about the public's goals should take place within a planning agency. By definition, planning was something done within planning agencies.

The increasing intensity and frequency of opposition to decisions made by local public agencies involved in housing renewal and redevelopment in the early 1960s led to the next step—the creation of a connection between anti-establishment planners and urban movements of the poor and of racial minorities. Some planners found themselves participating more and more politically in challenging the right of established planning and renewal agencies to carry out their tasks. They found themselves in the role of antagonists to the planning process, trying to give assistance to those who were what we called the bulldozee in urban renewal, those who were pushed out of their slums. Frustrated planners tried to find a way to offer assistance to that class of the citizenry because they felt the agency was failing to do it. At the same time they began to build up a theory to justify their own actions. They built up a theory of planning concerned with the development of a role for the planner who wanted to work outside the public planning system, to counter that system if necessary. The name given to it was "advocacy." Planners would serve as advocates for interests that were not being given fair consideration by government agencies.

EMERGENCE OF ADVOCACY AS A PLANNING THEORY AND PRACTICE

In the 1960s planners began to engage in open debate not only within their agencies but between planning professionals inside the agency and those who were outside advocating special interests, such as universities, trade unions, and minority groups. The debate led to a suggestion that the problem in planning had been the dominance of a theory that planning should be monolithic or unitary, that there was an agency of government — a planning commission (in our cities), or a national planning entity (the Bureau of the Budget, in the United States, or the national Planning Bureau, in other societies) — capable of making plans for a whole city or a whole nation. Planners realized that this conceptualization of the process of planning had seen it as a unitary process with one input, the agencies' input, and that this was particularly startling when compared with the political decision process. Political decisions were to be openly debated at least by two parties and frequently by many interests; but planners had not identified how those interests could become involved in their process.

The attack on single-agency, unitary planning was accompanied by development of a notion of pluralism in planning (Davidoff, 1965), by which it was meant that there should be more than one voice in the discussion of plans for the future of a community. Pluralism may have been conceptually of much greater importance than a concept of advocacy. What was urgently needed was a process by which there is created more than one plan for the community to consider – that there is at least one "counter-plan." Plural plans make it possible for the citizenry to understand something of the range of what is available to them and to compare alternative plans.

It was conceivable that plural plans could all be created by a single planning agency. The recipe for rational planning which preceded advocacy theory suggested that it was the role of the planner in the agency to identify a number of alternative plans, or at least alternative sets of means toward a goal. But, in the context of an opposition based in poor communities to the downtown renewal plans of the official agencies, the idea of an agency technician setting forth the available alternatives seemed remote and alien.

Municipal planners and renewal officers were upper-middle class, highly educated, and used to dealing with others of the same status; poor people and minority-group members viewed them with suspicion. A plan purporting to express the interests of the poor and the minorities could hardly emerge from such a source.

How could a poor, minority community obtain the technical expertise needed to produce its own plan in opposition to the official agency plan?

In an analogy to advocacy in law, the issue was posed: can you be advocate for your own case or should you obtain a disinterested professional who can do a better job of advocating another person's case? A recurrent problem in an agency advocating a range of alternatives was that the agency planner was not deeply committed to them, and many of the alternatives he would present would be straw men. A number of planning reports have put forth a set of alternatives and then selected one. A client carefully reviewing the argument behind each of the alternatives can see that alternatives have been set forth merely to show they existed and have then been knocked down very quickly.

The challenge to advocacy became the need to develop a process whereby an interest group whose concerns had not yet been voiced in the construction of an official master plan could obtain expert planning advice and proceed to develop an alternative plan. Poor and minority communities, civil rights groups, residents of land "needed" for slum clearance or highway construction, all needed a formal process by which they could rely on, or develop themselves, the ability to prepare elements of a master plan serving their own concerns.

Pluralism and advocacy were bolstered by the concept, developed in the early 1960s, of client analysis. Planners talked about a "client-oriented" approach (Reiner, Reimer, and Reiner, 1963) – an interesting contrast to today's emphasis on the "consumer" as the sovereign figure in social activism. The concept of client-oriented social services was a response to the paternalistic approach of which social workers were said to be guilty. It urged providers of social service to give respect and attention to the views and values of the people they served. It urged professionals to be wary of the imposition of their own values on their clients, and to give presumptive legitimacy to their clients' views.

Advocacy was seen as a way in which the planning profession could give assistance to the client. Planners would open offices in parts of the city accessible to ghetto residents; would make themselves available to meet with poor people and minority groups; would help members of these communities articulate their concerns with the physical shape of their neighborhoods and the ways in which city services were provided to those neighborhoods. Planners would help residents shape proposals or responses to official proposals, would appear as expert witnesses in suits opposing highway and renewal plans destructive to poor neighborhoods; would use their knowlege of urban planning, renewal and redevelopment, capital budgeting, service programming and budgeting, and other urban processes to advance the interests of their new clients.

The development of the idea and practice of advocacy led to a new issue: who dictates the terms of the discussion, the professional advocate or the client? What is the role of the professional working with a client organization, a neighborhood group, in trying to develop a plan? To what extent does the professional lead; to what extent does he follow?

The proper client-advocate relationship was, of course, simultane-ously a topic of debate and exploration in other professional fields, notably social work, medicine, and the law. In the law, a client hires a lawyer to advocate his case before the bar. The client is assumed not to have the ability to make a presentation of his/her own case, under the ground rules of the courtroom. In line with that analogy, the attack on advocacy has been presented that it leads to a form of professional elitism such as we have in the law in which the lawyer makes the argument and the case, even identifying for the client what the client's interests are.

As the idea of the sovereign consumer has developed in recent years, the elitism of the client-professional relationship has been tempered by the notion that the consumer-client should establish his or her own goals and should require the professional to state a method of achieving those goals within the consumer's cost constraints, which include money, pain (in medicine), risk of failure, time, and other factors. And if the consumer's goal is not achieved, he can lash back in legal attacks on his professional helper. The rising costs of malpractice insurance are a testimony to the increasingly high performance standards of what used to be a passive client body.

If, however, the client-professional relationship is based on mutual respect, sharing of goals, and an appropriate balance of consumerism and expertise, the planning advocacy of making it possible for a community to participate in developing its own range of options can become a tremendously powerful educative device. The citizenry becomes aware of its potential to create, to plan, to change its conditions of life. New vistas open up. People become aware that almost everything is possible at some given cost. An advocate plan could propose that New York City could become a potato field, its residents fully employed in a primitive form of agriculture. Any plan can be set out for discussion, as long as the costs of carrying it out are set forth. The range is not really free, however; society is limited and constrained by technology, the available resources, the natural environment.

A further theoretical constraint on advocacy is the inevitable problem of irreconcilably clashing interests. Successful advocacy requires the forceful expression, in planning terms, of particular interests: those of neighborhoods, interest groups, ethnic and social groups within an urban community. The issue then arises of what person, agency, or force is in a position to referee or judge the proper resolution of irreconcilable plans?

If the city of New York opens up a neighborhood planning office in Bensonhurst, and the Bensonhurst community decides that it wants to prevent more black families from entering the community, is the planner's job as a representative of the city of New York in Bensonhurst to give representation to the views of Bensonhurst or to the views of the black and other interests of the larger entity, New York City? The answer could lie in either direction. The city determines that there ought to be an advocate for each neighborhood; then the planner's job would be to represent the views of Bensonhurst, which are to exclude blacks. There would lie the ultimate extension of the advocacy viewpoint, that would professionalize the process of neighborhood exclusion and mutual antipathy.

The city also determines, however, that all community interests should be fairly represented in the planning process. By assigning staff planners to work with communities throughout a city, the central planning body assures expression of divergent views, engendering further debate and discussion, enlarging the fact that there is a clash of interests. An advocate's view of the democratic tradition is that those differences have to be explored as explicitly as possible so that all parties can take the most intelligent position.

A cynic might argue that the ultimate resolution of an elaborated process of conflict among groups over planning decisions will always result in the victory of the forces that were strongest in the first place (and that might have proposed a single plan "in the public interest"). We believe that even relatively weak groups fare better if allowed to organize, develop viable ideas, exert pressure, and search for points of leverage even within a lopsided balance of power (Mazziotti, 1974).

Thus advocacy as a process leads to an analysis of pluralism in describing the contending planning viewpoints: a planner can be placed in any number of advocacy positions, setting forth any number of possible alternative substantive views of proper urban policy choice. The planner can choose for whom to work, or be assigned to a particular interest group by a central agency concerned with full representation for alternative views.

ADVOCACY AND MONEY

One measure of the political viability of an interest is: can you find somebody who will support it? In American practice, there exist enough liberal and conservative foundations to sponsor both interests on the right and on the left of a relatively radical nature. But not every group gets support, and a continuing reliance on foundation or public support is antithetical to democracy itself; it is like saying that those who have great wealth can choose who they want to support.

In the end, taxpayers pay for foundations, because they supply the federal revenue that is foregone through giving tax exemptions to the wealthy families and corporations which establish foundations. And taxpayers pay for the more complex, and more expensive, operations of a public planning agency that chooses to elaborate its field staff, sending representatives and resources out to formerly underrepresented communities and groups. The near-complete reliance of advocacy planners on public funds controlled by political authorities, or on foundations controlled ultimately by public tax policy as well as more immediately by their boards and wealthy donors, produces further moral dilemmas of the actuality of control over the advocacy process by the clients of that process. In addition to concern for dominating the process through advantages of education, verbalization, and status, the advocate has to be concerned about distortion of the available planning choices by reliance on foundations or on elected authorities. (The moral dilemmas, however, seldom trouble us to the point of refusing the support.) The long-run, preferable form of action is to find a way to make advocacy self-perpetuating; to increase the advocates' and their clients' ability to raise money.

URBAN PLANNING ADVOCACY IN PRACTICE

As advocacy developed a body of theory, it also generated strategies and techniques for practice. These were disseminated and used in planning practice. Possibly the earliest examples of advocacy were the consulting projects of the Walter Thabit consulting firm, based in New York, beginning in the mid-1950s. Thabit's alternative proposal for housing University of Pennsylvania students in small, scattered residential units so as to avoid creating "student ghettos" and clearing large numbers of existing low- and moderate-cost housing units was commissioned by Powelton Village Associates, a pioneer group of university-based younger faculty and graduate students who had carved a rehabilitated residential neighborhood out of an old Victorian low-income district. The Thabit firm also conducted the studies that led to the West Village House in New York City, a new-construction, low-rise solution to a need for moderate-cost housing without extensive clearance or the creation of a single-income, high-density ghetto.

In the 1960s, advocacy practice flourished in a number of communities around the nation. Urban Planning Aid, an advocacy agency in Cambridge, Mass., carried through a number of sophisticated studies accompanied by intensive and successful community-organizing efforts that led to the halt of construction of a major highway project planned to go through inner-city residential neighborhoods.

In response to the increasing number and scope of advocacy projects and to demands for action within its membership, the professional society, the American Institute of Planners, established an advocacy office in the late 1960s. Planners for Equal Opportunity (PEO) was formed in 1964 and flourished through the rest of the 1960s as a gadfly to the planning establishment on issues of equal rights. Official agencies around the nation altered their staff structures to accommodate one or more professionals whose responsibility was to work with community groups to develop independent planning proposals and to respond to official proposals.

The federal Office of Economic Opportunity and the HUD Model Cities staff, imbued with the ideology of "maximum feasible participation" in the planning and delivery of antipoverty programs, contributed mightily to the creation of new forms of urban advocacy. Local antipoverty boards and Model City agencies, formed in response to federal funding mandates, hired planners. The antipoverty agencies and their staff soon became potent political and patronage organizations in big-city ghettos. The issues they dealt with came to involve city-wide questions of resource allocation – as well as their original mandate for determining the specific local direction of federal antipoverty resources.

Simultaneous with the development of the officially sponsored Planning Commission and antipoverty advocates in cities around the nation came the formation of privately organized advocacy groups. Soon it became impossible to carry out a major renewal or highway project in big cities around the country without dealing with community groups, staffed by volunteer professionals or public-interest planning concerns. Costly investment programs were slowed, redirected, or halted in the face of protests, publicity campaigns, and litigation programs. The late 1960s and early 1970s saw a flowering of advocacy in a climate of professional approval and support — but with a decidedly mixed set of results.

As in many areas of national life, the overwhelming electoral victory of Richard Nixon over George McGovern in 1972 set the stage for a rapid decline in antipoverty urban advocacy. The federal funds which supported professional staffs were cut or eliminated. Private advocacy agencies found themselves subject to IRS audits. The public climate of support for minorities and the poor in efforts to claim a larger share of national resources turned to hostility and the counter-assertion of the rights of the "silent (white, middle class) majority."

Urban advocacy in the early and mid-seventies was thus a lonelier and less protected activity than before. One area of continued, and even expanded, growth was in the formation of community advocacy groups in lower middle-class and working class, often white ethnic neighborhoods in cities around the country. These groups are to an extent reflective of concerns for home, school, and community apparently threatened by the expansion of blacks' and poor peoples' claims to greater shares of urban resources. Nonetheless they share many of the concerns of the antipoverty advocacy groups: the need for more federal resources for city housing and job programs, the need for greater representation in city-wide resource allocation.

We will discuss in some detail only the two advocacy agencies with which we have been closely connected, Suburban Action Institute and Garden Cities Development Corporation. Both were launched in the heyday of urban advocacy, the period from 1969 to 1972. One, having survived the lean times, continues. The other fell victim to overexpansion, the cut-off of federal funds, and the recession of 1973-1975.

SUBURBAN ACTION INSTITUTE

Our organization, Suburban Action Institute, grew out of an interest in opposing a public policy toward urban development in the late 1960s, the policy of rebuilding ghettos. In the mid-1960s, under the Johnson Administration, as a part of the war on poverty and a reflection of the growing civil rights movement, the urban policies of the nation shifted to some extent towards an increasing concern with the well-being of the low-income and nonwhite families of our cities. This was in contrast to the earlier days of slum clearance, primarily concerned with regenerating downtowns and attracting new capital to the cities. The new approach was a clear, conscious recognition that a decade of urban renewal had if anything been counterproductive; had led to increased social tension in our cities, such that the minority groups that had been pushed around under urban renewal were reacting violently against the Establishment because of their maltreatment under these specific programs.

One of the results of the new approach to urban development seemed to be an increasing concern with the well-being of those who had the least — the nonwhite and low-income families. Simultaneously, movement towards increased citizen participation in the planning process was taking place as Congress recognized that it was essential that those whose neighborhoods were being affected by development would have the opportunity to participate in making choices about what was appropriate development within their communities. Our reaction to citizen participation was mixed. As advocates of democratic practice, we believe that anything that involves the citizenry in more participation involving how resources affecting them directly will be allocated and employed is highly beneficial. But aspects of the early days of citizen participation were rather mechanical. To be eligible for federal funds, it was necessary for a local planning agency to show that it had a citizen group organized to serve as an advisory board; one never knew really whether that group represented "the community." The Model Cities program called for active participation by the community in the development of the plan, and took planning's concern with citizen participation beyond formalism into a functioning process by which citizens in the community receiving funds would play a strong role in the development of their plans. There remained many problems as to who represents a community, who speaks for a community, whether the people who are elected through official ballots in the communities (in extremely low-turnout elections) did in fact speak for the community. The elections were held; there was a political opportunity for people to speak out and to run for office in the Model Cities communities and to begin to play a role in the development of the Model Cities plans.

Our primary complaint with the Model Cities programs — with Title II of the original OEO Community Action Programs and with other socially oriented programs concerned with the eradication of poverty and discrimination — was that they tended to focus on a place. They established an identifiable physical place as the area in which solutions could be found to these social problems. In the Model Cities program it was the Model Cities community, a delineated area having a host of social problems, which was the arena for programs to operate. The existence of enormous social problems in the area were the very standard that HUD required for a community to qualify for assistance. Although the statutory language never explicitly said so, the solution to the problems of families residing in model cities communities had to be within the model cities community itself (Davidoff, 1967). The communities that received these funds, as physical places, desperately needed the infusion of dollars. But, insofar as federal grants limited the opportunity of the model city resident to choose whether to find opportunity where he lived presently or to find enlarged opportunity outside of his area, we felt that they were highly discriminatory programs. We accept the definition of a ghetto in its older meaning as a place to which a class of population is restricted. If this is a proper definition, then the whole idea of ghetto rebuilding would be anathema, because it meant a class of the population was restricted, in finding opportunities, to a very limited physical area.

We were opposed to a public process that restricted choice to a small area, particularly because it restricted choice to an area that was worn out. What we were seeking was a public program that offered opportunities to impoverished families, families discriminated against because of race, to make a choice of location within the regions in which they lived, based on where they thought they could find the greatest opportunities. Our studies of metropolitan regions indicated that the greatest opportunity for economic advancement rested not within the center city, but within our suburbs.

This was the case for a number of reasons. First, America has for many decades been decentralizing its metropolitan population; population has been flowing at a rapid rate from the cities to the suburbs. The suburbs have been attractive to American families for many reasons. Families did not like the congestion of the city. They found economic opportunity in the suburbs. They wanted more open space, more privacy, for themselves and for their children. They thought that the education offered in the suburban schools would be preferable. They fled the inner cities because the inner cities had more and more blacks, and they ran out of hate or out of fear. Objective and external forces were also at work; land was available in the suburbs.

There is some room in our cities for redevelopment, but in terms of total amount of vacant land in our metropolitan areas it is a very small percentage. Ten to twenty percent of the land available is in our inner cities, the rest being in the jurisdictions outside. There is a second fact of metropolitan development which is at least as important as the existence of vacant residential land, and that is the fact that American industry has for many years now been moving to the suburbs. Headquarters operations, service operations, manufacturing operations — the overwhelming bulk of the new jobs have been created in the suburbs. As the jobs have grown in the suburbs, our public policy for advancing opportunities for low and moderate income families has not looked to the suburbs. That policy has looked to the inner city. While our public policy on urban development speaks now of rebuilding and revitalizing the center city, in the postwar period tremendous subsidies have been given to the suburbs to allow their development to take place. Daniel Patrick Moynihan used to point out that had President Eisenhower wanted a conscious policy to develop our suburbs, he couldn't have proposed anything better than the federal interstate highway system. Meanwhile, F.H.A. housing policy has made possible the development of single-family homes in the suburbs. The federal income tax system operates to the advantage of home owners by granting a set of deductions from tax liability. Thus the federal government has sponsored the development of the suburbs, but that development has essentially been for the middle class. It has not been conscious federal policy to enlarge the opportunities of working class, moderate or low income families to take advantage of the resources that the suburbs provide.

While federal policies for ending poverty and discrimination were being focused on delimited portions of inner cities in the Model Cities program, suburban communities were growing in jobs, tax base, and quality of service — and erecting ever higher barriers to the immigration of nonwhites and the poor. These barriers include zoning restrictions and other controls on building; subdivision regulation; and building codes restrictions. Zoning — employed originally as a means of assisting communities to enhance public health, safety and welfare — has increasingly become a mechanism employed by localities to preserve the fiscal base of the community by prohibiting the forms of residential development which would heavily tax the community. The relatively low priced forms of housing are prohibited or restricted to a tiny area of the town. In addition, suburbs may require that the single-family homes that are permitted be developed on excessively large tracts of lands. It is not unusual for a town to require a home to be on a half acre, one acre, two acres, four acres or in Bedminister, New Jersey, five acres of land. What happens throughout a region when the land is under the control of one acre, two acre, four acre zoning? The potential supply of available units in the region sharply decreases. What happens to land price at a time when you have a sharp decrease in supply and a tremendous demand for development? Land price shoots up. In the suburbs, land prices are tremendously high for a single tract upon which a home can be constructed. It is our concern that with job opportunities growing in the suburbs, suburban community, corporations, and governments should see to it that the workers associated with those jobs have an opportunity to live close to those jobs.

It is important that a suburb not be able to reap the rewards of the taxes from an industry while foisting on the cities the jobs of educating and servicing the working class families who may have to shift to a new job or commute at great cost to that job. What Suburban Action has been doing is to put pressure on the corporations, the suburbs and state and national governments to change their practices.

Since its establishment in 1969, Suburban Action has made some important strides in dealing with its issues:

— It has contributed to an increased public awareness of the issue of suburban exclusion and the need for regional sharing of solutions to problems of race and class. One of the early goals we met was to have these issues treated on Page 1 of the New York Times. Our publications have been widely distributed to both planning and lay readerships. Our access to electronic media has been good.

— It has brought a number of legal actions to challenge suburban exclusionary practices, with some important victories to its credit in state or federal courts.

— It has successfully challenged the proposed move of one large corporation, RCA, from New York City to New Canaan, Connecticut. A number of other actions against corporate moveouts are pending.

— It has helped to focus the concern of civil rights agencies and official planning bodies on the issue of suburban exclusion.

— It has survived. Suburban Action's funding level (based primarily on foundation grants and research contracts), while never large enough to sustain even a small part of the effort needed to mount a major attack on the problems it deals with, has been able to maintain a staff, stay in operation, and weather the hard times of the past five years.

GARDEN CITIES DEVELOPMENT CORPORATION

As the first small victories were won in the battle against suburban exclusion, and in the expansive economic and public climate of the late 1960s and early 1970s, Suburban Action's staff gave a great deal of thought to the necessity for creating a housing and new-community development agency that could move beyond a theory of "suburban contributions to metropolitan problems" and into the reality of such.

Our hypothesis was that as court victories against suburban exclusionary practices were won, the development of new housing at moderate cost in the formerly exclusive suburbs should not be left solely to the private for-profit market (Davidoff, Davidoff, and Gold, 1971). Private developers generally realize their greatest profits from their highest-priced units. In addition, the usual form of nonprofit development agency — the urban public housing agency — usually did not exist in suburban municipalities. Suburban Action's staff believed that a nonprofit development corporation specifically geared to purchase vacant suburban land; apply for the right to build moderately priced and subsidized housing; where necessary, to litigate to gain that right; and carry through with the construction of the units, was urgently needed.

Garden Cities Development Corporation came into existence at a time when credit was widely available and relatively inexpensive; when tax shelters made a variety of private investors eager to go into partnership with nonprofit agencies for housing development; when federal housing subsidies were flowing at the fastest pace in their 50-year history; and just before a sharp jump in the cost of building materials took place.

By 1973, GCDC had pyramided millions of dollars' worth of land and completed apartment buildings onto a base of zero capital and a good basic concept. Working with the skilled and imaginative architectural firm of Callister, Payne, and Bischoff (the designers of Heritage Village) and other design firms, GCDC had prepared plans and submitted proposals for more than a dozen suburban mixed-income communities, ranging in size from a few hundred to a few thousand units. The flagship proposal was for a 6,000 unit new community, complete with recreation, commercial development, health, education, and welfare services on an 800 acre site in Mahwah, New Jersey, a town which is home to a mammoth Ford assembly plant of whose 6,000 workers fewer than 100 lived in the community, as a result of inflated house prices based on severely restrictive acreage zoning.

Victims of optimism and good times, GCDC and SAI moved from relatively modest quarters in their home community of White Plains, N.Y. to extensive and well-equipped new offices in Tarrytown. The two organizations expanded sharply.

Then came a series of crippling blows. The Nixon Administration cut off housing subsidy funds. The cost of credit and of building materials rose sharply. The business climate darkened as the economy slid into a massive recession. Along with the UDC, the state and City of New York, and other large and small concerns, GCDC went under, succumbing to a falling-domino syndrome as loans were called in. Having attempted to stay alive and keep functioning while warning signs accumulated, both GCDC and SAI slid under mountainous debts.

SURVIVAL AND RENEWED PROSPECTS

SAI was kept afloat by the simple, and Draconian, device of payless paydays and the reduction of staff and facilities far below the minimum necessary for normal operation.

Over the years from 1974 to 1976, SAI struggled to obtain continued funding and to pay off immense debts.

With the success of its efforts at retrenchment and survival, SAI has turned to a renewed analysis of the requirements of successful advocacy in its field. The following principles seem clear:

1. Planning advocacy on behalf of the interest of the poor and of minorities can be carried out on a sustained basis and at a high level of professionalism. Doing this requires sustained funding, and, as lines of inquiry and efforts are explored and continued or abandoned on the basis of their satisfactory payoffs, requires expanded funding to permit full pursuit of promising approaches.

2. Achieving a high and sustained level of funding through foundation appeals, fundraising events, and the search for research grants directly related to our areas of concern, requires a great proportion of staff time.

3. The original GCDC thesis, while it failed in execution, was substantially correct. Further, the nonprofit development corporation, if successfully put in operation, promises the creation of a self-sustaining (and possibly expanding) funding mechanism

as "nonprofit profits" are put to use in maintaining staff, acquiring land, and carrying through development projects.

4. Any advocacy effort should maintain a close relationship between advocate and client. In the case of Suburban Action, this relationship has been especially difficult to maintain because of the physical and temporal separation of our purported beneficiaries — inner city poor and working class people and minorities — and the resources we hope to offer — jobs and homes in suburban areas. The abstractness and remoteness of our operating hypothesis keep us from appearing particularly useful in the daily struggles of families in the inner cities to survive.

Consequently, SAI has a particular need to establish an independent base of financial and organizational support. With a new national political and economic climate, we expect to be able to create this base.

NEXT STEPS IN ADVOCACY PLANNING

Around the nation, a period of relative quiescence in public discussion of forms of advocacy within the profession has nonetheless seen a continued growth in advocacy practice, whether labelled as such or not. A comprehensive view of grass-roots urban organization around the country, much of it outside the aegis of organizations formally labelled "advocate planning," is given by Perlman (1976).

We believe that the organizational principles laid down by Saul Alinsky (1969, 1972) for community organizers are valid and important for the next stage in development of urban advocacy. Advocates and clients must be able to:

— Outline coherent tactics and strategies to advance their aims

— Achieve satisfying victories, however small, to maintain a spirit of optimism and hope

— Reach out to form working coalitions with groups that share significant interests

— Maintain independence and internal democracy; avoid cooptation.

In the next several years, these organizing principles may lead to increased stress by urban advocates for the poor and for working class communities on:

(1) Educating and enlarging the capacity of citizens to become effective advocates. The long-range goal of advocacy should be to reduce the dependence of the citizen-client on the skills of a professional advocate. The aim should be to enlarge the capacity of citizens to be their own advocates.

(2) Developing economic autonomy. Community self-help institutions in the form of sweat equity and urban homesteading, shared ownership of production facilities, and forms of cooperative ownership are proliferating in urban and rural communities. Misplaced utopianism and mismanagement are constant dangers, but when they are weathered these institutions hold out great hope for community autonomy and for increased leverage in the larger community.

(3) Refining and disseminating community organizing techniques.

(4) Acquiring political power. The experience of groups such as La Raza in the Southwest and of neighborhood groups in a number of urban wards presages the development of specifically political forms of advocacy. The low voting turnout of poor communities is the major roadblock to effective urban advocacy. It cripples the low-income and minority communities' efforts to obtain leverage over public resources.

It remains an important fact of life in professional planning that the wealthiest and most powerful interests in metropolitan communities have the resources to hire advocates who can present skillful and well-argued cases for community development that will advance those interests. Our kind of advocacy planning, advocacy on behalf of the relatively less wealthy and less powerful, can use community organization; political leverage over elected officials; foundation grantsmanship; media skills and other forms of community outreach — to try to narrow the gap in expertise and in effectiveness.

In a new national political climate, and building on the strengths achieved over the past ten years, urban planning advocates of redistribution both within and outside the national government may have the resources required to promote and implement the plans urgently needed.

REFERENCES

Alinsky, S. (1969) *Reveille for Radicals*. New York: Random House.

———. (1972) *Rules for Radicals*. New York: Random House.

Davidoff, P. (1965) "Advocacy and Pluralism in Planning." *Journal of the American Institute of Planners*, 31: (January): 12-21.

———. (1967) "A Rebuilt Ghetto Does Not A Model City Make." in *Planning 1967*. Chicago: American Society of Planning Officials: 187-192.

———, and L. Davidoff (1974) "Response to Mazziotti." *Journal of the American Institute of Planners*, 40: 41, 48.

———, Davidoff, L., and Gold, N. N. (1971) "The Suburbs Have To Open Their Gates." *New York Times Sunday Magazine*, November 7, 1971.

Gans, H. J. (1962) *The Urban Villagers*. New York: Free Press.

Goodman, R. (1971) *After the Planners*. New York: Simon and Schuster.

Hajek, F. (1944) *The Road to Serfdom*. Chicago: U. of Chicago Press.

Mazziotti, D. F. (1974) "The Underlying Assumptions of Advocacy Planning: Pluralism and Reform." *Journal of the American Institute of Planners*, 40: 38, 40-47.

Meyerson, M. and E. Banfield (1964) *Politics, Planning, and the Public Interest*. New York: Free Press, 1964.

Perlman, J. (1976) "Grassrooting the System." *Social Policy* 7:

Reiner, J., Reimer, E., and Reiner, T. (1963) "Client Analysis and the Planning of Public Programs." *Journal of the American Institute of Planners*, 29 (November): 270-282.

Simon, H. (1976) *Administrative Behavior* (rev. ed.). New York: Free Press.

Sussman, C. (1976) *Planning the Fourth Migration*. Cambridge: MIT Press.

5

ADVOCACY AND APPLIED ANTHROPOLOGY

Stephen L. Schensul and
Jean J. Schensul

This chapter attempts to define and describe advocacy-oriented activities in the discipline of anthropology. One constraint in this objective is that the term "advocacy" has not generally been used as a labeling device to delimit a specific set of activities, methods or approaches in anthropology. For this reason we must look to those fields in which there is a developing tradition under the concept of advocacy and use their criteria and definitions as guideposts in the search for advocacy in anthropology.

There is an apparent consistency in the way in which the concept of advocacy has been defined and used in such practitioner-oriented fields as social work and urban planning. Blecher (1971: 17), an urban planner, states that, "advocacy planning provides citizens and client groups with their own resources, especially technical and professional, to enter, in a new way, into the activities underlying the urban decision process." Peattie (1970: 80), an anthropologist in urban planning, sees advocacy planning as helping "people make their interests felt, especially [those] that seem to be underrepresented in the planning process." Brager (1968: 6) sees the advocate social worker as a "political tactician." The advocate "sees as his primary responsibility the tough-minded and partisan representation of [the disadvantaged's] interests."

Both Peattie and Blecher see advocacy as pluralistic, partisan and political: "Advocacy planning also recognizes the existence of a pluralistic society and the need for restructuring the nature of the urban decision-making process" (Peattie, 1970: 82); "It moves . . . from public interest to a process of 'community dialogue," negotiation and decison making that produces an amalgam of private or client interests" (Blecher, 1971: 19).

Advocacy in these terms has come to mean:

— Strengthening the representation of economically and politically marginal groups who have been denied a voice in societal design and action in the past.

— Helping lay people to overcome the technological and professional barriers to effective participation in societal issues.

— Professionals taking an overt value and political stance in support of the needs and perceptions of specific sectors of the society who have been consistently denied a voice in the past.

— The recognition that science and professional practice, in their attempts to develop "objective truth" and actions in the "public interest," have served the socio-politically dominant sectors of the society to the exclusion of those that are marginal.

— The use of professional expertise to support or enhance plans and actions developed by lay people rather than the development of plans and programs imposed upon people "in the public interest."

The usual definition of advocacy — "to plead the cause of another," emphasizes the professional as a broker between the client and the system within which the client seeks a voice. Here the professional expert — lawyer, social worker or planner — speaks for the client community. While the professional may assess the client's needs and consult in potential courses of action the responsibility for representation falls not to the client but to the advocate.

The procedures of a court of law require the presence of such a professional advocate. However, the role of the outside professional as spokesman on behalf of the poor, ethnic minorities, and a range of other special interest groups in our society has declined as these people have seen it in their best interests for indigenous members to speak for and represent their own needs. The presence of these lay advocate groups requires new adaptations and objectives for the advocacy-oriented professional. In our view the aim of the "expert" must be to increase the capability of client group members to speak for themselves in political, planning and service arenas. In this perspective the professional is not a leader or a pleader but plays a background and supportive role. Courses of action, and decisions, are made by the indigenous lay advocates. Such a role requires a facilitative and nondirective approach, as the professionals contribute their skills to action organized, developed, and run by lay people.

This paper will attempt to show that anthropology can make a significant contribution to advocacy — particularly to the more facilitative approach described above. While anthropology is a discipline rooted in a theoretical and academic tradition it has also sought its data from intensive involvement in local cultures and communities. This "within the community" research tradition has given anthropology:

- Methods, theories, values, and research interests that are ideally suited for advocacy activities.

- A slender but significant thread of action involvements which, while not labeled as advocacy, provide a basis upon which advocacy anthropology can build for its future development.

- An impetus, as a result of the political strains of the 1960s and the economic decline of the 1970s, and the self-identified needs of local communities to create a value explicit social science located "beyond the University" (Redfield, 1973) and addressing issues central to the society.

A consideration of the potential of advocacy in anthropology must rest on an understanding of the nature of anthropology and of anthropological values. In the following section some of the features basic to anthropology will be considered — both in terms of their historical development and their adaptation to contemporary society.

THE NATURE OF ANTHROPOLOGY

Anthropology has existed as a discipline for over a century. It arose at a time of expansionism and colonialism in the domination of non-Western societies and peoples by Western nations. Since that time it has undergone significant changes in theory, method and membership, both as a result of intellectual and factual development and its articulation to the changing times. There are however certain basic features of anthropology which have deeply influenced and shaped the field since Boas defined its major lines of development in the late 19th and early 20th century.

ANTHROPOLOGY IS PRIMARILY AN ACADEMIC DISCIPLINE.

The historical development of anthropology, particularly in Great Britain and the United States, has seen anthropology's interest and involvement in practical issues continually superseded by an academic and theoretical orientation. To support this view we will cite three instances in which significant efforts toward practical involvements lost to the domination of basic research and theoretical interests in anthropology.

The earliest origins of anthropological activity in England began with advocacy. In 1838 the Aboriginal Protection Society was established in London in response to the reports of massacres and other excesses inflicted by colonists on the native peoples of colonial dependencies. Early in its history the society split over methods of protection — one faction supported direct intervention while the other maintained the need for research and study of the native races. Unable to resolve the split the latter left the organization and formed the Ethnological Society of London in 1843. This society split once again over the popularization of anthropology and the issue of slavery in 1863. In 1871 the new association recombined with the Ethnological Society to form the Anthropological Institute of Great Britain and Ireland. This new organization specifically avoided policy issues and directed its attention toward research, respectability and academic recognition (Reining, 1962). Reining states that "for about thirty years after the establishment of the Anthropological Institute the practical value of anthropology was rarely mentioned. The efforts of anthropologists were primarily aimed at getting anthropology accepted by universities" (p. 598).

Another instance of academic domination occurred in relation to the Women's Anthropological Society — founded in 1885 as a result of the exclusion of women from the Washington Anthropological Society. The aims of the Women's Anthropological Society were both theoretical and practical: "They chose to stress the need to understand social problems if such problems were to be alleviated . . . they sought to analyze as well as to break bread with the needy brother" (Helm, 1966: 38).

In 1896, at the instigation of the Women's Anthropological Society, the Washington Sanitary Improvement Company was formed to construct 808 low rent dwellings. However, when the Women's Anthropological Society merged with the Washington Anthropological Society, there was little continued emphasis on societal issues.

The use of "applied anthropology" as a tool in the understanding and manipulation of native cultures had long been a part of colonial tradition in Britain, France, and the Indian Administration in the United States. It was not, however, until 1941 that the Society for Applied Anthropology (SAA) was formed. The SAA was not enthusiastically welcomed into the world of anthropology. The new-born organization was regarded by most anthropologists as something of a monstrosity and as a consequence it began its first growth in the limbo of illegitimacy (Spicer, 1976: 335). It was not until 1971 that the American Anthropological Association (AAA) included the Society as one of its sister associations.

An interesting transformation occurred in the Society between its establishment and its acceptance by the AAA. The association and its journal, *Human Organization,* changed from concern for practical to theoretical issues. By 1971 a new trend had been set in the journal. Steadily the pages were being filled with the work of academically oriented anthropologists and other social scientists. Their take-over was nearly complete by 1970 when it was reported that more than 90 percent of the articles published were by anthropologists and sociologists holding academic positions (Spicer, 1976: 337).

The academic orientation of anthropology has had considerable impact in the following areas:

— Beyond the narrow research oriented role of "government anthropologist" in colonial administration no practitioner roles were forged for anthropologists within their own society.

— Because basic research and academic anthropology were the most valued endeavors in the discipline, anthropologists who engaged in applied and advocacy activities tended to avoid discussing or publishing their work. As a result there is only a limited body of materials to represent the application of anthropology to societal issues. Many anthropologists outside of academia "lost contact" with the discipline.

— Anthropological research has been primarily directed at theoretical questions that have developed in the discipline rather than through the examination of issues facing our society as a whole. Thus a great deal of anthropological research bears little relevance to contemporary issues.

There are signs, however, that the dominant academic orientation of the field is changing somewhat. The boom in academic anthropology that occurred in the 1950s and 1960s is on the decline. Overproduction of anthropology Ph.D.s, combined with a severe reduction in the academic job market, is forcing anthropologists to look to nonacademic realms of employment. At the same time the number of anthropologists seeking nonacademic jobs through a commitment to the application of anthropology has increased significantly. Anthropologists are now employed as researchers in community mental health and health programs, drug and education programs as well as other human service and planning entities. Subfields of anthropology, in particular medical and educational anthropology, have led the way in linking anthropological skills to human service efforts.

ANTHROPOLOGY HAS BEEN A FIELD DEALING WITH SMALL, ISOLATED AND "EXOTIC" CULTURES.

The tradition in anthropology has been to focus research attention on cultures "very different" from the anthropologist's culture. For the westernized and urbanized anthropologist in the world academic community, ethnographic interest centered on small and isolated societies that could be studied on a local basis. Even when anthropologists shifted their attention to Western societies, it was the ethnic minorities rather than the majority to which they turned their attention.

The research questions with which anthropologists studied these locales were drawn from current theoretical issues in the discipline. It is no surprise then, given the tradition within which the discipline developed, that anthropologists were guided to emphasize:

(1) the reconstruction of traditional culture rather than an assessment of contemporary social issues,

(2) "exotic" customs rather than everyday behavior essential to group survival;

(3) local phenomena rather than the political and economic factors that linked these local cultures to a wider national system.

Thus, anthropologists focused their attention on less than vital questions among populations which for the most part were not concerned with making them accountable either in terms of the research process or ethnographic content of research monographs. There have been, over the past two decades, considerable signs that anthropology's sphere of action may be changing:

- Non-Western nations are increasingly closing up to American anthropologists.

- American ethnic minorities are making anthropologists more accountable for the results of their ethnographic reports (see Vaca [1970] and Romano [1968] for Chicanos, Valentine [1968] and Szwed [1974] for Blacks, and Deloria [1969] and Ortiz [1973] for American Indians).

- The political awareness and research priorities of the 1960s have turned anthropological attention toward urban communities and national issues both in this society and abroad.

Anthropological method and theory has not fully caught up with world transformation and politicization of the Third World. However, the mainstream of anthropology seems to be slowly shifting to an incorporation of these contemporary world issues in its research.

ANTHROPOLOGY HAS STRIVEN FOR OBJECTIVITY AND A VALUE-FREE SCIENTIFIC APPROACH.

Anthropology, in its drive to establish itself as an academic science, has encouraged the "myth of value-free research" and "objectivity" in ethnographic observation. This "value implicit" approach, so antithetical to advocacy, seems to be on the wane in the discipline. Berreman (1968: 391) has sharply attacked this myth of value-free research:

The dogma that public issues are beyond the interests or competence of those who study and teach about man is myopic and sterile professionalism and a fear of commitment which is both irresponsible and irrelevant. Its result is to dehumanize the most humanist of the sciences. . . . That neutrality in science is illusory is a point which has been made often and well.

ANTHROPOLOGY HAS BEEN DOMINATED BY THE PERSPECTIVE OF CULTURAL RELATIVISM.

The principle of cultural relativism as articulated by one of its most active advocates, M. J. Herskovits (1949: 64-66) is that "judgments are based on experience and experience is interpreted by each individual in terms of his own enculturation . . . . The very definition of what is normal or abnormal is relative to the cultural frame of reference."

The cultural relativistic approach was a reaction against the ethnocentrism and racism of the anthropological evolutionists (Tylor, Morgan, and others) as well as that of the colonialists, missionaries, and others who had contact with non-Western peoples and ethnic groups other than their own. Herskovits goes on to say that "cultural relativism is a philosophy which, in recognizing the values set up by every society to guide its own life, lays stress on the dignity inherent in every body of custom and on the need for tolerance of conventions though they differ from our own" (p. 76).

The tradition of cultural relativism has been one of anthropology's greatest contributions to social science and to human affairs. It has made anthropologists the major advocates for cultural pluralism, ethnic identity, and maintenance of cultural traditions. It has provided the philosophical and methodological base for consideration of native culture in programs of technological development and change.

However, this philosophical position, along with attempts at objectivity, has kept anthropologists from making judgments, from intervening into the actions and issues of the real world and developing a conception of "universalistic" values and moral positions. Such a position is "in basic contradiction to the very claim of applying anthropological science to the solution of human problems" (Batalla, 1966: 90).

The extreme point of view is expressed by Edwin Smith (cited in Batalla, 1966: 90):

> As men and women we may have our opinions about the justice or unjustice of certain acts and attitudes, but anthropology as such can pronounce no judgment, for to do so is to invade the province of philosophy and ethics. If anthropology is to judge and guide, it must have a conception of what constitutes the perfect society; and since it is debarred from having ideals it cannot judge, cannot guide and cannot talk about progress.

Despite these enforced limitations, anthropologists have made at least implicit judgments concerning their visions of a just and healthy society. In the following section we will examine some of these concepts and the recent attempts of anthropologists to be more overt in their vision of a good and just society.

ANTHROPOLOGICAL CONCEPTIONS OF A JUST SOCIETY

Anthropologists have spoken out strongly for a vision of society marked by equality for and understanding of racial and cultural differences. Boas (1928: 83) made an early stand for racial equality, for the distinction between race and culture, for the negative effects of war and the excesses of nationalism.

> The interests of mankind are ill served if we try to instill into the minds of the young a passionate desire for national power; if we teach the preponderance of national interest over human interest, aggressive nationalism rather than national idealism, expansion rather than inner development, admiration of warlike, heroic deeds rather than the object for which they are performed.

The concepts of cultural relativism point to a just society in which different cultural traditions contribute productively to a pluralistic society. It also emphasizes the need for people to freely change or retain their culture and customs without outside interference or constraints.

These values have made anthropologists more aware and concerned about the rights of ethnic and cultural minority communities in national systems for self determination. They have also tended to admire those cultural groups that have retained their traditional life despite the onslaughts of industrialization, nationalization and a cash economy.

Other dimensions of a just or good society have produced more controversy. Some anthropologists, perhaps because they tended to study "simple societies," have always had a "Rousseauian" preference for the, as they perceived it, harmonious, small, slow-to-change community. Sapir (1924: 410) in his search for "genuine culture" sees it as:

> inherently harmonious, balanced, self satisfactory. It is the expression of a richly varied and yet somehow unified and consistent attitude toward life ... A genuine culture refuses to consider the individual as a mere cog ... The greatest cultural fallacy of industrialism, as developed up to the present time, is that in harnessing machines to our uses it has not known how to avoid the harnessing of the majority of mankind to its machines.

Other anthropologists have strongly disagreed with the inherent harmoniousness of these traditional small societies.

Anthropologists have argued on both sides of several questions concerning the good and just society. Are cultures and societies better off under slow or rapid culture change? Some anthropologists have seen the insistence on a slow, integratable pace for change as conservative, status quo-oriented and antirevolutionary (see Batalla, 1966).

Are societies better constructed with rigid role expectations and little flexibility in behavior (tight) or high flexibility in roles and individual freedom of behavior (loose)? The debate over the merits of assimilation vs. nonassimilation vs. an integration of the best of both worlds has concerned anthropologists both as basic and as applied researchers (see Gearing, 1970).

The last decade has seen the development of Marxist or "Radical" anthropology. This is a value explicit approach which uses Marxist theory as a framework for anthropological analysis. K. Gough (1968: 405) states, "the question tends to become: what does an anthropologist do who is dependent on a counter-revolutionary government in an increasingly revolutionary world?" Gough argues for the kind of anthropology that opposes racial, class, sex and ethnic discrimination, and unequal distribution of resources, labor and capital. It is her feeling that anthropology should conduct research which seeks to understand these phenomena and supports efforts to transform them into more egalitarian forms of social, economic and political life.

Anthropologists have sought to change society by the contribution of their research, models and ideology to the world of ideas. In the next section we will review some of anthropology's approaches to societal change which, while not within the scope of advocacy, have sought to affect and broaden the societal "mind."

ANTHROPOLOGICAL STRATEGIES
FOR SOCIETAL CHANGE

While anthropologists have been primarily concerned with generating data to answer theoretical questions raised in the discipline, they have also sought to achieve societal impact through the anthropological message. Students in universities have been the primary recipients of that message but, as we will see in this section, anthropological participation has also extended to mass communication and political realms and to programs of social and technological change both here and abroad.

TEACHING AND TRAINING

Anthropologists have seen their primary sphere of influence as resting within the university and their impact achieved through affecting the world of ideas and theories.

For people imbued with . . . the anthropological ethic, it was not immediately necessary to go out and work for the betterment of individual peoples. The bigger task was in spreading the message of cultural relativism in the universities, among people who would soon take their place as the legislators and executors of the Establishment (Pelto and Pelto, 1976: 539).

For thousands of introductory anthropology students the evils of ethnocentrism and the value of different cultures was the major message they could carry to all walks of life.

APPLIED ANTHROPOLOGY

The utility of anthropology for "indirect" colonial rule became apparent to anthropologists and administrators before the turn of the century. By the early 1900s anthropologists were training colonial administrators in Britain and by the 1920s there were civil service positions for "government anthropologists." In the United States the first formal applied anthropological work began in 1934 when John Collier, Commissioner of Indian Affairs, brought anthropologists into the Bureau of Indian Affairs and the Soil Conservation Service to carry out research in conjunction with innovating programs.

Since that time, anthropologists have played a significant role in the Indian Service, the relocation of Japanese during World War II, the occupation of captured territories after World War II, and administration of the trust territories of Micronesia. Anthropologists have also been involved in the Peace Corps and technical aid and development projects in "developing countries."

These activities can and have been looked at in two ways. In the first perspective anthropologists have played an ameliorative role in curbing the ethnocentric tendencies of the administrators of these programs. Many have claimed, on a sound factual basis, that their efforts have been directed toward "advocacy" for the populations that are the "targets" of these programs. Data collected on cultural and community life have been used by anthropologists as a base from which to block destructive legal sanctions, curb inappropriate technology and explain, in ways not derogatory to the native culture, the rationale behind the failure of outside imposed innovation. A second perspective on these activities would maintain that anthropologists have collaborated in the colonial process no matter how benign their intentions. Bastide (1973) sees anthropological involvement in technological development projects as another form of ethnocentrism, as influence seeking world powers impose these projects on underdeveloped Third World countries.

ANTHROPOLOGISTS AND MASS COMMUNICATION

Over the last two decades anthropology has become a popular subject as concepts of evolution, prehistory and ethnic and cultural differences have been "interesting" to the public. Several anthropologists have carried the anthropological perspective into the mass media. Foremost in this regard is Margaret Mead, who has "advocated" for three-generation extended households and a range of other societal issues on the "Tonight" show, in her *Redbook* column and in numerous interviews and articles. Other anthropologists in the public spotlight have included Ashley Montague and Oscar Lewis.

Another mass communication input of the anthropological message has been "Man; A Course of Study" — a part of the curriculum in hundreds of schools around the country. This multi-media project has received considerable input from anthropologists as it transmits the socio-environmental and cultural relativistic messages to young people.

Radical anthropologists have also been active in publicly attacking U.S. policy in Vietnam, racism in universities and other institutions and a range of other issues.

SOCIO-POLITICAL POSITIONS OF THE
AMERICAN ANTHROPOLOGICAL ASSOCIATION

The notion that contemporary world events are irrelevant to the professional concerns of anthropologists was laid nearly to rest when, at the meeting of Fellows of the American Anthropological Association in Pittsburgh in November, 1966, Michael Harner rose to challenge the ruling of the president elect that a resolution . . . condemning the United States role in the war in Vietnam was out of order because it did not "advance the science of anthropology" or "further the professional interests of anthropologists." Harner suggested that "genocide is not in the professional interests of anthropologists." With that the chair was voted down and the resolution was presented, amended and passed (Berreman, 1968: 391).

Through the years the American Anthropological Association as the body representing the discipline of anthropologists has taken a number of positions in resolutions passed by its Fellows. In 1946 a resolution was passed on the use of atomic energy, encouraging "efforts to make appropriate social inventions to guard against the dangers and utilize the promise, inherent in atomic use." In 1952 the Association passed a resolution recommending a commission to review Bureau of Indian Affairs policy in light of the "great and irremediable harm and injustice" of those policies. In 1962 a resolution "reaffirms the fact that there is no scientifically established evidence to justify the exclusion of any race . . . from equality before the law." Resolutions in 1970, supported fair claims settlements for Indians, investigation of the use of U.S. military weapons in Latin America, and opposed sex discrimination, secret or classified research, disclosure of informant data (cited in Weaver, 1973: 43-45).

The overall impact of all these anthropological strategies on societal policies and citizen attitudes and behavior is difficult, if not impossible, to measure. Certainly anthropology has contributed to the intellectual development and "relativistic" perspective of many people in our society. However, some anthropologists have felt that this is not good enough — they are concerned with the direct application of anthropology to the needs of the people they study. In the next section we will deal with those activities in which anthropologists have sought to use their information and skills on behalf of a specific community, culture, ethnic or special interest group.

DEFINING AND TRACING ANTHROPOLOGICAL ADVOCACY ACTIVITIES

We began this chapter by considering advocacy as the use of professional skills and information to facilitate representation and participation of a specific group in societal plans and programs which affect them. Such an advocacy approach requires the practitioner to take a value-explicit stand with the group and to facilitate rather than impose group directions and actions. In line with this definition we have identified four types of advocacy-oriented activities:

1. **BASIC RESEARCH AND ADVOCACY**

   Those situations in which the anthropologists were able to advocate for groups under study even though their primary activities were oriented toward basic research;

2. **POWER BROKERAGE AND ADVOCACY**

   Those situations in which the anthropologists were able to

control power and the political process sufficiently to create changes which would permit greater representation for the group;

3. APPLIED ANTHROPOLOGY AND ADVOCACY

Those situations in which anthropologists based in "outside controlled" change and development programs facilitated the input and representation of the group to be affected by the program;

4. ACTION ANTHROPOLOGY AND ADVOCACY

Those situations in which the primary activities of the anthropologists centered on facilitating plans and programs concerned with and developed by the group to be affected by these efforts.

BASIC RESEARCH AND ADVOCACY

The earliest activities involving "advocacy" in American anthropology center around the religious use of peyote among American Indians. In these activities anthropologists used the results of ethnographic research on traditional cultures to support the legitimacy of Indian religious freedom. James Mooney, ethnologist in the Bureau of American Ethnology of the Smithsonian Institution, used the data he collected on peyote use to win a case for a group of Indians arrested in Clinton, Oklahoma, and to get an antipeyote law repealed in Oklahoma. In 1918, because of his efforts in behalf of peyotists to legally incorporate the Peyote religion as the Native American Church, Mooney was recalled from Oklahoma (Stewart, 1973).

In 1937, an organized attempt to outlaw peyote on the national level was counteracted by a report entitled "Documents on Peyote" submitted by a group of the most famous anthropologists of the time, including Boas, Kroeber and Hrdlicka (Stewart, 1973).

Stewart states that:

> In the last 20 years . . . I testified in a half dozen court cases involving peyote . . . Anthropologists have been actively concerned in protecting the religious freedom of the Native American church and will continue to be, and this is because we were given opportunity and assistance by the Indians when we were interested in the study of the Peyote Religion. (Stewart, 1973: 38-39)

The involvement of anthropologists in Indian land claims issues may also be seen as advocacy stemming from basic research enterprises. Anthropological contributions have included historical data and testimony in court. In many cases anthropologists have been hired by the tribe to collect data to establish the legitimacy of land claims (Stewart, 1973; Lurie, 1955).

Three other cases serve to illustrate this type of advocacy anthropology. James Spillius (1957) was doing basic research on Tikopia when a devastating hurricane hit the island. He played a crucial role in advocating for community needs to outside authorities and his knowledge of community organization and culture helped him in bringing aid to the people.

John A. Hostetler's basic research (1972) into the Amish educational system helped to protect the Amish right to separate schooling for their children. His work showed that:

(1) Pupils in Amish schools have a positive self image.

(2) Amish pupils manifest trusting rather than alienated relationships.

(3) Amish pupils scored higher than pupils in rural public schools in arithmetic, spelling, and word usage.

This data enabled him to contribute testimony to a recent Supreme Court decision that made it possible for the Amish to resist compulsory secondary level public education.

Paredes (1976) found that ethnography contributed significantly to community action among the Eastern Creeks despite the fact that his goals were basically research oriented. After a year of part-time research in the community he moved into the role of "publicist" — writing newspaper articles, using his data to write a community history which was sold at the Thanksgiving pow-wow, and making speeches at schools and local associations concerning Creek culture. As he continued his fieldwork stay he helped the Creeks draft proposals, acted as an informal consultant to the chief and developed data to get official recognition of the tribe from the federal government.

The reciprocal helping relationship between the anthropologist and the community underlies this type of advocacy. As Pelto and Pelto (1976: 539-540) state, "the ethics of the complex exchange relationship of fieldwork require that researchers be prepared to use considerable amounts of their financial resources, skills and information for the benefit of the people who supply them with data in the long hours and days of the fieldwork enterprise."

POWER BROKERAGE AND ADVOCACY

Anthropologists are most usually marginal figures in their socio-political systems. They specifically avoid the pressures of leadership and value judgments inherent in positions of power. Such responsibilities are viewed as "nonanthropological" and individuals who assume such positions risk alienation from the mainstream of the discipline. While there are some anthropologists who have taken positions of power they find that the issues in which they are involved are not easily communicated to the discipline while the issues current in the discipline are not relevant to their work.

The most significant exception to this pattern involved the efforts of a team of American and Peruvian anthropologists to link control of power and resources with anthropological research to create positive change on behalf of a community of Peruvian peasants. This "research and development" approach led to the well-known Vicos project, directed by Alan Holmberg and sponsored by Cornell University and the Institute for Indigenous Affairs of the Peruvian government.

As a public manor, the *hacienda Vicos* and its people would be leased to the highest bidder from periods of five to ten years. The renter would become the *patron:* "He was the maximum authority within the system and all power to indulge or deprive was in his hands" (Holmberg, 1971a: 36). After five years of ethnographic study, Holmberg and associates decided to assume the power role. The project leased the hacienda and Holmberg became the *patron* of the hacienda.

In this power role the goal was to:

> Assist the community to shift for itself from a position of relative dependence and submission in a highly restricted and provincial world to a position of relative independence and freedom within the larger framework of Peruvian life. (Holmberg, 1971a: 22)

> From the very first day the process of power devolution was initiated. (Holmberg, 1971b: 47)

With full power over the decision-making process and with five years of ethnographic data on Vicos, Holmberg and associates were able to make broad and sweeping changes in the socioeconomic system. The steps that were taken were aimed at changing the image of the patron to one of "friendly consultants and observers and ... developing independent problem-solving and decision-making organizations among the indigenous population which could gradually assume the control and direction of community affairs in a rational and humane manner"

(Holmberg, 1971a: 26). Specific steps included organization of a self-governing and decision-making body, weekly discussion meetings of the labor force, cooperative development, new agricultural practices and profits reinvested in community development. The result was that new community political organizations were developed, economic production was increased and the hacienda was eventually taken over by the residents themselves ten years after the initiation of the project.

Another example of the research and development approach was Kuyo Chico, a project growing out of Vicos, directed by the Peruvian anthropologist Oscar Nunez del Prado. The objectives of the project centered on creating a political situation in which the Indians could assume political control: "We knew that the Indians would not be able to improve their situation alone, that someone was needed . . . with a knowledge of the laws who could see to it that they were enforced and the rights of the Indians recognized, until the Indians were capable of exercising their power" (Nunez del Prado, 1973: 47).

Using his link with the national government as a lever, Nunez del Prado was able to reduce the economic and political exploitation of the Indians and was initiating extensive economic and political development in Kuyo Chico. Income in Kuyo Chico tripled as a result of a number of independent economic projects, and the community became "recognized," entitling it to independent leadership and legal protection: "We believe that an initial period of protection and aid or 'paternalism', if you wish, is necessary, until little by little the Indian learns to walk alone" (Nunez del Prado, 1973, p. 54).

These projects spanned the fifties and early sixties – a different time politically within Peru and in the relationship between the United States and Peru. Nevertheless, these projects are important in exemplifying the use of cultural and community data to facilitate the ability of communities such as Vicos and Kuyo Chico to become integrated into the national culture from a position of power. In addition, they illustrate the explicit value stance anthropologists took in defining a good and just society characterized by democratic participation in decision-making, community control over economic and social development and an effective voice in national politics.

APPLIED ANTHROPOLOGY AND ADVOCACY

Much of what has been termed applied anthropology falls within the scope of anthropological work in colonial administration, and technical aid and development projects. For the most part we would not consider these efforts under the rubric of advocacy, since anthropological input tended to focus on the discovery of cultural factors which facilitated or offered barriers to innovations developed by national and international agencies, introduced into communities which had not asked for them (Foster 1969; Barnett 1956; Spicer 1954). Anthropologists committed to the success of such nonindigenously controlled programs and administrations are not usually doing advocacy anthropology for the following reasons:

a) Their focus is on facilitating the successful integration of a program considered to be important and beneficial by the wider society rather than by the "recipient community." An advocacy position would focus on strategies for developing programs generated by the community.

b) The program is usually relatively clearcut; it does not modify easily to the needs of the community because of its predefined and extra-local character. An advocacy position would attempt to maintain considerable flexibility and ability to change the direction and character of the program based on the self-defined needs of the people and the unique events in the community.

c) The broker position of most applied anthropologists places them in a position which makes it difficult to do anything more than speak for the community or serve as a medium for indirect communication between the community and the program or administrative unit. The advocacy approach would call for supporting and clarifying the community position so that community groups could deal directly and from a position of power with the innovating program.

d) The anthropologist's position is one which supports the rights of the innovating program and the need for accommodation on the part of the community. The advocacy position argues for the right of less powerful communities to negotiate their own program development and/or to play a significant participatory role in extra-locally derived programs.

Nevertheless, applied anthropologists can offer input into these programs which we would consider to be advocacy as the counter to those forces who impose change by such activities as:

— giving voice to community interests and concerns;

— changing the nature of program services to more effectively meet client needs;

— encouraging joint planning between the group to be affected and the change program.

In our experience, however, most programs tolerate such advocacy activities only so long as they do not threaten the basic framework and philosophy of the program and approach.

In general, it is difficult to assess from the literature into which category a particular applied anthropological activity should fall. It is perhaps more important to keep in mind that:

a) Applied anthropologists in development programs are frequently not able to adequately represent the target population's attitudes and interests or affect program change on their behalf because of the anthropologists' marginal status in the program.

b) The program may be bound to an inflexible intervention strategy which is nearly impossible to change and which violates indigenous power and control.

c) Anthropologists who are committed to advocacy strategies may have to carry out such activities outside the bounds of their programmatic responsibilities.

The activities of applied anthropologists in these settings can be distinguished from what has been termed the action anthropology model. In this model, guidance for action derives from the community itself, and the work of the anthropologist is to facilitate this process. In the view of the action anthropologists, working with community-derived change programs avoids the pitfalls and ambiguous allegiances of outside directed programs.

ACTION ANTHROPOLOGY AND ADVOCACY

Perhaps the most discussed applied project in anthropology has been the Fox Project — emerging from the direction of Sol Tax and the implementation of a number of his students. Out of this project came the idea of "action anthropology." Tax (1960: 168) states that the action anthropologist has two goals: "he wants to help a group of people to solve a problem *and* he wants to learn something in the process."

Tax and his students started out to do traditional anthropological research on the Fox reservation in Iowa: "The malaise of the community and sympathy with individual Indians . . . conspired to turn us into actionists" (Gearing, et al., 1960: 10).

The project facilitated the development of a cooperative farming effort, an education project, a scholarship program and a traditional crafts project. In doing so, they participated in discussions with residents around these community development projects, suggested strategies for carrying them out, linked the community with outside resources and acted as negotiators with relevant outside agencies.

The significance of Tax's efforts for anthropology lay less in his community accomplishments (which were relatively limited in relation to the project's length) than in a model of nondirective facilitation. This facilitation model allowed suggestions for development to emerge from the community residents themselves, rather than from the framework of an imposed change program. In addition, it involved a constant consideration of the meaning and ethics of "helping" people solve a problem as the project moved through several facilitative strategies.

Lurie (1973: 6-7) has described the key facets of action anthropology in the following ways:

(1) The definition of problems and decisions to implement solutions is honestly left up to the people whose lives will be affected. The action anthropologist acts not as a planner or expert but as a catalyst.

(2) ... from an action anthropological perspective goals are open ended, subject to revisions as the people may see need to reassess and redirect effort.

(3) The action anthropologist usually has to run some interference so the community can run with the ball.

(4) ... The action work demands ... humility about one's own pretensions to any expertise and total conviction that action anthropology really works.

Sue Ellen Jacobs, in an article entitled "Action and Advocacy Anthropology" (1974), describes her work, saying that, "my students and I provide diagnostic research and therapeutic and supportive action for this grass roots program designed to improve quality of life for low income — especially Black — people in the country."

Van Willigen (1976) in classifying different types of applied anthropology identifies a category he calls "The Community Advocacy Model." In this approach, research problems and data collection revolve around community-identified needs and issues. The data is then analyzed and incorporated in a variety of different forms such as community-initiated efforts to advocate for particular programs or social changes, to write proposals, and to develop and implement community-controlled programs. The work of the anthropologist in this approach involves collaboration with community activists to carry out the above activities.

Several other anthropological efforts bear significant relation to action anthropology in their nondirective, facilitative approach. Three projects in particular that have developed this approach used or are associated with the use of the term "advocacy." One of these efforts revolves around the work of John Peterson who became a staff member of the Choctaw tribal council in 1972-1973. Peterson (1974: 316) describes his role as one of "advocate." "My relationship with the Choctaw tribe is that of a brief lawyer who is responsible for an analysis of possible courses of action suggested by the client and who, after the decision among alternatives is made by the client, proceeds to prepare the best possible case for the client along the lines of the alternative chosen."

Leonard Borman, an anthropologist, and a student of Sol Tax, has been involved in action research with a wide range of self-help groups and at attempts to define the self-help movement. Such groups have included those centered on physical handicaps, substance abuse, child abuse, psychiatric disorders, cooperatives and others. He has played a significant role in facilitating cooperative strategies among these groups, in advocating for their effectiveness and legitimacy to institutions and professionals and in establishing better working relationships between these groups and the professional establishment. Lieberman and Borman (1976: 461) stress the collaborative relationship between the researcher and the self-help group:

> The kind of research findings that emerge and the way in which they are learned, we believe, will be the product of a genuine partnership between the researcher and members of the self-help group. Realistic collaborative arrangements that involve important payoffs to the groups as well as to science are essential. Such close collaboration may help to translate research questions and findings into language and concepts intelligible to the self-help groups. This may also be one important way to narrow the usual gap between research findings and implementation.

In summary, the essential feature of the action anthropology model as it continues to develop involves facilitation of independent community organization and citizen action groups. Thus, action anthropology comes closest to the supportive, nondirective approach within advocacy described in the beginning of this paper.

The meaning of the term facilitation in relation to indigenous advocacy groups is a complicated one for the advocacy-oriented professional. Facilitation includes such activities as raising with community and lay citizen activists important issues emerging out of participant observation and involvement in community action; generating situations in which such issues can be addressed; offering suggestions and analyzing alternatives in developing action strategies; preparing materials to be used by community members as they "make a case" to the wider society for particular needs and helping to plan, develop and evaluate indigenously run programs. The key factors that differentiate facilitation from other types of involvements are the following:

(1) In facilitation, the anthropologist avoids making decisions for any sector of the community.

(2) In facilitation, the anthropologist does not speak at any time for the community or for any sector of the community.

(3) In facilitation, the anthropologist may disagree and voice disagreement with a direction taken by the community but has no direct influence over that decision.

Obviously, the distinction between facilitation and more directive forms of community involvement is a thin one, conditioned by circumstances, personality and other factors. The term is currently in frequent use, and a more accurate definition awaits further applied research and community experience.

Over the years there has been considerable discussion of action anthropology and the facilitation model has had an effect on the thinking of some anthropologists. Nevertheless there are very few case materials available which describe and analyze its application and evaluate its impact. While the rhetoric of the action anthropology approach shows it to be the most advocacy-oriented of the range of anthropological pursuits, its limited empirical base and dearth of operationalized concepts have left applied anthropologists with few procedural guidelines. The impact of this promising approach in structuring the actions of advocacy-oriented anthropologists therefore has been limited.

In this section we have examined some of the theoretical models, methods and experiences associated with activities that fall under the definition of advocacy. To further develop a perspective on advocacy, we will present two community action projects in which we have been involved — one in the Chicano community in Chicago and the other in Puerto Rican and Black inner city communities in Hartford. Using these two case studies and the activities discussed in this section, we will then examine themes which cross-cut advocacy-oriented activities in anthropology.

THE CHICANO EXPERIENCE

In 1967, a Community Mental Health Program was organized at Chicago's West Side Medical Complex. A segment of the lower west side composed of Chicanos, Blacks and Middle Europeans was chosen as the area to be served by the program. The objective of the program was to provide free and highly accessible mental health services to these residents. A second goal of the program was preventive in orientation, calling for involvement in and change of those factors in the area productive of mental illness. S. Schensul was hired in 1968 to direct the Community Research Unit (CRU) of the program. The task was to:

> collect information on the "natives" of the area so that plans, policies and therapeutic methods could be developed to meet the special needs and cultural requirements of the Black, Mexican and Middle European populations in the area . . . This . . . parallels the traditional role of the applied anthropologist — that of providing information to facilitate social-service programs established by the dominant policy-making and power sectors on behalf of economically and politically marginal groups in a society (Schensul, 1973: 107).

This role depended on the willingness of the program's service and outreach staff to respond by changes in attitude and clinical procedure, to the implications of the unit's socioeconomic and cultural data on health and mental health adaptations among Chicanos. We found they were unwilling to make these changes. With the support of the director of the program, we reoriented ourselves to focussing on the community "both as the object of study *and the most important recipient of the results of that study*" (p. 119). This change marked a transition into advocacy-oriented activities, by moving toward a commitment to community-generated plans for its own development.

Work was geared in two directions: the collection of basic data on demographic patterns, organizational development and Chicano health and mental health; and the identification of situations, events and planning in the community for which such data could be useful. The unit's strategy was to become involved in participant observation and other forms of data collection in the community setting, to seek for ways of involving the unit in action situations and to watch for emerging action potential in the community context.

The first year in the community was marked by participant observation, attendance at public meetings, key informant interviewing, formal interviews with community leadership, and two school-related surveys of parents. This initial entry process allowed the research team to identify existing community agencies and service organizations, to delineate a range of community issues and problems and to begin to gather preliminary data on these concerns; and to meet community activists involved in service provision and community action.

During the beginning of the second year of work in the community, several opportunities opened up. The first involved the decision by a neighborhood settlement house to develop summer block clubs to provide recreation and community organization. Members of the research team were assigned to the blocks where they helped organize activities while they engaged in participant observation, identified potential leaders, carried out block censuses and surveys, and used block data and community data earlier collected by the unit to support issues such as the lack of garbage collection, the press of urban renewal and lack of educational activities. These data were used to justify positions block residents wished to take and they were also made available in the context of ongoing discussions and planning in block club meetings.

A second and related opportunity involved a confrontation between a community group and the city, over rezoning of a residential block in which 40 families were living, for commercial enterprises. The research unit worked with the block club and other area residents to develop strategies for opposing the rezoning. The members of the unit documented the needs and situation of the residents, helped gather signatures and assembled data on the visibility of the community, to be presented to the zoning commission of the city council.

These early cases involved the collection of data around social issues, community needs, and community leadership. They illustrated the importance of being on hand when interesting action situations arose and the necessity for becoming involved in order both to understand the situation and to be able to offer data to facilitate it in the community's favor. Finally, they demonstrated the importance of understanding and being able to manipulate wider society institutions and political processes to the advantage of inner city residents.

By 1972, the brown power movement had begun to influence the community as various sectors turned their attention to community development. The one generalized Chicano community organization gave way to a number of voluntary groups of a more specialized nature. Some of these organizations were oriented toward short-term confrontational action in the areas of education, immigration and urban renewal. Others directed their attention to institutional change and the development of community services in the areas of health, jobs, youth activities, drugs and others.

With the development of these more specific and stable groups the research unit began to link research plans and questions directly to their informational needs. The research team had, by the beginning of our third year in the community, developed good working relationships with most of these newly emerging activists. Thus, members were called upon to discuss strategies for community development, to attend planning meetings, and to present data to "make the case" around particular issues, such as the need for more community responsive social, educational and medical services.

When a community strategy to push service institutions serving the community to provide more relevant services failed, the next step was to develop parallel services, designed, directed and staffed by community people. Several groups began to look actively for outside funding.

The research unit's skills and data pool were then applied to the development of "grant proposals." It supplied extensive portrayals of community problems on the basis of available survey and ethnographic data and designed new data collection operations to support the community case in these proposals. In addition, members of the unit worked with community activists to decide what kinds of services to develop, in line with federal funding guidelines, accompanied activists and program developers to local and federal funding agencies in search of contacts and information concerning funding, and learned with the activists a great deal about the politics and process of getting proposals funded.

The submission of proposals for the development of Chicano

community-run services resulted in the funding, from public and private sources, of programs including a health clinic, a mental health paraprofessional training program, an employment program, a drug abuse program and a youth services-community center. In the year 1971, the area had zero dollars in community-controlled funds. In the year 1973, it had $625,000 and commitments in succeeding years for over $1.5 million.

July 1, 1972 precipitated a new phase in the development of the community. Almost overnight programs had to be organized, staff hired, plans and decisions formulated. CRU staff participated in the development of these programs by:

— Helping in planning and organization;

— Supplying relevant data;

— Designing internal service data systems;

— Setting up evaluation procedures;

— Training Chicano staff in research and data analysis skills;

— Conducting surveys of potential consumers of services;

— Working on program expansion and broadening the base of program funding.

The involvement of the community research unit continued in these programs until the termination of the Community Mental Health Program in 1975. The commitments of individual unit staff to community research and facilitation in Chicago have continued to the present, through ongoing discussions with community activists and program directors and the development of new action research projects. One such project funded by NIMH through a local community organization with S. Schensul as principal investigator is examining the sociocultural aspects of health and mental health problems among expectant and new mothers and infants. The results of this project will be used by a newly formed Mother-Infant Committee to argue for more relevant health and mental health services in the community. Over 40 Chicano women are participating in all stages of the research project. Our role in this project centers on research design, analysis of data, the training of lay researchers and participation in the development of strategies for new and more culturally specific services.

Advocacy in the Chicago context involved the following set of skills and techniques:

1. A good understanding of basic research techniques, both qualitative and quantitative, and a flexible adjustment of these techniques to the demands and contingencies of each action situation;

2. Familiarity with community organizations, activists, political, economic and social issues, gained through participant observation and the willingness to become involved in these action situations;

3. An understanding from the residents' perspectives of the community's relationship with the broader political and institutional structure;

4. An understanding of the service institutions, including schools and mental health facilities, social service agencies, and community structures that serve the community;

5. An understanding of the various sectors of the community, identifiable through cultural, economic, age and other dimensions; and the ways in which these sectors relate differently to political issues and social services;

6. Skills in proposal writing and report development which include using relevant data to support community positions, plan innovative programs in collaboration with activists, and negotiate the politics of proposal writing, submission and review;

7. An understanding of the ways community-based and controlled organizations operate, and skills in program planning and implementation in such programs;

8. Technical expertise above and beyond research competence, in health and mental health, educational programs, administration, community organizing and other areas;

9. The ability to build linkages between the community and outside resources such as universities, hospitals, educational networks, church services, etc., which can be drawn in by the community for collaborative action.

Three basic assumptions underlie these advocacy-oriented activities in the Chicano community in Chicago:

(1) "Anthropological research should provide information to the population under study which contributes to the development of the community and the improvement of community life.

(2) "Programs for community development and improvement are

most successful and effective when they are conceived and
directed by knowledgeable community residents.

(3) "It should be the goal of our applied anthropological unit to
facilitate indigenous social action programs by supplying data
and results which can make significant contributions to the
effectiveness of their efforts" (Schensul, 1973: 111-112. For
more information see Schensul 1974a, Schensul 1974b,
Schensul and Bymel, 1975).

THE HARTFORD CASE

The Hartford situation involves a group of anthropologists of which
S. Schensul is a member based in the Department of Community
Medicine and Health Care at the University of Connecticut. This group,
under the direction of Pertti J. Pelto, seeks to link the department into
health action in Connecticut and provide outside the clinic training
experiences for medical and social science students in the community.[2]

Our approach in the summer of 1976 was to seek out health-related
action being carried out by nonmedical people in the Hartford area. We
looked for community groups seeking more health services, community
health facilities seeking more outreach and ethnic activists seeking
linguistically and culturally appropriate health care for their people. We
felt that our anthropological group could provide:

(1) Research and information gathering capabilities essential to
documenting health care needs, identifying types of health
adaptations in the community and increasing health activists'
knowledge of the health system and particular health problems;

(2) Links with community-oriented medical service resources at the
University of Connecticut Health Center so that community
and medical expertise could be used collaboratively to deal with
health problems;

(3) Techniques for the use of this information in reports, proposals
and presentations which could support the community position,
maximize its exposure to health decison makers and attract
funding and resources for community-controlled programs.

After following a number of leads, we centered our attention on
two potentially highly productive situations. The first was a group of
Puerto Rican health activists committed to rectify what they perceived
as a failure of the Hartford medical system to adequately serve Puerto
Ricans. The second situation was a Puerto Rican and Black housing

project in which the Visiting Nurses Association (VNA) proposed to establish a clinic. In consultation with the VNA, staff of the housing project and members of residents' organization, we began to examine the potential for preventative and research activities in the community that would support the efforts of the clinic.

Each of these health action cases offered the potential for facilitation for the following reasons:

(1) Citizens had organized their own advocate groups to deal with health issues.

(2) Each of these groups was medically underserved as a result of a complex interaction of cultural, linguistic, economic and geographic factors.

(3) The nature of the health problems required not simply clinical services but a comprehensive community mobilization, involving systems change and preventive health programs.

The focus of these groups on systems change, community action, prevention and socio-cultural factors were issues to which we as anthropologists could contribute as professionals, and identify with as individuals.

a) **Puerto Rican Health Action.** The major immigration of Puerto Ricans into Hartford began in the early 1960s and has sharply increased over the last decade. A survey of Puerto Ricans leaving the island conducted by the Archdiocese of San Juan (1970) showed that Hartford ranked third in all cities of destination in the U.S. The Puerto Rican population of Hartford is now estimated to number 40,000 people — close to 25 percent of the total population of the city.

While this new population seems to be making its fair share of demands on the health system, the system's response has been inadequate in the Puerto Rican view. They have documented that there are:

(1) Few Puerto Rican health care providers in the city;

(2) Insufficient interpreters available in clinics and emergency rooms;

(3) Very limited efforts in health care outreach into Puerto Rican neighborhoods;

(4) Limited programs for training of health care providers on cultural and social aspects of Puerto Rican health adaptations;

(5) Too few recruitment programs for developing Puerto Rican health care professionals.

In response to the deficiencies of the health and mental health system, a Health Committee was organized in 1974 by the key Puerto Rican organization in Hartford. In 1976, it was expanded to include a number of other Puerto Rican organizations and individuals and members of the anthropological team of the Department of Community Medicine.

The Committee directed its primary attention toward documenting the health and mental health adaptations of Puerto Ricans in Hartford and using this information to develop Puerto Rican health programs and create medical systems change. With the help of the anthropological team, information was collected on:

— Staff and programs serving areas in Hartford with high concentrations of Puerto Ricans. Such information included the percentage of Puerto Rican clients, translation resources, types of problems presented and evaluation of the care received.

— Uses of indigenous resources in the community to deal with health and mental health problems. These "folk practitioners" include *espiritistas, curanderas* and *santiras*. In addition to these folk medical practitioners, the committee has begun to assess the role of the clergy, relatives, neighbors, and police and fire department emergency services in medical and mental health problems.

— Schistosomiasis (Belharzia) and other pathological parasites as one of the medical problems with which Puerto Ricans must cope but which has not received attention in the Hartford health system. The anthropological team helped to assess the literature on this disease, and contacted and met with staff in New York with experience in its identification and treatment.

This information provided a base for:

— expanding the health committee to include Spanish-speaking health professionals and other health personnel committed to Puerto Rican community needs;

— supporting Puerto Rican participation in health and mental health planning agencies in the Hartford region;

— initiating efforts to recruit bilingual, bicultural health personnel;

— meeting with the ambulatory care directors of the major health facilities in Hartford to present a report written by the health committee discussing the significance of schistosomiasis among Puerto Ricans in Hartford and seeking a joint program to deal with the problem;

— organizing a research and screening project for schistosomiasis and other parasitic diseases among recent arrivals from Puerto Rico in a Hartford Middle School;

— the development of three grant proposals seeking funds for training Puerto Rican agency personnel in health problems and health care and research projects assessing Puerto Rican adaptations in health and mental health.

— These proposals were submitted by the Puerto Rican health committee with the support of the anthropological team of the Department of Community Medicine. The funding of this research will give the Health Committee an ongoing capability to use research and information as a tool in health systems change.

The role of the anthropological research team in these activities has been a diverse one. It has variously involved primary research, literature reviews, processing of secondary data, participation in health committee strategy design, arranging meetings with health personnel, designing interview schedules, writing proposals, and identifying potential sources of funding. The anthropologists are now well integrated into the health committee — contributing to all aspects of its activities with an emphasis on accumulation of informational resources — but remaining relatively non-directive in selecting courses of action and objectives.

b) The Housing Project. The housing project in which we became involved consisted of approximately a thousand units. About 55 percent of the community is Puerto Rican, 40 percent Black, and the remainder white ethnic senior citizens. Housing is dilapidated, crime is high, city services are poor, and many consider it the worst project in the city. From the aspect of medical services, the project is "indigent." Hospitals, clinics and private physicians are located at some distance from the area and public bus transportation is minimal. As a result, most people in the housing project have little involvement in Hartford's health care system.

As we became involved in the housing project, we found that the city was delaying in funding the health clinic. In consultation with the housing project staff and residents, it was decided that we would jointly organize a "Health Fair" in conjunction with "Community Day," an annual celebration at the Housing Project. The objectives of the health fair included:

- Raising consciousness concerning health issues in the community;
- Collecting data on health problems that could add further support to the need for a clinic;
- Linking in resources from the health center and the voluntary health agencies — putting the housing project on the "medical map" so that the system could recognize its lack of access to services and develop their own outreach plans for providing those services;
- Developing a residents' health committee which could plan preventative projects and have a voice in the organization of medical services in the community.

The Health Fair was a considerable success with an attendance of over 500 people. Of the hundred people screened, the great majority had significant health programs. Over 20 voluntary health agencies participated, providing screenings, information and consultation with physicians.

The anthropological team:

- Drew up and distributed a medical survey which was used as part of the screening process;
- Collected, analyzed and wrote up the screening data;
- Conducted follow-up interviews to evaluate the effectiveness of the referrals made to medical services. The results of these interviews showed that there were significant health care delivery problems even when specific arrangements were made in Hartford's hospitals to receive housing project residents.

In January of 1977, we learned that the VNA clinic would not be funded. However, the health fair and the information resulting from the follow-up had raised the health consciousness of several active residents and the new manager of the housing project. A housing project health committee was organized which now includes residents, housing project staff, several health providers who were involved in the fair, and members of the anthropological team. This committee is now in the process of organizing preventive and clinical services in a location it has received from the housing authority. The anthropological team is now working on the organization of screening, monitoring and prevention programs and helping to train volunteer residents to fill positions in these programs.

Our presence in the community gave us the opportunity to identify another housing project group involved in health action. This group, incensed at the infestation of rats in their area of the housing project, dramatically presented the rats to the director of the city's department of public health. The day after the demonstration, S. Schensul visited the group. On the basis of the positive image the anthropological team had developed in relation to the health fair, we were asked to participate. The first job as outlined by the group was to document in less dramatic but more comprehensive terms the rat problem in the housing project. The next day, members of the anthropological team and residents systematically located rat holes, found violations in the equipment and process for garbage removal, and interviewed residents concerning the health hazards, particularly to children, of rat infestation. The results were presented in a meeting which included the housing project manager, the exterminators, public health officials and residents. While improvements have not been dramatic, there have been some changes made. A further result of the anthropological team's involvement with this group was in their more active participation with other residents in the health fair and in the subsequent health committee.

The involvement of the anthropological team in Hartford's community health action is still at the initial development stage. However, drawing from the Chicago experience, we expect to learn a great deal as we become increasingly involved in the health activities of the Puerto Rican and housing project communities.

The goal of collaborative action in the Hartford experience is helping Puerto Rican and housing project residents:

(1) To get their fair share of medical and health services;

(2) To have significant input in determining the nature and type of services;

(3) To effect changes through organized action in their communites and in the relationship of their communities to the wider political system which can promote health among residents.

CROSS-CUTTING FEATURES OF ADVOCACY
APPROACHES IN ANTHROPOLOGY

FIELD WORK IN THE COMMUNITY

At the heart of advocacy-oriented activities in anthropology is the anthropologists' presence in the field, the local community. Anthropological tradition is rooted in the method of "participant observation." The object of this approach is to see things from "the inside-out" — to understand the behavior and world view of the residents of a community through participating as much as possible in the life of the community. This involvement in community life is increased by living in the community, developing a personal and reciprocal network of friends and blending in unobtrusively in community activities. This approach has several implications for advocacy:

— Anthropologists begin to share the world view of the residents and identify with their values and perspectives.

— Anthropologists see on a firsthand basis the community's relationship to the wider political system and the inequities that exist in that relationship.

— Anthropologists get a close-up view of community needs and problems.

Since this approach is a basic part of the anthropological tradition, it is not surprising that anthropologists such as Stewart, Hostetler, Spillius, Paredes, and Tax and associates went into the field as basic researchers and came out as advocates. For those that do go into the field with an action and advocacy perspective, the field work process ensures that anthropological activities directed toward change and advocacy will be grounded in the community and will be linked into the personal and reciprocal relationships that result from that process. Even the Vicos and Kuyo Chico projects, in which anthropologists directed change, were rooted in fieldwork and personal network development before and during the implementation of the project. Foster (1969: 61) sees the anthropologists as developing in fieldwork "a personal element that is poorly developed or lacking entirely in other social sciences. The social anthropologist must experience total immersion in the system he is studying ... he lives in the community ... comes to know well a great many people ... [has an] emotional involvement with the people he is studying." This "grassroots" approach is the cornerstone of the advocacy-oriented activities we have described in this section.

Another underlying feature of these advocacy activities is that the anthropologist is oriented toward building innovation and change on the culture resources and felt needs that exist in the community. The anthropologist through the very nature of the field work process is concerned about understanding what peoples' views, needs and concerns are and starting at that point rather than with a preconceived notion of where the people "should be." Nunez del Prado (1973: 10) states that "If the ideas and programs we introduced [in Kuyo Chico] were related to already existing meaning in the culture, rather than based solely on our own point of view, the receptivity of the group would be greatest, since those 'innovations' would be in accord with the group's own mode of thought." Tax suggests that these needs and priorities emerge through listening, observing and questioning in the field work process.

It follows that the anthropologist considers it absolutely necessary to devote considerable time before and during a project to collecting data on the behavior, attitudes, and perceived needs of people in the community. All of the projects described in this section have carried out extensive community research in association with their action activities. These research efforts have been directed both at baseline data and the impact of change and advocacy efforts.

CONTINUED ADAPTATION OF GOALS AND STRATEGIES

Communities are subject to rapid changes from internal and external factors. Citizen action groups can change direction in response to "hot" issues or changes in key personalities. A plan accepted by all one week is rejected the next, or becomes impossible to implement. Such shifting contingencies, and changes in group structure and organization, must be taken into account if the input of the advocacy-oriented professional is to be useful.

The anthropologists involved in advocacy-oriented activities have been on an intimate basis with the "action and reactions" both in response to their inputs and the ultimate success and impact of the action taken. They have developed this intimate view both through the formal research process and through their ongoing presence in the community or citizens' group.

As a result, we find the anthropologists who have been involved in the activities described in the preceding sections willing to change and adapt their procedures and goals to new data, unforeseen events and new directions taken by community residents. Both Holmberg and associates and Nunez del Prado describe their shifts in program and goals in response to unforeseen events and unaccounted-for cultural and community factors. Tax and associates, in their work with the Fox, emphasize the need for flexibility and responsiveness of anthropological approaches and goals. Flexibility is essential if anthropologists are to be "where the action is" and to continually revise their strategies so that they are in line with the action objectives of the group.

ADAPTIVE RESEARCH METHODOLOGY

The primary tool of the advocacy-oriented anthropologists is their ability as researchers to generate information that will be useful to the activities of an advocacy group. The idea of "useful" research data in the action context is evaluated in terms of its positive contribution to plans, programs and action of the advocacy group. If, at the same time, such information contributes to knowledge accumulation in the social sciences, the action researchers yield an added but secondary "payoff." These advocacy research goals are, of course, the reverse of the standard academically-oriented research objectives.

Producing "useful" research in advocacy activities requires research methodology that can conform to shifting contingencies, urgent time limits and the informational needs of "nonresearcher" activists. Unfortunately, most anthropologists in advocacy-oriented activities have not provided a detailed statement of their methods and techniques. The result is that each of these anthropologists have had to "reinvent the wheel" as they seek to produce better advocacy-related research data. Some of the key principles we have developed out of the Chicago and Hartford experiences are methods undoubtedly used by many of these anthropologists:

1. Research questions need to be worked out collaboratively between researchers and lay advocates. This process will increase the likelihood that the most appropriate questions will be researched, and will also insure that the resulting information will be understood and usable by those who are the implementers of the action.

2. Research operations must fit the time frame presented by the action and advocacy activities. Late results, no matter how scientifically obtained, are not useful for the action at hand.

The advocacy-oriented researcher must operate on the idea of doing the most legitimate research within the time available. This principle calls for effective use of secondary data, special sampling techniques, and rapid data analysis.

3. The one-shot, written research article or report is inadequate for advocacy-oriented research. To maximize the impact of data on action, the data must "live." By this idea, we mean that the dissemination process must be ongoing — mining the same body of data with new perspectives developing out of current action — initiating new research to update old data. Unlike standard research there is no end-action structured research which feeds into action which raises new research questions.

It is not appropriate here to fully discuss advocacy-oriented research methodology. It may be enough to say that for the advocacy researcher research is a tool — a means to the objective of providing a set of skills and information which can make advocacy groups more effective.

RECIPROCAL LEARNING IN THE ACTION CONTEXT

Many of the anthropologists involved in advocacy-oriented activities, particularly Tax and associates and S. Schensul, stress the growth and learning that occur on the part of both the anthropologist and the people with whom he works. Schensul (1974: 206) states that:

A key element underlying the skills we learned ... involved a reciprocal process ... between the researcher and the community action person ... We found that we began to develop increased skills, as a result of this training (in) political action, community organization, manipulating bureaucracies .... We also found that community activists became skilled in developing research questions, analyzing research data and generally knowing how to work with and use researchers for the benefit of their programs.

This collaborative learning is an important aspect of the anthropological approach to advocacy. It insures that the exchange of information between the professional and the lay person is not unidirectional — a situation which would threaten the very nature of the advocacy program.

Collaborative learning is also important in expanding the skills of the specialized professional — the researcher, the planner or the therapist. The advocacy-oriented anthropologist must also become or at least intimately know about being a political activist, a community organizer, a service program developer, an administrator and a range of other ubiquitous skills and roles imposed by the unfolding advocacy activities. Much of this learning can come only through reciprocal exchange with indigenous lay advocates.

SELF-CONSCIOUS REFLECTION ON GOALS AND VALUES

In addition to concern about the behavior, values and actions of the community, each of these anthropologists does a great deal of self-conscious reflection on their own behavior, attitudes and values. Anthropologists expect to react — to experience "culture shock" — as their own values and expectations confront a very different cultural and community environment. What makes this self-analysis so significant to advocacy is that it causes anthropologists to work hard to avoid imposing their own concepts of approapriate behavior, to question the "cultural boundedness" of their approaches and to clarify their value positions. The continuous interaction between the anthropologist and the people, in advocacy-oriented activities, creates considerable changes for the anthropologist as a professional and as a person and demands the thinking through of explicit and definable value positions.

THE IMPORTANCE OF FACILITATION

With the exception of the Vicos and Kuyo Chico projects, anthropologists in advocacy-oriented activities work hard to be facilitative and non-directive. Even in those "power brokerage" projects, the goal and the eventual result were a "devolution of power" into the hands of the Indians.

Anthropologists generally do not feel comfortable with the power roles assumed in these two projects. Their natural inclination is to play a background role, leaving the direction of actions in the hands of community residents. As Tax (1960: 110) states,

> we feel most strongly the value of freedom . . . for individuals to choose the group with which to identify and freedom for a community to choose its way of life . . . . All we want in our action programs is to provide, if we can, genuine alternatives from which to choose and to be ourselves as little restrictive as is humanly possible . . . . Such a program requires that we remove ourselves as much as possible from a position of power or undue influence . . . to impose our choices on the assumption that "we know better than they do what is good for them" not only restricts their freedom but is likely to turn out to be empirically wrong.

GENERATING A BALANCE OF POWER

Finally, in all these examples of advocacy, anthropologists are concerned about a "balance of power" between economically and politically marginal communities and the dominant sectors of regional and national society. Tax (1960: 109), in assessing the function of their scholarships and crafts projects, feels that "perhaps the greatest end served by these [projects] is removing obstacles that keep Indians from relating to functional white organizations and in trust groups." One of Holmberg's (1971a: 22) assumptions was "that the Indians themselves, *through the development of new organizations* (emphasis ours) would take over the operation of the community after our period of research and experimentation ended." Both Tax and Holmberg envisioned their activities as removing barriers and setting up new social and economic systems which would help local communities to face the wider world more effectively.

Another aspect of the balancing of power involves the transmission of the skills of the professional to the community and advocacy group members. Holmberg and Nunez del Prado stress this strongly in their work in Peru. S. Schensul (1974) describes the training of lay researchers in the Chicano community in Chicago. This educational and training process creates the indigenous resources which can allow the local community to deal with issues more independently in the future.

We began this paper with the view that anthropologists could make a significant contribution to advocacy — particularly in facilitating lay and community advocacy groups rather than as advocates themselves. In this section we have presented the ideological, methodological and procedural underpinnings of this contribution. Anthropologists are not unique in their employing of any of these elements. Yet we feel it is safe to say that these factors are "built in" to anthropology to a greater extent than any other discipline. However, we will in the future still be discussing the "potential" of advocacy in anthropology unless we generate more cases and advocacy projects, and draw from these experiences the training procedures, the institutional supports and the literature to support advocacy and action in anthropology.

THE TRANSMISSION OF SKILLS TO THE COMMUNITY

In addition to helping to remove the negative factors and building positive ones the anthropologists in several of these projects have worked to pass on their skills and those of other "experts" to the local group. This educational and training process creates the indigenous resources which can allow the local community to deal with issues more independently in the future.

CONCLUSION: THE FUTURE OF
ADVOCACY IN ANTHROPOLOGY

The anthropological approach to advocacy we have outlined in this paper involves a reasonably long-term commitment to a specific group or a community, flexibility in time and issue orientation and a base of activities which will support the political nature, the time and the flexibility of these commitments. Most anthropologists do not have such advocacy-oriented bases. The primary thrust of the university requires an emphasis on teaching, serving on departmental and university committees, advising students, and publishing in response to the pressures of tenureship. Anthropologists based in extra-local human innovating programs and other directed change projects are often limited in their range of issues and may be linked to models of innovation not easily adaptable to the advocacy approach. Anthropologists, unlike those in other disciplines, have not to any great degree developed private corporate bases which could perhaps provide the economic support to do the kinds of independent free lance work that would fit into the advocacy model. While this analysis tends to be pessimistic, it is our feeling that with a clear vision of the need for advocacy activities anthropologists can create effective bases in the university, in human service programs and in noninstitutionalized settings.

Anthropologists can play a significant role in the development of advocacy activities from a university base. There are several models of service institutes within universities whose aim is to use university expertise to facilitate activities beyond the university. Very frequently, however, such institutes get over-committed to coordination within the university and do not make sufficient contacts within the wider community. Anthropologists can make a major contribution to these multidisciplinary "technical assistance" efforts by establishing their link to the wider community and by developing long-term involvements in those communities in which technical expertise in the university can be effectively used.

Anthropologists can also begin to develop advocacy-oriented activities from a department-of-anthropology base. While this does, of course, require some flexibility to escape the demands of the regular schedule, we feel that faculty "corporations," temporary appointments, applied research training linked to advocacy needs and departmental plans of action can contribute significantly to a link between academic and advocacy-oriented anthropology.

In the programs of the 1960s and the early 1970s, anthropologists often had considerable flexibility to define their jobs within medical, mental health and other human service programs. These programs, particularly those with a preventative and broad-based intervention strategy, continue to be potentially ideal locations for advocacy-oriented anthropologists. However, many of the community-oriented programs such as community mental health, community health, and family medicine have retreated from a past position of broad-based outreach to traditional clinical services. We might say that advocacy-oriented activities for anthropologists in this realm are directly related to the impetus of the new Administration in developing broad-based, community-oriented change programs.

In our desire to increase our own flexibility, the coauthors developed a private research corporation – *Community Research Incorporated*. The emphasis in our work involves contracting with ethnic- and community-based organizations to provide technical assistance and evaluation, research and community outreach. We find it a relief to be able to make professional and community decisions, apart from the constraints and demands concomitant with institutional affiliation. The possibility also exists for anthropologists to link up with advocacy-oriented private firms not only in anthropology but in law, urban planning and other fields as well.

If advocacy activities grow among anthropologists and if there are positions available for such activities, the nature of the training of anthropologists must be altered at least in some departments. At this time almost all anthropology departments in this country prepare students for only academic positions and basic research. To support a move toward action and advocacy research in anthropology, departments must emphasize:

(1) Learning by direct experience in departmentally sponsored advocacy projects;

(2) Integration of courses and seminars with community work;

(3) Multidisciplinary training in the range of skills needed in advocacy settings.

In addition to direct experience, training must also be based on a corpus of materials which describe multiple cases of anthropological involvement in advocacy and in which models, methods and cross-cutting features have been delineated. Thus, what is needed is not only more experiences but research which assesses the function and impact of the anthropological contribution to advocacy. Bastide (1973: 21-32) calls for a "science" of applied anthropology. We would expect in line with this view that as anthropologists become more involved in advocacy a role will develop for those anthropologists interested in studying and assessing their activities. Such a "science" of action and advocacy involvement in anthropology will serve to:

(1) undergird the training of students in these activities;

(2) more firmly establish such activities as a legitimate part of anthropology;

(3) identify a set of tested methods, procedures and experiences which can support anthropologists currently involved in such activities.

The development of an advocacy approach in the social sciences and related fields has implications for significant changes in the training process and the structure of the disciplines and the operations of the universities and human service institutions. Such changes can provide the beginnings of efforts to heal the schism between the university and the community, between the professional and the lay person, between the service program and the consumer. Advocacy and action involvement may also provide some answers to the continuing but relatively ineffectual debate concerning the conservatism and lack of relevance of anthropology and the other disciplines.

NOTES

1. Members of the Community Research Unit included Felipe Ayala, Santiago Boiton, Susan Stecknij, Mary Bakozysz-Bymel, Kay Guzder, Emile Schepers, Elias Sevilla-Casas, Gwen Stern.

2. Other members of the team include Joanne Allport, Lawrence Beede, Kathleen DeWalt, Douglas Goldsmith, Janice Hogle, Thomas Marchione, Susan Mesurick, Florence Mueller, and Kevin O'Reilly.

REFERENCES

Barnett, H. (1956) *Anthropology in Administration.* Evanston, Ill.: Row, Peterson.

Bastide, R. (1973) *Applied Anthropology.* New York: Harper and Row.

Batalla, G. B. (1966) "Conservative Thought in Applied Anthropology: A Critique." *Human Organization,* 25: 89-92.

Berreman, G. D. (1968) "Is Anthropology Alive? Social Responsibility in Social Anthropology." *Current Anthropology,* 9 (5): 391-396.

Blecher, E. M. (1971) *Advocacy Planning for Urban Development: With Analysis of Six Demonstration Programs.* New York: Praeger Publishers.

Boas, F. (1928) *Anthropology and Modern Life.* New York: W. W. Norton.

Brager, G. A. (1968) "Advocacy and Political Behavior Social Work." *Journal of the American Association of Social Workers,* 13 (2): 5-15.

Deloria, V. (1969) *Custer Died for Your Sins.* London: Collier-Macmillan Limited.

Foster, G. (1969) *Applied Anthropology.* Boston: Little, Brown.

Gearing, F. (1970) *The Face of the Fox.* Chicago: Aldine.

–––, R. McNelting, and L. Peattie (1960) *The Documentary History of the Fox Project.* Chicago: University of Chicago Press.

Gough, K. (1968) "New Proposals for Anthropologists." *Current Anthropology,* 9: 403-407.

Helm, J. (ed.) (1966) *Pioneers of American Anthropology.* Seattle, Washington: University of Washington Press.

Herskovits, M. J. (1949) *Man and His Works.* New York: Knopf.

Holmberg, A. (1971a) "Experimental Intervention in the Field." Pp 33-64 in H. F. Dobyn, et al. (eds.), *Power and Applied Social Change.* Beverly Hills: Sage.

–––. (1971b) "The Role of Power in Changing Values and Institutions of Vicos." in H. F. Dobyns, et al. (eds.), *Peasants, Power and Applied Social Change.* Beverly Hills, Sage.

Hostetler, J. A. (1972) "Amish Schooling: A Study in Alternatives." *Council on Anthropology and Education Newsletter,* Vol. III, no. 2.

Jacobs, S. E. (1974) "Action and Advocacy Anthropology." *Human Organization,* 33: 209-215.

Just, M., Bell, C. S., Fisher, W., and Schensul, S. L. (1975) *Coping in a Troubled Society.* Boston: Lexington Books.

Lurie, N. O. (1955) "Anthropology and Indian Claims Litigation: Problems, Opportunities and Recommendations." *Ethnohistory,* 2: 357-375.

———. (1973) *Anthropology and the American Indian.* San Francisco: Indian Historical Press.

Nunez Del Prado, O. (1973) *Kuyo Chico: Applied Anthropology in an Indian Community.* Chicago: University of Chicago Press.

Paredes, J. A. (1976) "New Uses for Old Ethnography: A Brief Social History of a Research Project with the Eastern Creek Indians or How to Be an Applied Anthropologist Without Really Trying." *Human Organization, 35:* 315-320.

Peattie, L. R. (1970) "Reflections on Advocacy Planning." *Journal of the American Institute of Planners, 34:* 405-410.

Pelto, G. and P. J. Pelto (1976) *The Human Adventure: An Introduction to Anthropology.* New York: Macmillan.

Peterson, J. (1974) "The Anthropologist as Advocate." *Human Organization, 33:* 311-318.

Redfield, A. (ed.) (1973) *Anthropology Beyond the University.* Athens, Georgia: University of Georgia Press.

Reining, C. C. (1962) "A Lost Period of Applied Anthropology." *American Anthropologist, 64:* 593-600.

Romano, O. (1968) "The Anthropology and Sociology of Mexican Americans." *El Grito, 2:* 13-26.

Sapir, E. (1924) "Culture, Genuine and Spurious." *American Journal of Sociology, 29:* 401-429.

Schensul, S. L. (1973) "Action Research: The Applied Anthropologist in a Community Mental Health Program." Pp 106-119 in A. Redfield (ed.), *Anthropology Beyond the University.* Athens, Georgia: University of Georgia Press.

———. (1974) "Skills Needed in Action Research: Lessons from El Centro de La Causa." *Human Organization, 33:* 203-209.

——— and M. Bymel (1975) "The Role of Applied Research in the Development of Health Services in a Chicano Community In Chicago." Pp 211 in S. Ingman and A. Thomas (eds.), *Topias and Utopias in Health.* The Hague: Mouton.

Smith, E. W. (1934) "Anthropology and the Practical Man." *Journal of Royal Anthropological Institute, 54:* xiii-xxxvii.

Spicer, E. (1954) *Human Problems in Technological Change.* New York: Russell Sage Foundation.

——— (1976) "Beyond Analysis and Explanations? The Life and Times of the Society for Applied Anthropology." *Human Organization, 35* (4): 335-344.

Spillius, J. (1957) "Natural Disaster and Political Crisis in a Polynesian Society: An Exploration of Operational Research." *Human Relations, 10:* 3-27; 113-125.

Stewart, O. C. (1973) "Anthropologists as Expert Witnesses for Indians: Claims and Peyote Cases." Pp 36 in *Anthropology and the American Indian.* San Francisco: Indian Historical Press.

Szwed, J. F. (1974) "An American Anthropological Dilemma: The Politics of Afro-American Culture." Pp 153 in D. Hymes (ed.), *Reinventing Anthropology.* New York: Vintage Books.

Tax, S. (1958) "Values in Action: The Fox Project." *Human Organization,* 17: 17-20.

———, (1957a) "The Bow and The Hoe: Reflections on Hunters, Villagers, Anthropologists." *Current Anthropology,* 16: 507-513.

———. (1975b) "Action Anthropology." *Current Anthropology,* 16: 514-

Vaca, W. (1970) "The Mexican-American in the Social Sciences." *El Grito,* 4: 17-51.

Valentine, C. (1968) *Culture and Poverty: Critique and Counterproposals.* Chicago: University of Chicago Press.

Van Willigen, J. (1976) "Applied Anthropology and Community Development Administration: A Critical Assessment." Pp 79 in M. V. Angrosino (ed.), *Do Applied Anthropologists Apply Anthropology?* Athens: University of Georgia Press.

Weaver, T. (ed.) (1973) *To See Ourselves: Anthropology and Modern Social Issues.* Glenview, Illinois: Scott Foresman and Company.

ADVOCACY AND SOCIOLOGY

James H. Laue

SOCIOLOGY AND THE JUST SOCIETY

The discipline of sociology grew out of a concern for reform and social justice, a belief in the possibility (and for some the inevitability) of progress, and the often unexamined conviction that rationality and truth-telling can (and usually do) affect social policy — in a positive direction. This legacy has been traced by numerous sociologists and historians, among them Barnes (1948), Shils (1948), Hinkle and Hinkle (1954), Nisbet (1966), Gouldner (1970), Lauer (1973), Ritzer (1975), and Williams (1976).

THE SOCIOLOGICAL WORLD-VIEW(S)

How do contemporary sociologies view "justice"? Explicit attempts to define justice or other desirable end-states toward which sociologists believe they should work are extremely difficult to find in the literature — especially in the contemporary self-conscious sociologies with their focus on method rather than outcome.[1] To approach an answer, we must first examine the nature of the world-view(s) of sociology. Such an examination has been the task of a number of the scholars noted above, and can be only briefly mentioned here.

The critical elements for understanding the discipline's conception of justice are the following:

1. While sociology was conceived in Western Europe, academic sociology (as contrasted with Marxist sociology) took root and achieved its more rapid growth in the United States (Gouldner, 1970: 20-24).

2. The American setting and ethic were particularly conducive to the development of a sociology concerned with change and progress. Williams (1976: 79) points to the role of "the American rationalists and deists in the generation of 1776" in preparing "a cultural setting favorable to the later nineteenth-century social science," noting especially the "faith in reason, in natural order and in potential human progress" among educated Americans in the nation's first century. These articles of faith are important in the conception of justice in the social sciences today, I believe.

3. There is no single paradigm governing sociological activity today. One recent analysis identifies three operating paradigms in the field, each linked to specific methodological approaches: social facts, social definition, and social behavior (Ritzer, 1975).

4. There are "domain assumptions" shared by all sociologists, however, the most important of which is the assumption of the autonomy of social structure from the individual and the collectivity (Gouldner, 1970: 51). Society is external, and tenacious in its determination of individual behavior, covert and overt. Stated in strongest terms, there are no persons in sociology — only role- and status-occupants within social structures.

5. "Sociology for whom?" and "how?" are the most frequently asked questions by sociologists of themselves and their discipline today. The answers to the first question range from "all of humanity" to "underdogs" (rarely is "overdog" the appropriate answer). Answers to the second question also vary — from methodological pluralism to strict experimentalism to near-journalistic qualitative approaches.

6. The justice question — "Sociology for what?" — is rarely addressed directly. Answers must be inferred from examining the other questions and answers.

From these roots and from the practice and writings of sociologists in the United States today, the following concept of the "just society" emerges:

A just society is a macro-social system in which:

— resources are allocated on the basis of equality rather than equity;

— interest groups (especially non-elitist groups) are sufficiently empowered to negotiate their own rights (i.e., power is diffused rather than centralized);

— decision making is orderly, patterned, democratic, and based on rationality and good data;

— the population is pluralistic in base and tolerant of pluralism in outlook (the world-view is cosmopolitan rather than local); and the ultimate aim (and, ideally, outcome) of the society's existence is maximum personal fulfillment of all persons in the system.

SOCIAL JUSTICE AS MAXIMUM PERSONAL FULFILLMENT

The last characteristic — fulfillment of persons — emerges as the basis of most of the theories of justice — Aristotelian, Judaeo-Christian, Lockean, Marxist, and, most recently, Rawlsian, to name a few — which I believe to have influenced the development of sociology. Personhood, rather than gods, pure ideas, or structures, is the criterion for pursuing and evaluating justice. Rawls' massive review of western theories of justice and development of his advocacy of "justice as fairness" begins with the underlying assumption of "the inviolability of the person" (Rawls, 1971).

In the only two articles by sociologists in a recent *Journal of Social Issues* symposium on "The Justice Motivation in Social Behavior" (Lerner, 1975), an equality conception of justice is favored over an equity conception. Walster and Walster (1975) elaborate on Aristotle's distinction between two major types of social justice: equal justice (based on equality) and distributive justice (based on equity). Under the equity principle, resources are allocated in proportion to inputs or merits; the authors reject this principle, noting (as does Deutsch, 1975) that virtually any value may serve as the basis for evaluating inputs and that such values are essentially conservative in that they represent prevailing power arrangements and norms. Under the equality principle, resources are allocated to persons based on documented need and all get what they need.

Sampson (1975: 49) explores equity and equality principles, and concludes that equality-based justice, "by contrast [to equity-based justice], is based on a principle that divides resources equally, arguing that differential investments do not provide a legitimate basis for making claims to differential outcomes." Sampson believes the equality theorists' claim which he cites: "All persons deserve much the same."

In the same issue, Morton Deutsch, a social psychologist, poses the question, "Equity, Equality or Need?" in order to understand what value(s) will be used in determining the basis for just allocation of resources. He concludes that "the concept of justice is concerned with the distribution of the conditions and goods which affect the well-being of individual members of a group or community (1975: 142).

The only formal, official statement of the American Sociological Association which addresses the issues around which this book is focussed is the most recent Code of Ethics, adopted in 1971. The Preamble ultimately rests on a doctrine of persons which calls for: "respecting the integrity," "promoting the dignity," and "maintaining the autonomy" of the persons the field touches through research, teaching or other activities. The Preamble exhorts, "Persons are to be considered – in the renewable phrase of Kant – as ends and not as means" (American Sociological Association, 1971).

So, somewhat ironically, a discipline which often ignores individual persons in its practice comes to rest its ethical code in a doctrine of persons as ends in themselves. A person-centered sense of justice emerges in a field where persons are less important than structures. Perhaps equality-based justice emerges precisely because each single individual is equally unimportant to the sociologist-qua-actuary. All persons become curiously equal in their claim on the resources of the social system – each deserving "much the same."

SOCIOLOGISTS AND INJUSTICE

TRUTH-TELLING

A review of various segments and schools of the sociological literature (and of the activities of more innovative and, to some extent, less publishable sociologists) reveals no clear consensus on modalities for applying the discipline to social injustice. But one fact emerges clearly from an analysis of what a wide range of sociologists do, talk and write about: Most sociologists are unreconstructed rationalists, devoted to truth-telling as the major practice modality for the field.

By "truth-telling" I mean that mode of behavior which consists of gathering data, organizing and interpreting them, then communicating the results through speaking, print or electronic media with the belief that this form of activity will influence important decisions (as defined by the truth-teller) in a positive direction (again, in the view of the communicator). Truth-telling is a practice modality in that its practitioners generally: (a) identify target audiences (whether academics, public officials, or perhaps the mass media); (b) believe they are pursuing positive goals; (c) learn and attempt to adhere to standards accepted by their disciplinary peers; (d) are somewhat subject to peer review and evaluation (and even less so to client influence); and (e) constantly seek to upgrade their practice competence and, therefore, their professional standing.

The use of the term "truth-telling" does not even assume that there is a truth – or several truths – to be told, or that sociologists could find it – or them. The phrase is phenomenological rather than epistemological.

The major underlying assumptions of the truth-telling mode of practice flow directly from ideologies regarding justice and a just society: human dignity, rationality, and progress. Across a wide range of forms, forums, levels of methodological sophistication, ideological positions, ages and institutional locations, sociologists show a remarkable tendency to act alike when trying to "practice" their craft: they talk and write about sociology, society, and truth, with the usually tacit but sometimes explicit assumption that somehow good data, careful research, and clever and/or correct conceptualization affects policy. Ahistorical young radicals, respectable conflict theorists and apparently pure science structural-functionaries choose the same weapons to pursue their particular vision of applied sociology – words. Even Friedrichs' prophetic doers-of-change (1970) for the most part try to do it through classroom teaching, lectures, congressional testimony, resolutions, action research, policy research, evaluation research, letters to the *New York Times,* books on radical sociology, and articles in *Social Problems* and the *Insurgent Sociologist.* Only the ideologies and distribution outlets are different from the priestly keepers-of-truth.

The tradition of the truth-telling modality is not unique to sociology; nor are other modalities involving, for example, agency administration, case work, policy-formation roles or political or legal action. While one can find support for, and examples of these more "active" modalities, sociologists primarily act out their academic socialization, as do their colleagues in the other social sciences.

OPTIMISTIC RATIONALITY

In summary, the dominant — almost exclusive — self-conception of the sociologist as practitioner is the researcher/scholar who communicates what he or she knows to appropriate audiences. It is curious that the social scientists who pride themselves on professional debunking of values and questioning of societal assumptions should have been so blind to the ramifications of their own tenacious optimistic rationality. The Nazis, the Holocaust, assassinations, civil rights resistance, Southeast Asia, Watergate ethics, terrorism and other 20th century correlates of the rise of the social sciences should have tempered continued reliance on rational models of social influence.

Yet naively optimistic truth-telling remains the dominant mode of sociological intervention in human affairs.

SOCIOLOGY AS ADVOCACY:
THERE ARE NO NEUTRALS

I have tried to indicate that sociology's dominant conception of both "the just society" and of intervention approaches to achieve justice are grounded in doctrines of persons and society which stress human fulfillment as the ultimate goal, and rational, data-based social decision processes as the appropriate means.

Now we come to an analysis of sociology's conception of advocacy, which must begin with the assertion that all human social action (including the doing of sociology) is (a) value-laden and (b) political. That is, all action (a) requires choice among alternatives (whether conscious or not, with not deciding being as value-laden as deciding) and (b) exercises power and affects the power configuration of the social systems involved.

I shall argue in this and subsequent sections that doing sociology in all its forms is social intervention, and that all intervention is advocacy of one of three types — of party, outcome or process. Given these conditions, there are no neutrals in terms of their impact on given power configurations, and any sociologist claiming to be "neutral" in anything other than the strictest technical sense is naive, misinformed, and/or devious. The conceptions of intervention and advocacy developed here are intended to be applicable to all forms of discipline-based and professional action.

SOCIAL PROBLEMS: THE ROOT OF SOCIOLOGICAL ADVOCACY

The concept of social problems is at the basis of virtually every contemporary conception of sociological advocacy. "Social problems" is the most firmly established sub-field of sociology, as evidenced by the 25-year existence (and contemporary strength) of the Society for the Study of Social Problems, and its journal, *Social Problems.*[2] Most of the 24 recognized specialties and sections within the American Sociological Association deal with issues or institutional systems that are considered to be problematic for one reason or another — medicine, education, aging, deviance and world conflicts, for example.

The viability of the sub-field of social problems is visible in the comprehensive and useful issue of *Social Problems* devoted to "SSSP as a Social Movement" (Colvard 1976). Hundreds of persons, most of them sociologists, worked in task forces and other research arrangements to analyze the field, the Society, and the journal *Social Problems.* A thorough review of the issue leaves one with a feeling of the vitality of social problems theories, networks and research efforts.

Definitions of social problems abound as textbooks and articles continue to proliferate. While the definitions differ, it is clear that most sociologists agree that there does exist a class of phenomena which may be appropriately labeled "social problems." With Kohn (1976: 94) in the *Social Problems* special issue, my preference is for "a broad definition . . . that includes any social phenomena that have a seriously negative impact on the lives of sizable segments of the population."

Different approaches to the etiology of social problems may provide at least implicit guidelines for meliorative attempts by sociologists and other problem-definers. Rubington and Weinberg (1971) analyze five different sociological perspectives on social problems, each with its own practice implications: social pathology, social disorganization, value conflicts, deviant behavior and labelling.

"Social problems," then, is the label for the cluster of ideologies and conceptions that is at the root of sociological efforts at advocacy. Two other traditionally valued orientations in sociology provide the vehicle and conception-of-outcomes for responding to social problems (in some rubrics, "solving" them) — social policy and social change.

SOCIAL POLICY AND SOCIAL CHANGE: THE PURSUIT OF JUSTICE

There seems to be an emerging consensus in the field that social policy is the most appropriate vehicle for applying sociological understandings to the amelioration of social problems (Freeman and Sherwood, 1970; Etzioni, 1973; Rainwater, 1974; Horowitz and Katz, 1975; Lee, 1976). Social policy research is critical, comprehensive, reality-testing, alternatives-generating, and appropriate for small demonstration or quasi-experimental field projects. Sociologists are among numerous social scientists currently benefiting from the need of governmental agencies to know, to plan, to evaluate and to traffic in expertise.

Freeman and Sherwood's view of the "key role of the social-policy scientist" is precisely what would follow from the human fulfillment criterion for justice noted in the first part of this paper:

> The social-policy scientist seeks to mold a social order that is more consistent with human needs and human dignity. He searches for the causes of social problems and attempts to specify the conditions which will achieve a better state of affairs. He views any particular social arrangement as only one of many. Thus, he often challenges the status quo. Perhaps most important, he asks what institutions and what course of action are most likely to meet the needs and enhance the dignity and self-fulfillment of man (1970: 22).

Social policy, adequately researched and planned by the sociologist-reformer, is believed to create new social arrangements and to redistribute resources — which, therefore, "solves social problems," i.e., moves the system toward justice. This is social change — the third cornerstone of sociology's predominant conception of its advocacy role.

But sociologies' conceptions of social change still suffer, for the most part, from an Enlightment hangover. "Social change" has a generally positive ring to the sociologist: Bash argues (1977) that in its earliest conception, social change "was almost unanimously construed as 'progress'." Students prepare for careers in social change; agencies promote social change. But social change means the continually shifting patterns (sometimes dramatically so) of distribution of power and resources, and those redistributions may take a variety of forms, ranging from revolution to consciousness-raising and institutional reform on the left, to increased social control, status quo-ante conditions, or political repression on the right.

This is the scenario of advocacy (often implicit) on which sociologists base their activities: research on social problems which interest them, which is expected to influence the development of social policies which will produce desired social change. The uni-directional scenario becomes a loop, of course, when social changes engender new social problems — usually unintentionally — to which policy solutions must be addressed.

MODALITIES FOR SOCIOLOGICAL ADVOCACY

Numerous specific activities have been undertaken by sociologists in their advocacy of truth and specific policies. It is important to record at least some of them to indicate the range and diversity of the discipline's practice approaches beyond the traditional teaching, research and publication. They include community organizing, training, passing resolutions, picketing and other forms of direct action, formation of radical and ascription-based caucuses in professional associations, other internal political action within professional associations (the write-in victory of Alfred McClung Lee for the Presidency of the ASA in 1975 is the best example), signing petitions, making videotapes rather than publishing findings (for greater accessibility to "the people"), conscious institution-building, networking (see Duhl and Volkman, 1970), and lobbying and litigation.

It is clear, then, that sociology is "practiced" in a variety of ways and settings (i.e., the members of the discipline advocate, at the minimum, their ways of viewing social phenomena as "better" or "more truthful"), with wide-ranging conceptions of appropriate outcomes for the host systems. The dominant ways may be summarized as truth-finding (research) and truth-telling (teaching, consultation, testimony and various forms of policy advice). The dominant settings are the university, the professional journal, the private or public agency program, the legislative hearing, and the popular media. The dominant desired outcomes are, in Kelman's (1968: 9-10) terms, "the advancement of human welfare, the rationality of social decisions, and the achievement of constructive social change."

How is it possible to organize and understand the wide range of methods and forums utilized by sociologists in expressing their advocacies? We approach the problem in two ways: first, through examining several formulations of the social roles and functions of sociologists and other social scientists, and, second, through an analysis of the three types of advocacy — party, outcome, and process.

Social Roles and Functions of Sociologists. Herbert Kelman (1968), 1976-77 chairperson of the Social Psychology Section of the American Sociological Association and a major spokesman for a systematic ethics of social science, proposes three analytically distinct roles in which the social scientist "practices:"

— Producer of social forces (through research findings and other activities that may affect social policy);

— Experimenter and social thinker (the classical scientist/scholar role); and

— Participant in social action ("a role defined in nonprofessional terms, but to which his standing and knowledge as a social scientist have obvious relevance.")

Most sociologists see their "practice" as centering in the first or second roles, whether in the classroom, in publication or in the field.

In another formulation, Gans (1967: 443-448), noting "that the sociologist ought to be more than a detached researcher and that he should participate more directly in social-action programs," delineates the "role of sociology in planning against poverty" into four categories that can apply to sociological (or other social science) advocacy regarding any problem:

— Developing a theoretical scheme to guide planning;

— Determining appropriate and feasible goals;

— Program development;

— Evaluation of action programs.

This scheme accurately describes the major roles of the sociologist-practitioner in a program agency, I believe, and is discussed in connection with an analysis of types of advocacy later in this section.

Howard Becker answers the question of what social scientists can contribute to dealing with social problems with the following list of five activities — all of them squarely within the truth-finding/telling modality:

— Sorting out the differing definitions of the problem;

— Analyzing the assumptions made by the interested parties about the problem;

— Testing various assumptions about the problem against empirical reality;

- Discovering strategic points of intervention in the social structures and processes that produce the problem;
- Suggesting alternative moral points of view from which the problem can be assessed (in Rainwater, 1974: 10-11).

Becker's 1966 SSSP Presidential Address clearly framed sociology as an advocate for the subordinate and less powerful members of the social systems in which sociologists work (Becker, 1967). His argument may be summarized as a plea for "evening up the odds," especially between client underdogs and service agency overdogs (who, in Becker's words, "usually have to lie" because they are responsible for services which "are seldom as they ought to be"). By explicating the points of view of subordinates, minorities, or deviants, sociologists help move them up the "hierarchy of credibility." With perhaps unintentional symmetry, sociology thus reflects its own underdog status among the disciplines in its practice roles and orientations.

Alvin Gouldner has contributed a wide range of insights to understanding the place and purposes of sociology, notably through *The Coming Crisis of Western Sociology* (1970) and *For Sociology* (1973). He joins the argument with Becker by questioning "blind advocacy" for underdogs, and in essence accuses Becker of being a lower-level reformer aiming at the managers of service-providing institutions which are structurally corrupt by nature. Gouldner wants the sights of sociological advocates set on the real overdogs who maintain the traditional liberal's welfare state for their own interests — corporate financiers and policy-makers. His own SSSP Presidential Address in 1962 argued against the tradition of objectivity, "charging the value-free researcher with being socially irresponsible" (Freeman and Sherwood, 1970: 21), and calling for professionalized disrespect of the existing order and for advocacy of change.

Sociology as Intervention: Three Types of Advocacy. Each of these formulations is useful in categorizing the advocacy positions and activities of sociologists. What is needed now, I believe, is a more general theory of social advocacy which can help explain the nature and impact of the practice of sociology (as well as other disciplines) on the clients, colleagues, administrators, politicians, and other publics it touches.

I began by asserting that all activities of sociologists are a form of social intervention. Intervention may be defined as follows:

1. A deliberate and systematic entering into a social setting or situation (often a conflict situation) —

    (a) By an outside or semi-outside party or parties;

    (b) With varying degrees of legitimation conferred by the first and second parties;

    *(c) With the aim of influencing the course of events toward outcomes which the intervenor defines as positive.

*2. Every act of intervention alters the power configuration in the social systems in which it takes place and, therefore:

*3. Every intervenor is an advocate — for party, for outcome and/or for process.

The last three elements of the definition deserve elaboration.

*1(c) Intervenors aim to influence the course of events in the intervention setting in a direction which they define as positive. Each intervenor has tolerance limits for acceptable outcomes; just any outcome will not do. Family therapists, architects, lawyers, and college professors, for example, operate from different world views, but each "knows" the range of conditions within which outcomes of intervention must fall to be acceptable — whether the coinage is family dynamics, buildings, litigated settlements, or concepts. All intervention is thus value-directed; there are no "neutral" intervenors.

*2. Human social life is the process and product of decision. Social decisions allocate scarce resources among persons and groups. Power is the control of decisions. Every act of intervention affects the configuration of negotiable power in a given social system, increasing the power of some parties, decreasing that of others. Therefore, every act of intervention — and especially the activities of conscious, goal-directed professionals — is an exercise of power, with positive consequences for some in their pursuit of their interests.

*3. Every intervenor, therefore, is an advocate, despite self-perceptions or public claims of "neutrality." Most intervenors advocate particular outcomes or advocate the case of one of the parties (typically their client). The third type of advocacy is for a particular kind of process to be followed in arriving at the outcome (see Laue, 1975b).

Analysis of the three ideal-types of advocacy proposed here can provide an organizing framework for the various activities of practicing (i.e., all) sociologists. But first definitions and qualifications regarding advocacy are in order.

Advocacy and advocates have received considerable treatment in the nonsociological literature in the last ten years. Among the elements which have been defined as crucial to the role of advocate are:

— Alignment with the interests of disadvantaged subgroups who heretofore have not been in a position to articulate their needs in the process of community decision-making, with the objective of effecting a redistribution of public resources from the most advantaged sectors of the community (Davidoff, 1965).

— Provision of leadership and resources directed toward eliciting information, challenging the stance of service institutions, and arguing issues in behalf of disadvantaged clients (Grosser, 1973).

— Utilization of the expertise of professionals to defend the interests of low-income community groups in the policy process . . . Assisting the poor, black and Third World minorities to compete successfully in the influence process as a way of compensating for "an imperfect pluralism (Guskin and Ross, 1974)."[3]

But a much broader conception of advocacy is required if the concept is to have utility beyond the limited settings described in the preceding definitions. For, in fact, every act of intervention by every professional affects the power configuration in the target system — whether that system is a classroom, agency, legislative body, neighborhood, courtroom, or intergroup conflict. Modern dictionaries offer derivations and definitions that cast the analysis of advocacy in the comprehensive terms that are most productive for our purposes. Here advocacy means "to speak or write in favor of," "to plead or argue for something," "support," and "active espousal," in addition to the term's technical application to lawyers in litigation:

Advocacy, as utilized in this paper, means acting in support of a particular party, outcome and/or process in a social situation.

Acting encompasses writing, talking, and other forms of overt human social action. Support may take the form of any of the activities engaged in by practicing sociologists. A social situation may include social systems or processes of any size, structure, duration and dynamic.

The central focus of the analysis contained in this paper is on the three types of advocacy — party, outcome, process. Every act of sociological practice represents one or a combination of these three advocacies. Dimensions of the three types of advocacy are summarized in the accompanying Table 6.1.

Table 6.1 attempts to systematize some of the characteristics and activities I have observed and practiced as a sociologist. It is intended to delineate some of the categories for a general theory of advocacy for social scientists — not only for sociologists. Sociology is no different than the other social sciences in its approach to advocacy: the practitioners' worldviews and the subject matter may vary, but the structural characteristics of intervention situations and the range of loyalties available to the advocate for party, outcome or process are similar.

So, structural characteristics rather than self-conscious choice are the major determinant of the impact and, therefore, the type of advocacy employed in any intervention situation.

We start with the assumption that there are elements of all the three types of advocacy in every interventive act; one cannot choose to limit his or her impact to only one of the three areas. The table focuses attention on the predominant mode of advocacy employed by the practitioner, and proposes correlative conditions and characteristics. We also assume that most sociologists — especially those in the truth-telling mode — generally are unaware of their work as advocacy, for their professional training imparts values to the contrary.

Most of the cells in the chart are derived in response to questions about the actual impact of social science intervention on actors, outcomes and processes in the target systems. Regarding "Goals (A)" and "Targets (B)," for example, activities which improve the perceived or actual advantage of a client or target group may be labeled "party advocacy." The production of a considerable volume of research findings by sociologists regarding the negative impacts of racial discrimination have been a form of party advocacy — for blacks and other minorities.

Perhaps the most typical form of advocacy represented in the research activities of sociologists conducted outside the academy is "outcome advocacy." Here the target is social policies and the goal is to influence them in a direction that squares with the values of the researcher.

TABLE 6.1
A Typology of Social Advocacy Goals, Targets and Practice Characteristics

	Predominant Mode of Advocacy		
	PARTY	OUTCOME	PROCESS
A. GOAL	Improve the perceived or actual advantage of a client or target group – individual or class.	Achieve a decision or policy the advocate defines as positive.	Institute and/or follow a process meeting important value criteria of the advocate in achieving an outcome.
B. TARGET FOR INTERVENTION	Clients and/or their opponents.	Social policies.	Social systems. [a]
C. PRACTICE CHARACTERISTICS			
1. Truth Orientation			
a. Predominant Practice Setting:	a. Academic Institution, Professional Journal		
b. Predominant Roles:	b. Advocate researcher.	b. Policy researcher; summative evaluator.	b. Pure researcher.
c. Major Practice Approach:	c. Research, writing and teaching.	c. Research, writing and teaching.	c. Research, writing and teaching.
d. Primary Product(s):	d. Position paper; opponent analysis.	d. Position paper; research report; evaluation report.	d. Article or book.
e. Effectiveness Criterion:	e. Client acceptance.	e. Colleague acceptance.	e. Colleague acceptance.
2. Change Orientation			
a. Predominant Practice Setting:	a. Public or Private Agency, Popular Media [b]		
b. Predominant Role(s):	b. Community organizer; trainer; agency field worker.	b. Policy-maker; administrator.	b. Mediator; advocate mediator; program developer; formative evaluator; action researcher; trainer.
c. Major Practice Approach:	c. Political action.	c. Legislative or administrative action.	c. Third-party action.
d. Primary Product(s):	d. Client empowerment.	d. Laws; budget allocations; administrative guidelines or regulations.	d. Action memorandum; evaluation report; programs; consultation.
e. Effectiveness Criterion:	e. Client gets bigger share of power, resources.	e. Policy influence.	e. Win-win, jointly-determined, rational outcomes (i.e., the result of "good process").

a. All the parties, intervenors, structures, processes and outcomes in the social systems affected.
b. And, on rare occasion, elected office.

The focus of process advocacy is on the totality of interaction in a system, with the sociologist always holding values about the most productive ways of viewing the system and its processes, and often, in addition, about the process or procedure that should be followed in ongoing decisionmaking and problemsolving in the system. While in the first case the major impact of the intervention ultimately falls on a party or parties (i.e., actors) in a social system, and in the second case the impact is on social policies, in the case of process advocacy the impact is on the way in which parties achieve outcomes — namely, the entire range of social interaction.

The most important distinction made in the table is between the "Truth Orientation (1)" and the "Change Orientation (2)" under "Practice Characteristics (C)." After examining the role formulations of Kelman and others, I concluded that virtually all distinctions in practice approaches in sociology are best understood by first determining whether the practitioner is primarily oriented to truth-finding and truth-telling or to promoting social change. Kelman's three role types may be condensed into these two; Friedrichs' "priestly" and "prophetic" paradigms represent the same distinction.

Applying this distinction does not imply that truth-oriented practitioners are uninterested in doing change — only that they see their roles as predominantly involving discovering and communicating social reality, usually coupled with the unexamined assumption that truth somehow directly translates into good policy. Similarly, the change-oriented sociologist is not disinterested in finding and telling truth; indeed, his skills in doing so usually are at the base of his ability to be an effective change-agent. But the ultimate professional and personal reward for him is more likely to be found in particular client, policy and process outcomes (see C.2.e.) than in the professional approbation which is the lifeblood of all who see truth rather than change as their predominant mission (C.1.e.).

The predominant practice settings are consistent within the two orientations: truth-tellers are most at home in academic institutions and in the pages of professional journals (C.1.a.); and change-doers are more likely to gravitate to the public or private agency, to the popular media, and, on rare occasion, to elected office (C.2.a.).

The predominant roles associated with the two orientations (C.1.b. and C.2.b.) vary within advocacy types in this scheme. In each case for the truth orientation, the role is related to research, whether as advocate, policy and pure researcher. The range of roles is greater for the change orientation. Typical client advocate roles include community organizer, trainer and field worker, and the sociologist who chooses to direct his work toward actively influencing change in favor of a given group will inevitably find himself assuming these types of roles. The sociologist predominantly committed to policy change would find high administrative or policy positions the most cordial practice setting.

The most innovative and potentially influential roles for the sociologist/change-agent cluster around process advocacy, where the commitment is to promoting a process of social interaction that reflects such values as win-win social exchanges, rationality, and democratic decisionmaking. The mediator assists in negotiations between disputing parties. The advocate mediator uses his skills and base to empower the less powerful in preparation for fuller participation in the process. A variety of agency and social movement-related roles attract process-oriented change agents with sociological training: program developer (the activities of sociologists in poverty, population, crime, and delinquency program development is noteworthy), formative evaluator, action researcher and trainer, for example.

Regarding the major practice approach of advocates, the distinctions again are more complex for the change-oriented in contrast to the truth-oriented practitioner. Research, writing, and teaching is the basic modality for all truth-telling (A.1.c.). The different requirements for effective advocacy in the change-oriented mode (C.2.c.) call for different kinds of approaches, skills, and risks. Party advocacy requires political (i.e., power-related) action if the relative advantage of groups is to be altered. Policy changes require legislative and/or administrative action. And the most effective way of promoting "good process" is through the types of third-party activities listed in C.2.b. — mediation, action research, training and the like.

Primary products of sociologists in the truth-telling mode (C.1.d.) are written materials. Again, the requirements for effective advocacy are more complex for the change-oriented roles (C.2.d.); for the practitioner is committed to real-world outcomes in contrast to writing or talking about real-world outcomes. Hence, client empowerment is the primary product of the change-oriented party advocate, and various forms of policy statements (laws, budget allocations, administrative guidelines and regulations) are the principal intended products of change-oriented outcome advocates. The primary products of change-oriented process advocates include various forms of action and evaluation documents, programs, and consultation activities.

SUMMING UP: SOCIOLOGICAL ADVOCACY

In structure and impact, then, sociological advocacy is much the same as other advocacies. The worldviews and the content may differ, but the practice modalities and impacts cover the same range of alternatives. All sociological activity is advocacy — whether for an intellectual viewpoint on social reality, for the rights of a given set of actors, for a desired policy outcome, or for a specific set of social processes.

From the early days of the field — especially in the United States — the subject matter of sociology and the values of sociologists have kept sociological "practice" (of even the most isolated/scholarly type) closely related to the ongoing issues and problems of the host social system. So the history of sociology is a history of advocacy: at the minimum, advocacy for certain ways of viewing society and its "problems," often in sharp contrast to the views of politicians, ecclesiastics, secular humanists, agency bureaucrats, journalists and the electorate.[4]

APPLICATIONS: TELLING TRUTH, DOING CHANGE AND/OR TAKING CREDIT

Now we turn to an examination of two examples of sociological advocacy — one of them from a predominantly truth-telling stance, one from an explicit change orientation.

SOCIAL SCIENCE AND SOCIAL POLICY: Schools and Race[5]

Cohen and Weiss (1976) explore the interrelationships of research and social policy formulation in their analysis of the advocacy of sociologists and related social scientists in school desegregation since 1954 — when, for the first time, social science data were cited as sufficient evidence for establishment of precedent in the *Brown v. Board of Education* decision.[6] The theme of their paper is that

> for the most part, the improvement of research on social policy does not lead to great clarity about what to think or what to do. Instead, it usually tends to produce a greater sense of complexity. This result is endemic to the research process. For what researchers understand by improvements in their craft leads not to greater consensus about research problems, methods and interpretations of results, but to more variety in the ways

problems are seen, more divergence in the way studies are carried out, and more controversy in the ways results are interpreted (56).

Cohen and Weiss trace the involvement of social science research with race-and-schools policy through several stages since 1954:

(a) The *Equality of Educational Opportunity Survey* (1966), sponsored by the U.S. Commission on Civil Rights and directed by sociologist James Coleman, reported that racial segregation had no independent impact on black achievement in schools — but social class did. Class integration thus seemed important. The *Survey* (commonly called The Coleman Report) also found no consistent relationship between school desegregation and racial attitudes.

(b) Thomas Pettigrew, a social psychologist, reanalyzed some of the Coleman data and used new data to produce a Civil Rights Commission report entitled *Racial Isolation in the Public Schools* (1967). Coleman's findings on the noneffects of schools' racial composition were confirmed, but it was determined that racially desegregated classrooms had a positive effect on achievement — at the high school level. Pettigrew also found no consistent improvement of racial attitudes associated with desegregation. Thus, the social science bases for the 1954 decision came to be called into question.

(c) Many smaller, system-specific studies of desegregating schools followed, with inconsistent results.

(d) With the shifts of white populations to the suburbs and the blackening of central city public schools, social scientists began to propose and research metropolitan and other cross-district solutions to racial segregation in the schools. But black politicians and some social scientists reacted negatively to the "dilution of black student bodies in mostly white settings."

(e) Enter the black community control movement in the late 1960s, and the subsequent conflicts with white-controlled administrations and teachers unions, especially in New York City.

(f) "Increasingly, social scientists held that the central problem in matters of education and race was no longer segregation; rather they argued that the racism which had engendered segregation also made desegregation a demeaning and humiliating experience for blacks. Desegregation had come to seem as much a problem as segregation."

An important parallel development during this period was the debate over testing and standardized achievement scores, fueled by the studies of Jensen, Garrett, and Shuey, who held that lower black scores were manifestations of innately lower intelligence. Coleman's data were analyzed and reanalyzed. "Reading the *Survey* analysis was hard enough," write Cohen and Weiss, "but umpiring debates over the correct regression statistic taxed the brains of even rather sophisticated researchers."

The controversy continued and continues, currently focussing on the debate over bussing as a technique for ending racial isolation in the schools. The courts are wavering on bussing. Coleman has become a kind of egghead folk hero for parents opposing desegregation since he concluded (from limited data, charge Pettigrew and Green, 1976) that bussing is fostering white flight and subsequent resegregation of the schools. School districts try magnet schools, educational parks and other approaches (some of them suggested or at least later supported by sociologists) to desegregate without massive bussing. A federal judge in St. Louis tries a consent decree as an alternative to a court order – and, as of this writing, is moving toward issuing a court order.

Cohen and Weiss (1976: 68) conclude that "on the evaluative criterion advanced by most advocates of policy research – does the research contribute more precise guidance for particular decisions? – most research would fail miserably."

The activities of the social scientists described by Cohen and Weiss are in the mainstream of the truth-telling orientation: researching, writing, imploring, arguing, testifying. While many of them no doubt have seen themselves as advocates of change, their "practice" by and large has not included political action per se and the other approaches associated with the change orientation in our chart. The driving faith seems to have been that the quality and the power of the truth will, in the end, make the direction clear. Yet Cohen and Weiss conclude that the escalating complexity of the research and the rising temperatures of the social scientist/debaters had, by the 1970s, made social science research findings far less useful as a policy guide than in 1954.

This account illustrates all three types of advocacy within the truth-oriented practice approach proposed in the previous section. Some researchers and policy analysts (indeed the Court itself in 1954) advocate for particular parties (in this case, black students). Others have as their goal particular outcomes (desegregation, integration, metropolitanization, etc.). Still others are process advocates (focussing on community control and related strategies).

SOCIOLOGISTS IN THE PUBLIC SCHOOLS:
PROBLEMS AND ROLES IN CRISIS MANAGEMENT

Sociologist Mark Chesler pioneered the development of an Educational Change Team in the University of Michigan School of Education, which worked in a number of public schools throughout the United States in the late 1960s and early 1970s in response to interracial and other kinds of educational conflicts. His predominant orientation was and is toward the promotion of positive social change, and he operates from the traditional base of the university as well as that of the social action consulting agency. Aspects of the roles and values of the sociologist-intervenors involved in this work are summarized in a paper with the above title (Chesler and Crowfoot, 1975).

The Educational Change Team carried on in-school consultation to schools (carefully working with and for all the interested parties and not just the administration or board), participated in direct mediation and management of school crises as they arose, and published a number of manuals (as contrasted to books for professional peers) for use by schools facing crisis and conflict (Wittes, 1970; Bryant, et al., 1972; and Chesler, et al., 1972).

Chesler and Crowfoot address the issue of the appropriate roles for intervention of sociologists in the public schools, examining such related questions as:

— What values shall the sociologist pursue in this setting? (tension-reduction? orderly management? redistribution of resources? empowerment of weaker parties?)

— What constituencies shall she/he serve? (students? parents? administrators? faculty? board? larger community? professional peers?)

They understand that no intervention approaches are neutral — including the provision of factual information. Chesler and Crowfoot conclude that school intervenors should promote social justice values in schools through a variety of techniques that encompass virtually every practice role and approach contained in sections C.2.b and C.2.c of our advocacy typology:

— Encouraging elite values and actions consistent with social justice priorities.

— Helping organize oppressed groups.

— Challenging elites.

— Heightening differences and unclarities among elites.

— Creating alternative schooling forms.

— Training intervenors and parties in these types of justice-based intervention concepts and techniques.

Each of these approaches stands in startling contrast to the research, publication, and rational policy influence approaches described by Cohen and Weiss. These interventions are predominantly political rather than cognitive-rational in their thrust.

Chesler and associates are clear, conscious and explicit in their attempts to achieve justice through reallocation of power and resources. They are primarily outcome-advocates standing squarely in the charge-oriented approach. Justice (a policy outcome) is their goal, and empowerment of weaker parties (party advocacy) and due process (process advocacy) are the required means. While they appreciate and conduct sound scholarship, their ultimate goal is social justice rather than sociological truth, and their success criteria have more to do with empowered clients, just policies and due process than with the judgments of their professional peers.

NEXT STEPS: THE ETHICS OF ADVOCACY
AND THE FUTURE OF SOCIOLOGY

In this brief final section, I want to put aside the standard next-step questions about theoretical development, research projections, and the need for further refinement of practice techniques. I shall not even offer the requisite urging for sociologists to resolve their pure-versus-applied argument and get on with integration of the discipline. These issues are important, and I believe this paper has offered sufficient leads for dealing with such questions.

Instead I want to focus on what I consider to be two more general and more difficult questions, one squarely within the truth orientation (the ethics of advocacy) and the other concerned predominantly with institutional change (the future of sociology). The most crucial needs, I believe, are (a) the development of a self-conscious, prescriptive set of ethics for the practice of sociological advocacy, and (b) dramatic

changes in the institution of sociology predicated on service as well as
survival needs of the discipline.

TOWARD AN ETHICS OF ADVOCACY

The personal decision is the unit act of social ethics. Every action of
every person represents a decision — however unexamined, unintended
or programmed. Virtually every decision is a political decision, i.e.,
exercises power or affects the power configuration of a social system.

Sociologists' practice of their discipline consists of a series of
decisions among alternatives through time, however clearly or vaguely
framed: In whose employ shall I be? Or — who will ultimately control a
good deal of my time and possibly my value choices if a confrontation
comes between me and the institution? For what goals will I work?
Tenure? Prestige? Survival? Truth? Justice? With what client groups?
Students in my classes only or disempowered community groups as
well? Shall I publish my research findings? If so, where? In professional
journals for peer judgment? In popular media? In underground media
for underdogs? Or shall I disseminate my research findings through
workshops, or videotapes, or through community organizing?

The list of questions could go on. The point is clear: every
professional decision of every sociologist affects the relative advantage
or disadvantage of some group(s), and those decisions ought to be
explicit and self-conscious. This assertion is the basis of any system of
ethics regarding the practice of sociology.

This principle of political and decisional self-consciousness for the
sociologist must be paired with a principle of support for proportional
empowerment of client groups. If indeed sociologists believe in
promoting maximum individual fulfillment, due process, and democratic decisionmaking, then the first question they ask about any social
system in which they work or which their work touches should be: Are
there great power disparities between the various parties in this
situation? If the answer is yes, then the sociologist-advocate is faced
with the question of how those power disparities may be reduced, for
he knows that none of the values for social process and individual
fulfillment noted above can be achieved unless all persons and parties in
a social system have some operational power with which to negotiate
their own rights. Charity is no basis for justice; ultimately all advocacy
must be aimed at the goal of every party possessing sufficient power to
represent its own interests. Sociology — with its emphasis on openness,
underdog advocacy and debunking — is in a unique position to develop

and implement strategies for reducing power disparities. Often simply elucidating the control mechanisms of the established party in a situation or assisting a disempowered party in assessing its strategic options can change the power balance dramatically.

Because we understand power and its dynamics as sociologists, we often act as process advocates in our work, whether consciously or not. We may appear to be party advocates in our espousal of underdog causes, but this is but a strategic step in the process: because we know the powerful will have their needs and interests represented, we work to empower out-parties precisely so due process can operate. Otherwise, unilateral outcomes are likely to take place instead of multilateral, win-win outcomes.

To summarize, I believe that a solid body of prescriptive sociological ethics (do's for sociologists, rather than only proscriptive don'ts) must begin with the following framework, adapted from Laue and Cormick (1977):

1. All sociological activity is intervention, and all intervention is advocacy — whether for party, outcome or process.

2. There are no "neutral" intervenors in terms of their effect on the parties and the processes of social interaction.

3. Sociologist-intervenors are under an ethical obligation to make their basic values and ethical criteria for decisionmaking explicit — to themselves and especially to the intervened-upon (whether students, poor people, bureaucrats or corporate managers).

4. The three core values which provide the basis for the ethics of decisionmaking for the sociologist in practice are:

   (a) Proportional Empowerment. A condition in which traditionally disempowered groups have developed their latent power to the point where they can advocate for their own needs and rights; where they are capable of protecting their boundaries from wanton violation by others; where they are capable of negotiating their way with other empowered groups on the sure footing of respect rather than charity.

   (b) Justice. The nature of the social order resulting only from the interplay of proportionally-empowered interest groups, in which power (control of decisions) is diffused, decisionmaking is participatory, accountability for decisions is visible, and resources are adequate and equitably distributed.

    (c) Freedom. The ability of an individual to responsibly choose among the maximum number of options consistent with the common good in determining his life conditions, in a context in which he is held accountable for those decisions. The fully just social system would provide for every member the maximum degree of freedom consistent with the common good — and, therefore, the maximum potential for human fulfillment, which is the end purpose of every system of social ethics.

5. Empowerment of Out parties is an ethical mandate when power disparities among affected parties are great.

6. Regarding work in social conflict situations, tension-reduction or "settlement" per se is never an adequate goal. Intervenors who hold such an outlook virtually always strengthen the interests of the status quo, often with the best of intentions.

I believe that sociologists as a professional group will not set out to deal seriously and systematically with the ethical system-building advocated here until or unless they feel a sense of collective threat to their current situation. The rewards for such activity are neither plentiful nor systematically dispensed. The market mechanism will force many more sociologists into change-oriented rather than truth-oriented settings — out of the academy and into the street and the agency. Then there will be more pressure for dealing collectively with the everyday ethical issues of empowerment and resources allocation which are so much more a part of sociological practice "outside."

ADVOCACY AND THE FUTURE OF SOCIOLOGY: A MODEST PROPOSAL

With academic jobs for sociologists dwindling and sociologist-taxi drivers proliferating, the time is ripe for the discipline to rethink its position and future in more conscious change-oriented terms than ever before. This analysis of sociology and advocacy concludes with a proposal which emerges from my own ongoing work in becoming a sociologist and building a field of community conflict intervention.[7]

I begin with the assertion that there is a pressing need for institutional change in the United States, particularly as it affects minorities and other disempowered groups. Conflict often is the dynamic through which such change may be accomplished. A body of community conflict intervention theory and techniques is emerging which can promote needed change, and intervention services are becoming increasingly institutionalized in the public sector (see Laue, 1975a; Laue and Cormick, 1977).

The implications for sociology and sociologists should be clear. The profession is in trouble, for reasons too numerous and well-known to recite again. The trouble relates not only to our inability to consistently demonstrate our worth as a policy science, but with the fiscal malaise of American higher education — which historically has employed more than 90 percent of all sociology Ph.D.'s, a percentage that is dropping rapidly. There are ways out of the troubles, and I am proposing that the development of praxis around community conflict intervention may be one such path.

Many factors lead me to the conclusion that sociology is well-suited to lead in the development of the field of community conflict intervention.

1. Sociology, more than any other discipline with the possible exception of some strains of political science, provides the appropriate conceptual framework for the in-depth understanding of community disputes required for appropriate intervention. Power and conflict models of social systems (which have enjoyed a renewed interest in the discipline in the wake of the 1960's) are the essential elements of the worldview of effective, change-oriented intervenors in community and racial disputes.[8]

2. In the interest of its own survival as a discipline, sociology needs to demonstrate its usefulness both as an analytical framework and as a basis for effective policy development. Sociologists can and do shape policy and promote social change through their work. Society appears to be less and less willing to allow disciplines like sociology the luxury of arm's-length analysis without returning the investment through constructive action. Sociologists need to learn how to do something other than talk and write about sociology and society, or the market may force many graduate sociology programs to atrophy or extinction.[9]

3. But there is a more persuasive argument than simply the survival of the field: that through development of work in conflict intervention or other action-related fields, sociology has a chance to recapture the imagination and commitment of the thousands of mired mid-career practitioners whose "help-people-and-change-society" motivation for entering the field has been replaced by professional and personal alienation. Further, I want to provide a way for sociology to stem the continuing

loss of bright potential sociologists — current students — to such disciplines as public administration, urban planning, social work and law.

We can expect racial and community conflicts to escalate in number and intensity — if not in public visibility. Disputes between providers and recipients of basic human services may reach epidemic proportions in some areas as the resources situation continues to worsen (or, in the case of health care, as national health care legislation is passed and the long struggle for advantage in its implementation begins). Dramatic community conflict events such as Wounded Knee in 1973, the Boston school crisis in 1975, and Kent State in 1970 and 1977 continue.

So it is clear that intervention will continue to occur, often by unskilled, insensitive and/or ill-motivated persons and organizations. I charge sociology and related disciplines with an obligation to shape the field of community conflict intervention in humane directions. Models drawn from community mental health, international peace and conflict studies, sensitivity and encounter approaches, intergroup relations, and labor negotiations are not appropriate for wholesale application to community and racial disputes. "Adjustment," "personal growth," "peace," "good communication," and "good feeling" are not appropriate goals for the outcome of community and racial disputes. Intervenors with those goals in mind will harm already disempowered groups despite their high ideals. A sociology rooted in power, conflict and social change must replace these approaches, and the replacement will not happen without substantial efforts on the part of individual sociologists and the profession.[10]

The need is present, and sociology is capable of supplying the leadership and the resources. The next step is the vision and the willingness of individuals and institutions to take the necessary innovative risks. Curricular designs and resources are becoming available.[11]

The entire curriculum should be based in — and point toward — the ethics of social intervention and social change. The development of the professions in the Western world has been marked by a focus on the technical/rational to the exclusion of ongoing, explicit ethical analysis — much lipservice to the contrary. Watergate-inspired catch-up seminars on "The Ethics of the _____ Profession" will not do. Ethical development must proceed apace with technical development in this and other emerging policy fields.

Development of innovative curricula in accordance with the principles espoused in this paper will require a rejection of business-as-usual
for sociology departments — especially low- and medium-prestige
departments with a substantial investment in producing doctorates. The
market for persons skilled in talking about sociology and society is
dwindling rapidly, since that market is almost exclusively within
academic institutions. In a period of dwindling societal resources and
eroding public confidence in higher education, sociology departments
need to turn out students who can do sociology in response to the
continuing and dramatic need for eradication of social and racial
injustice — to which community conflict intervention can make an
important contribution.

Rejecting business-as-usual for the majority of graduate programs in
sociology means developing a concentration on the master's level with
training that takes students beyond a practice degree in preparing them
for conceptualizing, research and, potentially, administration of human
services programs. Would-be change agents and agency personnel who
do not have this combination of skills are severely handicapped today,
and often further handicap their clients and allies.

Community disputes intervention offers an ideal meeting ground for
theoreticians, researchers and change agents of every sociological
persuasion. I advocate its development by the profession as a logical
next step in making explicit, systematizing, and applying the various
advocacies of sociology.[12]

NOTES

[1]Sociologists' values and beliefs concerning social justice must be inferred
from a variety of sources, published and otherwise. I have examined the American
Sociological Association's Code of Ethics, the problems sociologists choose to
study, specialties and interest groups within the field, canons of research, the
ongoing debates over the role and scope of sociology raging in professional
meetings, the ASA publications *Footnotes* and *The American Sociologist,*
newsletters and journals published by various departments of sociology and
groups of graduate students, the journals *Social Problems* and *Sociological
Practice* (established in 1976 at Boston College), and section newsletters of both
the Society for the Study of Social Problems and the ASA.

[2]The SSSP and *Social Problems* were formed in a time of intense and often
rancorous debate within the ASA's forerunner, the American Sociological
Society, regarding the relevance of sociology and the appropriate scope of
"applied" work. For an expanded discussion see I. L. Horowitz (1970).

[3]Additional recent efforts in systematically developing advocacy theories and techniques appear in other nonsociological sources, e.g., Berlin (1975) and Addison, Haggerty and Moore (1976).

[4]Space prohibits a review of the areas in which sociologists have practiced advocacy in the discipline's short history in the United States. A listing contained in an earlier version of this chapter (Laue, 1977) referred to activities ranging from the Western Electric studies to Footnote 11 in the 1954 U.S. Supreme Court decision on school desegregation and work in poverty, population, crime, and public opinion. Of most recent interest, dozens of sociologists have been among the consultants and staff members of such recent Presidential commissions as those on racial disorders ("the Kerner Commission"), campus unrest, television violence, and crime and delinquency, including several ASA presidents. See, in addition, Komarovsky (1975).

[5]This section is abstracted from the Cohen and Weiss article bearing the same title, "Social Science and Social Policy: Schools and Race."

[6]Cited in Footnote 11, along with the works of psychologist Kenneth Clark, were *An American Dilemma* (by Gunnar Myrdal with sociologist Arnold Rose and others, 1944), and *The Negro in the United States* by sociologist E. Franklin Frazier (1949).

[7]This section is adapted from Laue (1975a).

[8]Yet other disciplines with less appropriate models are further ahead in developing their role in the field. An example is the American Psychiatric Association's Task Force on Third Party Intervention, which resulted in publication of a monograph distributed to all APA members, entitled *Intervening in Community Crises: An Introduction for Psychiatrists* (Gant, 1974).

[9]A study in *The American Sociologist* (McGinnis and Solomon, 1973: 61) concludes that unless there are dramatic unforeseen developments, "in 1980 there will be somewhere between 1,200 and 2,000 sociologists who have earned the Ph.D. degree, but who cannot find a career in sociology" – in academy or agency.

[10]Substantial efforts have taken place in the past, but without the level of impact on the field envisioned here. Among these approaches have been the establishment of the now-disbanded Center for the Study of Conflict Resolution at Michigan, Robin Williams' pioneering effort for the Social Science Research Council in 1947, the applied work of the Russell Sage Foundation, Melvin Tumin's many years of compilation of the Anti-Defamation League's *Intergroup Relations Annual,* and the research and applied work of such sociologists as Lewis Coser, Ralf Dahrendorf, James Coleman, Ray Mack, Louis Kriesberg, Paul Hare, Elise Boulding, Richard Flacks, Irvin Horowitz, Herry Etzkowitz, Irvin Goldaber, Paul Wehr, and James Laue.

[11]The major sources of curricular materials include the Consortium on Peace Research, Education and Development (COPRED), the Community Conflict Resolution Program of the Center for Metropolitan Studies at the University of Missouri-St. Louis, the Institute of Behavioral Science at the University of Colorado, the Office of Environmental Mediation at the University of Washington, the Program in Nonviolent Change at Syracuse University, the Peace and Conflict Studies curriculum at Bethel College in Kansas, the Community Disputes Services Division of the American Arbitration Association, the Institute for

Mediation and Conflict Resolution in New York, the Community Relations Service of the U.S. Department of Justice, and a recent book, *Peacemaking: A Guide to Conflict Resolution for Individuals, Groups and Nations* (Stanford, 1975).

12A series of recent developments manifest increasing recognition and interest in the various forms of sociological advocacy, among them: designation of *Advocacy and Objectivity* (Furner, 1975) as the winner of the Society for the Study of Social Problems' 1975 C. Wright Mills Award; the appearance of such books as *Radical Sociology* (Colfax and Roach, 1971), *Roles for Sociologists in Service Organizations* (Trela and O'Toole, 1974) and *The Use and Abuse of Social Science* (Horowitz, 1975); birth of the journal *Sociological Practice* in 1976; books in preparation on *Clinical Sociology* (by Barry Glassner and Jonathan Friedman) and *Intervening in Community Conflict* (James Laue and Gerald Cormick); and the proposal from the ASA's Council Task Group on Dissemination for a new journal "emphasizing relevance, application and implications" of research findings for other fields *(ASA Footnotes,* 1977: 1).

REFERENCES

Addison, M. R., D. E. Haggerty and M. L. Moore (1976) "Advocates on Advocacy: Defining Three Approaches." *Amicus* 1 (May): 9-16.

American Sociological Association (1971) *Code of Ethics.*

ASA Footnotes (1977) "Council Ponders New ASA Journal." Volume 5 (May): 1.

Barnes, H. E. (1948) *An Introduction to the History of Sociology.* Chicago: University of Chicago.

Bash, H. (1977) "Conflict Intervention and Social Change: Sociological and Ideological Aspects of Professional Social Meddling." *Journal of Intergroup Relations,* 6 (July). (in press)

Becker, H. (1967) "Whose Side Are We On?" *Social Problems,* 14 (Winter): 239-47.

Berlin, I. N. (1975) *Advocacy for Child Mental Health.* New York: Brunner/Mazel.

Bryant, B., J. C. Huber and D. K. Stowe (1972) *Resources for School Change, III: A Manual On Issues and Strategies in Resource Utilization.* Ann Arbor: University of Michigan School of Education.

Chesler, M., B. Bryant, J. Crowfoot and S. Wittes (1972) *Resources for School Change, I: A Manual on Issues and Programs in Training Educational Change.* Ann Arbor: University of Michigan School of Education.

Chesler, M. A. and J. E. Crowfoot (1975) "Sociologists in the Public Schools: Problems and Roles in Crisis Management." Paper presented at National Conference of School Sociologists, Los Angeles.

Cohen, D. A. and J. A. Weiss (1976) "Social Science and Social Policy: Schools and Race." Pp 55-70 in R. C. Rist and R. J. Anson (ed.), *Education, Social Science and the Judicial Process.* Washington, D.C.: National Institute of Education.

Coleman, J. S., et al. (1966) *Equality of Educational Opportunity Survey.* Washington, D.C.: U. S. Government Printing Office for the U. S. Commission on Civil Rights.

Colfax, J. D. and J. L. Roach (eds.) (1971) *Radical Sociology.* New York: Basic Books.

Colvard, R. (ed.) (1976) "SSSP as a Social Movement." *Special Issue of Social Problems,* 24 (October): 142 pp.

Davidoff, P. (1965) "Advocacy and Pluralism in Planning." *Journal of the American Institute of Planners,* 31 (November): 331-37.

Deutsch, M. (1975) "Equity, Equality, and Need: What Determines Which Value Will Be Used as the Basis of Distributive Justice?" *Journal of Social Issues,* 31 (Summer): 137-49.

Duhl, L. and J. Volkman (1970) "Participatory Democracy: Networks as a Strategy for Change." *Urban Social Change Review,* 3 (Spring): 11-14.

Etzioni, A. (1973) "Policy Research." Pp 8-13 in N. Castleman and P. Doty, *Center for Policy Research: The First Five Years,* 1968-73. New York: Center for Policy Research.

Frazier, E. F. (1949) *The Negro in the United States.* New York: MacMillan.

Freeman, H. E. and C. C. Sherwood (1970) *Social Research and Social Policy.* Englewood Cliffs, N.J.: Prentice-Hall.

Furner, M. O. (1975) *Advocacy and Objectivity: A Crisis in American Social Science.* Lexington, KY: University of Kentucky.

Gans, H. J. (1967) "Urban Poverty and Social Planning." Pp 437-76 in P. F. Lazarsfeld, W. H. Sewell and H. L. Wilensky (eds.), *The Uses of Sociology.* New York: Basic Books.

Gant, H. M. (ed.) (1974) *Intervening in Community Crises: An Introduction for Psychiatrists.* Washington, D.C.: American Psychiatric Association.

Gouldner, A. W. (1970) *The Coming Crisis of Western Sociology.* New York: Avon.

——— (1973) *For Sociology: Renewal and Critique in Sociology Today.* New York: Basic Books.

Grosser, C. F. (1973) *New Directions in Community Organization: From Enabling to Advocacy.* New York: Praeger.

Guskin, A. and R. Ross (1974) "Advocacy and Democracy." Pp. 340-51 in F. M. Cox, et al. (ed.), *Strategies of Community Organization.* Itasca, IL: Peacock.

Hinkle, R. and G. Hinkle (1954) *The Development of Modern Sociology.* New York: Random House.

Horowitz, I. L. (1970) "Mainliners and Marginals: The Human Shape of Sociological Theory." Pp 340-69 in L. T. Reynolds, *The Sociology of Sociology.* New York: McKay.

——— (ed.) (1975) *The Use and Abuse of Social Science.* New Brunswick, N.J.: Transaction Books.

——— and J. E. Katz (ed.) (1975) *Social Science and Public Policy in the United States.* New York: Praeger.

Kelman, H. C. (1968) *A Time to Speak: On Human Values and Social Research.* San Francisco: Jossey-Bass.

Kohn, M. L. (1976) "Looking Back — A 25-Year Review and Appraisal of Social Problems Research." *Social Problems,* 24 (October): 94-112.

Komarovsky, M. (1975) *Sociology and Public Policy: Presidential Commissions.* New York: Elsevier.

Laue, J. H. (1975a) "The Intervenor in Community and Racial Disputes: A New Way of 'Being a Sociologist.?'" Paper presented at annual meeting of Midwest Sociological Society, Chicago.

——— (1975b) "Advocacy and the Ethics of Community Conflict Intervention." *Design Methods Group Journal,* 9 (October-December): 313-20.

——— (1977) "Sociology For ————————" Paper presented at annual meeting of Society for Applied Anthropology, San Diego.

——— and G. W. Cormick (1977) "The Ethics of Intervention in Community Disputes." in H. C. Kelman, D. Warwick and G. Bermant (ed.), The Ethics of Social Intervention. Washington, D.C.: Hemisphere. (in press)

Lauer, R. H. (1973) *Perspectives on Social Change.* Boston: Allyn and Bacon.

Lee, A. M. (1976) "Presidential Address: Sociology for Whom?" *American Sociological Review,* 41 (December): 925-36.

Lerner, M. J. (ed.) (1975) "The Justice Motive in Social Behavior." *Special issue of the Journal of Social Issues,* 31 (Summer).

McGinnis, R. and L. Solomon (1973) "Employment Prospects for Ph.D. Sociologists During the Seventies." *The American Sociologist,* 8 (May): 57-63.

Myrdal, G. with A. Rose (1944) *An American Dilemma.* New York: Harper.

Nisbet, R. A. (1966) *The Sociological Tradition.* New York: Basic Books.

Pettigrew, T. F. and R. L. Green (1976) "School Desegregation in Large Cities: A Critique of the Coleman 'White Flight' Thesis." *Harvard Educational Review,* 46 (February): 1-53.

Rainwater, L. (ed.) (1974) *Inequality and Justice: A Survey of Inequalities of Class, Status, Sex, and Power.* Chicago: Aldine.

Rawls, J. (1971) *A Theory of Justice.* Cambridge, MA: Harvard.

Ritzer, G. (1975) *Sociology: A Multiple Paradigm Science.* Boston: Allyn and Bacon.

Rubington, D. and M. Weinberg (ed.) (1971) *The Study of Social Problems.* New York and London: Oxford.

Sampson, E. (1975) "On Justice as Equality." *Journal of Social Issues,* 31 (Summer): 45-64.

Shils, E. (1948) *The Present State of American Sociology.* Glencoe, IL: Free Press.

Stanford, B. (1975) *Peacemaking: A Guide to Conflict Resolution for Individuals, Groups and Nations.* New York: Bantam.

Trela, J. E. and R. O'Toole (1974) *Roles for Sociologists in Service Organizations.* Kent, OH: Kent State University Press.

U. S. Commission on Civil Rights (1967) *Racial Isolation in the Public Schools,* Washington, D.C.: U. S. Government Printing Office. Vols. 1 and 2.

Walster, E. and G. W. Walster (1975) "Equity and Social Justice." *Journal of Social Issues,* 31 (Summer): 21-43.

Williams, R. (1947) *The Reduction of Intergroup Tension.* New York: Social Science Research Council.

——— (1976) "Sociology in America: The Experience of Two Centuries." *Social Science Quarterly,* 57 (June): 77-111.

Wittes, S. (1970) *People and Power: A Study of Crisis in Secondary Schools.* Ann Arbor: University of Michigan Institute of Social Research.

7

THE ADVOCATE SOCIAL SCIENTIST:
A CROSS-DISCIPLINARY PERSPECTIVE

George J. McCall

The preceding six papers present highly informed and very thoughtful analyses of the development, current state of the art, and projected future trends in advocacy within five applied social science disciplines and the profession of law. In preparing an analytical commentary on these papers, one is tempted by the richness of detail in these papers to focus on a highly systematic, point-by-point comparative summary of intriguing similarities and differences among the approaches to advocacy characteristic of various disciplines. I fear, however, that in this very wealth of detail, the larger picture of advocacy as a social science enterprise might be significantly obscured by that procedure. Accordingly, I have chosen instead to emphasize in my commentary an interpretative analysis of major and minor themes that emerge compellingly from these parallel papers as core concerns, conceptions, issues, and problems in advocacy as a social sciences enterprise.

The six papers document and analyze advocacy as one distinctive mode of performing applied social science — a mode which is numerically minor within each of the disciplines surveyed, fairly recently developed, and incompletely integrated with other modes.

Historically, applied social science has predominantly been linked with the social welfare movement. The advocacy mode, however, is closely linked with the more recent civil rights movement.

Perhaps the major impact of the civil rights movement on the social sciences has been to foster greater disciplinary concern for elaborating conceptions of social justice. In the applied social sciences, the centrality of the ideal of social welfare has been challenged by the ideal of social justice (Rawls, 1971; Rescher, 1966). More accurately, perhaps, the concept of justice traditionally associated with the welfare ideal (viz., the concept of equity) has been challenged anew by the concept of equality. In the 1960s, equality was taken to be the right to equal opportunity to strive for societal rewards; more recently, these papers indicate, equality has been viewed as the right to an equal share in societal rewards (construed rather distinctively by each author).

These challenges appear to have undermined, in some degree, the traditional role of the applied social sciences, viz., to utilize the technical expertise of the disciplines in analyzing and identifying the "public interest" (Charlesworth, 1972; Nagel, 1975). Clearly, a number of social scientists — including the Kutchins, the Davidoffs, and Laue — significantly doubt the capability of scientific disciplines to identify the public interest (Schubert, 1961), maintaining that the pluralism of interests instead requires policy determination through democratic political mechanisms.

On such a view, the role of social science experts is not to formulate that policy which is to the public interest, but (in the aggregate) to make available to each of the many competing interests, the expert services of their disciplines. The individual social scientist, then, would function as an advocate for one of these competing interests.

The foregoing papers cast important light on how social scientists might — and do — function as advocates within pluralistic decision-making contexts. In a classical vein, Kutchins and Kutchins state that "advocacy as a professional activity entails (1) pleading a case or a cause, one's own or another's, (2) in an appropriate forum, (3) to accomplish a specific goal (e.g., to resolve a specific conflict or to redress a specific grievance)." While endorsing this analysis, Laue further suggests that the advocate social scientist's interest may lie distinctively in only one or another of these three elements: (1) the case of some party, (b) some particular kind of process to be followed in arriving at the eventual outcome, or (c) some particular outcome.

Outcome advocacy is essentially the familiar and traditional role of the applied social scientist, i.e., the policy researcher committed to discovering, then pleading for "the best solution" to a perceived policy problem. Furner (1975) has thoroughly studied the contours of this role in the pre-professionalized, social ameliorationist era of social science. In the middle decades of this century, outcome advocacy has been pursued more professionally along the policy sciences, social engineering model (Lerner and Lasswell, 1951).

Process advocacy has been a less traditional role for applied social scientists, emerging significantly only since the Cold War years with the extensive interdisciplinary work on conflict and conflict resolution. The process advocate (e.g., mediator) is primarily committed to a particular conception of social process that will lead to just outcomes for all parties, rather than being committed to a particular party or outcome.

Party advocacy, however, appears to have been most central in the conceptual imagery underlying the recent social science interest in advocacy. The civil rights movement had dramatized the voicelessness and lack of representation of some significant segments of society relative to others. The climate of social activism in the 1960s prompted a number of social scientists to intervene directly on behalf of particular underrepresented segments, especially in their dealings with bureaucratic agencies.

PROFESSIONAL ADVOCATES AND ADVOCATE PROFESSIONALS

Since advocacy is virtually the entire stock-in-trade of the legal profession, the lawyer-client relationship was adopted as the central model for social scientists' advocacy for underrepresented segments. As Paul Davidoff has put it, every interest has a right not only to its own lawyer, but to its own anthropologist, sociologist, planner, etc.

It would appear from the foregoing papers, however, that the professional advocate (i.e., lawyer) has not proved such a ready model for the "advocate professional" (i.e., social scientist). The typical lawyer is a free professional in private practice, paid directly by the clients whose cases he advocates. The advocate social scientist typically is a salaried professional in the employ of an agency or university and thus has no true clients (Moore, 1970; Friedson, 1973; Abrahamson,

1967; Etzioni, 1969). In service agencies, the more clinical social scientists (e.g., social workers and psychologists) may, like salaried public defense lawyers, be paid in part to advocate the cases of "clients." More often, however, the duties of salaried social scientists are rather definitely taken not to include advocacy of "clients." (Accordingly, the foregoing papers note numerous attempts by advocate social scientists to set up private practices.)

For most advocate social scientists, then, "clients" may more adequately be conceptualized as simply one (relatively noninfluential) constituency within the social base of their professional activities. (Indeed, even in private law practice, true clients are but one type of constituency among several others.)

Finally, these papers indicate that, unlike lawyers, social scientists are typically not sought out by their "clients" but significantly serve as self-appointed advocates of "clients." This reversal in recruitment has significant implications for the practice of advocacy, discussed more fully below.

Aside from relationships with "clients," the analogy with legal advocacy importantly colors two major conceptions of social science party advocacy.

The first of these conceptions is advocacy as activity. On the analogy of ordinary case practice in the law, the advocate professional pleads the case of a "client" within a particular forum convened for a specific purpose. When that case is settled, the advocate relationship lapses.

The second conception is one of advocacy as role, on the analogy of a lawyer on standing retainer with a corporate client. The advocate professional represents his "client" in a variety of forums on a number of issues, even advising his "client" as to what the client's interests are, what issues might be advantageously raised and pressed, and in what forums.

Kutchins and Kutchins, for example, rather forcefully represent the first of these conceptions, but most of the papers clearly assume the second conception to be most germane to social science advocacy.

It is in such advocacy as role that the "client" cum constituency problems previously noted become most serious. After all, many professionals have occasion to advocate for a party on a "one-shot" basis through expert testimony in trials or legislative hearings; such services are seldom extensive and are not uncustomary even for salaried university professors. Advocacy on a standing basis, on the other hand, involves quite extensive time commitments which the employer is typically unwilling to subsidize and the "client" is unable to pay for.

In many of the instances described in the foregoing papers, the "client" is not only unable to pay, but has actually been created by the advocate professional. Frequently, the social scientist seeks to advocate for a diffuse social category that has no corporate social structure; in such cases the advocate first must organize the social category in order to have a corporate structure to represent. Even where some corporate structure does exist, the advocate professional most often must actively persuade the group that his advocacy of them would be beneficial. Consequently, his professional judgments as to the best course of advocacy are often seriously compromised by the "client's" reluctance to accede or lack of requisite social solidarity. (Of course, even within the free professions of law and medicine, the traditional client model — in which the professional is ceded authority — has been challenged increasingly by a consumer model — in which the client retains authority; witness the increases in malpractice suits against lawyers and physicians.)

Nonetheless, in having to "sell" himself as potential advocate to the "client," the social scientist must take stock of what he has to offer the "client" that might prove beneficial. Instances cited in the foregoing papers indicate that the distinctive social science expertise of his particular discipline, while important, may not prove paramount among what he has to offer. His credentials (degrees, job titles, etc.) and concommitant societal esteem and influence may be quite valuable to the "client" in many contexts. The advocate professional may have greater access to resources (e.g., libraries, government documents, Xerox machines) and valuable referral capabilities, through his institution and his own network of professional acquaintances. Less distinctively, he may through general higher education have greater sophistication in coping with and relating to bureaucracies and political organizations, more developed skills in policy formulation, and/or greater expressive skills (e.g., in debating, writing grant proposals, etc.). Least distinctively, he may offer additional legwork (time, energy, automobile transportation, etc.). It would appear that the would-be advocate professional must not assume these assets are necessarily in short supply to his potential "client," nor that the "client" will necessarily value or appreciate any of them.

The relative contribution of these various assets to his role of advocate professional may prove quite difficult to anticipate, since the shape of that role must be jointly negotiated with the "client." Something of the variety of negotiated roles of advocate social scientists is usefully described in the above papers by the Schensuls and by Laue.

One of the most striking lessons of the foregoing papers is the universality with which it is noted that the primary strategies and tactics of "advocacy as role" are often those of community organization. In some fields — especially social work and community psychology — the classical variety of community orgainization techniques (i.e., those of community planning) appear to be most heavily emphasized (Ecklein and Lauffer, 1971; Perlman, 1972). In anthropology and sociology, the more recent techniques of grass-roots organizing appear most appropriate (Grosser, 1976; O'Brien, 1976). Advocacy work in the urban planning field appears to be intermediate in this respect. But whatever the variety, community organization skills would appear to be a most appropriate item for consideration in the would-be advocate's stocktaking of what it is that he has to offer to his potential "client."

ADVOCACY ACROSS THE DISCIPLINES

My commentary thus far has emphasized those elements of advocacy which are rather general across the various disciplines. Yet one of the most valuable features of the above set of papers (and particularly of the descriptions of typical instance of advocacy) is the light they cast on distinctive features of advocacy as practiced in the different disciplines. Practice differs not only with respect to characteristic types of parties, issues, forums, and processes, but also the dominant models and conceptions of advocacy, strategies and tactics, and organizational locus. More than other disciplines, for example, the clinical fields of social work and psychology find practitioners advocating for individuals or families, in administrative appeals hearings, through advocacy as activity, and utilizing community planning techniques. Or, to take another example, process advocacy is much more likely to be encountered within sociology than any of the other social science disciplines. But, informative as these papers are, they do not permit a thorough-going analysis of characteristic differences among disciplines in the practice of advocacy. Rather, they serve to signal the potential value of a more ambitious and more empirically grounded comparative analysis.

The discipline of law, however, is deserving of some special comment in this context, not only because it is the only nonscience field represented in these papers, but because it has served as a key model for the other disciplines' conceptions of advocacy. Patner's paper dramatizes the seeming paradoxicality of twin historical developments that may bode well for interdisciplinary developments in advocacy. During the same time span in which a number of social scientists pronounced the futility of professional identification of the public interest and took up party advocacy, a number of lawyers tacitly abandoned the practice of case advocacy for its own sake and took up the pursuit of the public interest (albeit through the means of party advocacy). As Patner shows, these counterbalancing trends have led public interest lawyers to better comprehend the legal relevance of social science findings and, at the same time, led social scientists to better understand the peculiar constraints of case advocacy in legal contexts.

THE FUTURE OF ADVOCACY

These latterly observations lead directly to a consideration of the future of advocacy in the applied social science disciplines. What might be some important next steps in theory, research, practice, and training?

THEORY DEVELOPMENT

If advocacy as a mode of social science practice is a means of redressing social injustice, then clearly the further development of theories of social justice (or injustice) must rank as the central task in elaborating the theoretical basis of advocacy. Each of the papers casts significant illumination on the problems of justice (indeed, this may prove the major contribution of the present volume), yet none affords a truly usable theory. As Kutchins and Kutchins suggest, an adequate theory would serve to indicate for what, when, where, and why a social scientist should engage in advocacy.

Among the next steps in theory development, these papers would indicate, is the necessity for conceptual clarification of the relations among party advocacy, process advocacy, and outcome advocacy, explored so provocatively in Laue's paper. It would seem, for example, that although an applied social scientist might be primarily concerned with any one of these elements (say, a particular party), he must perforce be secondarily concerned with each of the other two (e.g., process and outcome), if his primary advocacy is to be successful in the long run.

Similarly, further conceptual clarification of the relations between "advocacy as activity" and "advocacy as role" would appear to be a major prerequisite for more adequate development of the theory of advocacy. Perhaps it is the case that "advocacy as role" ultimately represents that dimension of "championship of the underdog" that the Kutchins seek to detach from the concept of "advocacy as activity." If so, it would seem that further clarification is in order, since "overdog" corporate clients too have standing advocates.

The strategies and tactics of advocacy (Panitch, 1974; Knitzer, 1976) need to be differentiated and rationally related to (1) the various types and conceptions of advocacy and (2) typologies of combinations of forums, issues, parties, and processes. Relative to the first point, most discussions of strategy and tactics seem to have been directed toward party advocacy and "advocacy as role." Even there, characteristic choices between classical and more contemporary varieties of community organization strategies have not received conceptual justification. Relative to the second point, appropriate strategies and tactics have not been adequately linked even to first-order typologies of forums (e.g., administrative, judicial, political), processes (e.g., debates, hearings, disputes, trials, discussions, etc.), or parties (e.g., individuals, families, social categories, subcommunities, corporations, agencies, etc.), much less to even frequently encountered combinations of these elements.

Finally, it would appear to be a matter of some priority to develop in substantial conceptual detail the relations between party advocacy (as role) and the self-help movement. The current strains are evident in descriptions of "client"-advocate relationships and in occasional references to the goal of moving "clients" along the road toward self-advocacy, yet only one of the foregoing papers makes even passing reference to the self-help movement (Katz and Bender, 1976). Themes of client-determination (in the papers by the Kutchins and the Davidoffs) and of cultural pluralism and cultural self-determination (Davidson and Rappaport, as well as the Schensuls) would seem particularly relevant to the self-help conceptions.

RESEARCH

Many of these papers touch on the role of research in advocacy; despite a common charge to do so, only one paper (the Kutchins') was able to review any research on advocacy (and then only two studies). This low yield does not so much reflect on the diligence of the authors as it reflects the state of the fields; research — especially evaluation research — on advocacy efforts is woefully lacking (Kamerman, et al., 1972).

The descriptions within these papers of typical instances of advocacy practice clearly indicate the potential value even of descriptively oriented, empirical case studies of advocacy projects in their considerable variety. Within such studies, particular emphasis might well be placed on examination of the process through which the advocate-"client" role relationship is established, developed, and maintained.

Second, advocacy projects differing in type and/or conception might usefully be made the subject of comparative analysis of the mix of strategies, tactics, and techniques employed in each. Are the conceptually distinguished varieties of advocacy as operationally distinctive as has been proposed?

In a related vein, any contribution to the theory development task mentioned above — of codifying strategies and tactics of advocacy most appropriate to various typological combinations of forums, processes, parties, and issues — should be subjected to empirical demonstration and evaluation as a vital next step in the development of advocacy techniques.

PRACTICE

The papers reviewed here clearly indicate that the problems of constituencies and organizational base remain the principal obstacles to effective delivery of advocacy services. The free professional model fails because potential clients of interest to the advocate lack awareness of the availability of such services and/or lack the ability to pay for them (even, to a critical degree, in the case of public interest law practice). The salaried professional model fails because the interests advocated are not the employer's but the "client's." Further experimentation with forms of "private practice" through nonprofit public interest corporations, loosely linked to universities in many cases and dependent on grants and contracts, seems an inevitable and potentially viable next step. The more novel form of fee-based private practice described briefly by the Kutchins will surely receive close scrutiny also.

Similarly, more systematic attempts at multi-disciplinary "network building" by advocate professionals, to enhance their referral capabilities, appears to be an emerging trend that warrants explicit development. Some national association of advocate social scientists (providing for meetings and a newsletter or journal) might well be encouraged.

TRAINING

Relatively few training materials on advocacy have been developed, and it appears that formal university training in advocacy social science has been limited to sporadic efforts in schools of social work and urban planning. A plausible next step might be the development and evaluation of an experimental interdisciplinary course on an activist campus with a strong social science base.

As Patner indicates, in the area of "advocacy as activity," both lawyers and social scientists still have much to learn concerning one another's characteristic modes of advocacy. Since a number of good Law and Society training programs are already in operation around the country, it might prove cost-efficient to encourage practicing advocate social scientists and public interest lawyers to participate more extensively in such programs.

Similarly, with respect to "advocacy as role," it appears that a considerable proportion of practicing advocate social scientists (except in the discipline of social work) has had little or nor formal training in the techniques of community organization. Since (1) the centrality of these techniques to "advocacy as role" is well documented in these papers and (2) community organization is already taught in every school of social work, advocate social scientists should be strongly encouraged to upgrade their skills through formal instruction in community organization.

As both Laue and the Kutchins suggest, the need for training in the ethics of advocacy practice may be more critical than the need for training in relevant skills. Some university training is now directed toward the ethics of research and of casework, yet the much riskier and more uncharted activities of advocacy are typically undertaken in the absence of any clear principles of professional conduct.

The foregoing papers clearly convey the vitality — and the confusions — of advocacy as a contemporary mode of social science practice. The next steps in the development of theory, research, practice, and training in advocacy social science will surely prove critical to the determination of its eventual place within the repertory of social science practice.

REFERENCES

Abrahamson, M. (1967) *The Professional in the Organization.* Chicago: Rand McNally.

Charlesworth, J. D., (ed.) (1972) *Integration of the Social Sciences through Policy Analysis.* Philadelphia: American Academy of Political and Social Science.

Ecklein, J. L. and A. Lauffer (1971) *Community Organizers and Social Planners.* New York: Wiley.

Etzioni, A., (ed.) (1969) *The Semi-Professions and Their Organization: Teachers, Nurses, Social Workers.* New York: Free Press.

Friedson, E., (ed.) (1973) *The Professions and Their Prospects.* Beverly Hills: Sage Publications.

Furner, M. O. (1975) *Advocacy and Objectivity: A Crisis in the Professionalization of American Social Science, 1965-1905.* Lexington: University Press of Kentucky.

Grosser, C. F. (1976) *New Directions in Community Organization: From Enabling to Advocacy* (expanded ed.). New York: Praeger.

Kamerman, S. B.; Kahn, A. J.; and McGowan, B. G. (1972) "Research and Advocacy". *Children Today,* 1 (March-April): 35-36.

Katz, A. H. and E. I. Bender (1976) *The Strength in Us: Self-Help Groups in the Modern World.* New York: New Viewpoints, 1976.

Knitzer, J. E. (1976) "Child Advocacy: A Perspective." *American Journal of Orthopsychiatry,* 46 (2): 200-216.

Lerner, D. and H. D. Lasswell, (eds.) (1951) *The Policy Sciences.* Stanford: Stanford University Press.

Moore, W. E. (1970) *The Professions: Roles and Rules.* New York: Russell Sage Foundation.

Nagel, S. S., (ed.) (1975) *Policy Studies and the Social Sciences.* Lexington, Massachusetts: Lexington Books.

Panitch, A. (1974) "Advocacy in Practice." *Social Work,* 19: 326-332.

Perlman, R. (1972) *Community Organization and Social Planning.* New York: Wiley, 1972.

O'Brien, D. J. (1976) *Neighborhood Organization and Interest-Group Processes.* Princeton, N.J.: Princeton University Press.

Rawls, J. (1971) *A Theory of Justice.* Cambridge: Harvard University Press.

Rescher, N. (1966) *Distributive Justice.* Indianapolis: Bobbs-Merrill.

Schubert, G. A. (1961) *The Public Interest: A Critique of the Theory of a Political Concept.* New York: Free Press.

ABOUT THE EDITORS AND AUTHORS

GEORGE H. WEBER, a Ph.D. in sociology, is currently Deputy Director, Division of Special Mental Health Programs, National Institute of Mental Health. His experience has mainly been in applied sociology at the state and federal levels, including heading Minnesota's institutions for juvenile delinquents and youthful offenders, and serving as Executive Secretary of President Kennedy's Committee on Youth Employment. Considerable part-time teaching has involved him in a number of universities including an experimental course in *Law and Social Deviance*, team-taught at The Washington College of Law, American University.

GEORGE J. McCALL is Professor of Sociology at the University of Missouri-St. Louis, directing a special graduate training program in services evaluation. The author of several books, he served as Visiting Scientist in the Center for Studies of Crime and Delinquency at the National Institute of Mental Health.

HERB KUTCHINS is Associate Professor of Social Work at California State University, Sacramento, where he chairs the Social Justice and Corrections Concentration. Dr. Kutchins has helped organize a number of advocacy programs. He was Director of the San Francisco Bar Association's award-winning project to release defendants without bail; an organizer of the West Oakland Legal Switchboard; Research Coordinator of the Community Justice Center in Los Angeles; and one of the founders of the San Francisco Community Street Work Center. His research, which has centered around the impact particularly of the unanticipated consequences of social reforms, includes *Bail Reform and Preventive Detention; Pretrail Diversionary Programs: New Expansion of Law Enforcement Camouflaged as Rehabilitation; The Criminalization of the Mentally Ill: The Impact of Deinstitutionalization;* and *Social Work Malpractice.*

STUART KUTCHINS retired from a successful career as a business manager for rock musicians and now practices oriental healing arts including acupuncture at Black Mountain Medicine in Marin County, California. He is a staff member of the Postural Integration Institute.

He has attended the New School for Social Research in New York and the Graduate School of Letters at Indiana University.

MARSHALL PATNER practices law in Chicago and teaches in the Department of Criminal Justice at the University of Illinois at Chicago Circle. Among many other public interest activities, he was a founder and general counsel for Business and Professional People for the Public Interest.

WILLIAM S. DAVIDSON II is a 1976 Ph.D. of the University of Illinois at Champaign-Urbana. He is currently Assistant Professor of Psychology and Director of the Adolescent Diversion Project at Michigan State University. Previous works include numerous articles in the area of juvenile delinquency and a recent book (with M. Neitzel, M. MacDonald, and R. Winett), *Behavioral Approaches to Community Psychology,* published by Pergamon Press, 1977.

JULIAN RAPPAPORT, a 1968 Ph.D. of the University of Rochester, is Professor of Psychology and Director of the Community Psychology Training Program at the University of Illinois at Urbana-Champaign. He has recently been named Assistant Editor of the *American Journal of Community Psychology.* Previous work includes two books: the first (co-authored by J. M. Chinsky and E. L. Cowen) is *Innovations in Helping Chronic Mental Patients;* the second and most recent is a textbook, *Community Psychology: Values, Research and Action,* published by Holt, Rinehart and Winston, 1977.

PAUL DAVIDOFF is Director of the Suburban Action Institute, a nonprofit institute for research and action in the suburbs. He has taught at several universities, consulted widely, and received the Distinguished Service Award of the New York chapter of the American Institute of Planners.

LINDA DAVIDOFF is a Planning Associate of Suburban Action Institute, has been very active in state and local politics, and has taught at SUNY (Purchase) and the New School for Social Research.

STEPHEN L. SCHENSUL received his Ph.D. in anthropology from the University of Minnesota in 1969. He directed the Community Research Unit of the Community Mental Health Program in the West Side Medical Complex, Chicago, directed the Community Mental Health Program at Jackson Memorial Hospital in Miami, and is currently

Research Associate at the Department of Community Medicine, University of Connecticut. Dr. Schensul has also been on faculties of the University of Illinois Chicago Circle Campus (Department of Anthropology), the University of Illinois Chicago Abraham Lincoln School of Medicine (Department of Psychiatry) and the University of Miami School of Medicine (Department of Psychiatry). In addition to publications cited in the article, his publications include *Coping in a Troubled Society: An Environmental Approach to Mental Health,* with Just, Bell and Fisher, Lexington Books, 1974.

JEAN J. SCHENSUL received her Ph.D. in anthropology from the University of Minnesota in 1974. She directed the community component of an experimental education program at the Institute for Juvenile Research, Chicago, acted as Program Developer with the Dade County District Mental Health Board (Fla.) and since 1975, has been the director of Community Research Inc., a private research and technical assistance firm offering services in health and education. Dr. Schensul has been on the faculties of Middlebury College (anthropology and sociology), and the University of Kentucky (Department of Anthropology). She is currently affiliated on a part-time basis with the University of Connecticut Department of Anthropology. Her major publications include with Luz Maria Munoz Lopez, "Industry and Education in Highland Mexico: A case study in national planning and local change," *Revista de Estudios Educativos,* Mexico, D.F. 1976; and *Ensenanza para el Futuro y el Futuro de la Ensenanza,* Coleccion Sep-Setentas, Mexico, D.F. 1976.

JAMES H. LAUE is Director of the Center for Metropolitan Studies and Associate Professor of Sociology at the University of Missouri-St. Louis. Following graduate training at Harvard, he did field work, conducted research, and served as Director of Program Evaluation and Development for the Community Relations Service of the U. S. Department of Justice during the 1960s. His areas of research and publication are community conflict intervention, race relations, social change, and urban sociology. He is co-chairperson of a national campaign which secured legislation in the U. S. Senate and House Representatives for a Congressional commission currently studying the feasibility of a United States Academy of Peace and Conflict Resolution.